HOW TO DETHRONE THE IMPERIAL JUDICIARY

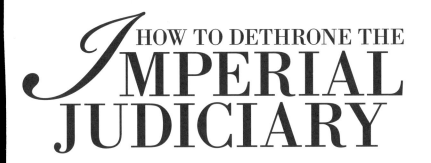

HOW TO DETHRONE THE IMPERIAL JUDICIARY

Dr. Edwin Vieira

VISION FORUM MINISTRIES
San Antonio, Texas

Vision Forum Ministries
4719 Blanco Rd., San Antonio, Texas 78212
www.visionforum.org

ISBN 0-9755264-1-3

Cover Design by Shannon G. Moeller
Typesetting by Joshua R. Goforth

PRINTED IN THE UNITED STATES OF AMERICA

Table of Contents

Foreword

According to Article I, Section One of the U.S. Constitution, "All legislative Powers herein granted shall be vested in a Congress of the United States."

It was intended that, insofar as legislative authority was delegated by the several states to the Federal Republic, such authority would be exercised by the Article I U.S. Senate and House of Representatives—certainly not by the Article III Judiciary.

It is made clear in Article III that "The judicial Power of the United States, shall be vested in one supreme Court, and in such inferior Courts as the Congress may from time to time ordain and establish."

Accordingly, while the size of the Supreme Court may be altered by statute, its existence may not be terminated. Nonetheless, Congress, which has power to "ordain and establish" the inferior courts, may also disestablish them.

Similarly, Congress can assert its primary authority by virtue of its control of the appropriations process.

Nowhere in Article III are federal judges granted "life tenure." To suggest such permanent, unchallengeable incumbency is as foreign to the actual text of the Constitution as are the words "separation of church and state."

Article III does explicitly provide that "The Judges, both of the supreme and inferior Courts, shall hold their Offices during good Behaviour." In other words, judges can be expelled from office by means other than impeachment. Section Two of Article III specifies:

> The judicial Power shall extend to all Cases, in Law and Equity, arising under this Constitution, the Laws of the United States, and Treaties made, or which shall be made, under their Authority;—to all Cases affecting Ambassadors, other public Ministers and Consuls;—to all Cases of admiralty and maritime Jurisdiction;—to Controversies to which the United States shall be a Party;—to Controversies between two or more States…between Citizens of different States,—between Citizens of the same States, claiming Lands under Grants of different States…
>
> In all Cases affecting Ambassadors, other public Ministers and Consuls, and those in which a State shall be Party, the supreme Court shall have original Jurisdiction. In all the other Cases before mentioned, *the supreme Court shall have appellate Jurisdiction, both as to Law and Fact, with such Exceptions, and under such Regulations as the Congress shall make.*

It is pure myth that the Supreme Court has the last word on the meaning of the U.S. Constitution. Indeed, Article VI makes clear that "This Constitution, and the Laws of the United States which shall be made in Pursuance thereof . . . shall be the supreme Law of the Land . . . and all executive and judicial Officers, both of the United States and of the several States, shall be bound by Oath or Affirmation, to support this Constitution."

In other words, the Judiciary is *under* the Constitution and not over it.

In years gone by, when constitutional literacy and discernment were more widespread, Presidents of the United States (including Thomas Jefferson, Andrew Jackson, and Abraham Lincoln) understood that, certainly insofar as the Executive Branch was concerned, their authority trumped that of the Supreme Court in determining constitutional meaning and authority.

It is no accident that the Legislative Branch is Article I, the Executive Branch is Article II, and the Judicial Branch is Article III under the Constitution of our federal republic.

It is time to put the Judiciary back in its proper place. Dr. Edwin Vieira, a Trustee of The Conservative Caucus Foundation (TCCF) and a brilliant legal scholar, has comprehensively addressed these and other issues in this study commissioned by TCCF, "Constitutional and Statutory Remedies for Judicial Usurpation and Tyranny."

As I am sure you will agree after reading this important work, Dr. Vieira has made an historically significant contribution to the public policy debates of the twenty-first century.

Howard Phillips
PRESIDENT
THE CONSERVATIVE CAUCUS FOUNDATION

Part I

The Illegitimate Insinuation of Foreign Law and Amorality into America's Constitutional Jurisprudence

Introduction

In a series of decisions culminating to date in, but (one may confidently predict) not ending with, *Lawrence* v. *Texas*,[1] a significant number of Justices of the United States Supreme Court, in majority or separate opinions, have employed *foreign* law as a ground for divining the meaning of, and applying, certain provisions of the Constitution of the United States. Although, so far, this reliance has not been admitted to be exclusive, in every case it has been effective in adding foreign law to the judicial armamentarium of techniques for "construing" the Constitution. Moreover, in *Lawrence*, a majority of Justices held—for the first time in domestic jurisprudence, and with very significant references to foreign law—that the promotion of traditional American morality will no longer constitute a constitutionally sufficient reason to uphold a statute that prohibits aberrant sexual conduct or practices. These developments raise numerous questions, including: Are these rulings consistent with the Constitution?

---

[1] 539 U.S. 558 (2003).

If not, what are their logical and likely consequences? What can and should be done to respond to them and to minimize their destructive potentials?

CHAPTER 1

The Supreme Court's Decision
in
Lawrence v. *Texas*

At issue in *Lawrence* v. *Texas* was the validity, under the Due Process and Equal Protection Clauses of the Fourteenth Amendment,[2] "of a Texas statute making it a crime for two persons of the same sex to engage in certain intimate sexual conduct" (to wit, sodomy).[3] Holding that "[t]he Texas statute furthers no legitimate state interest which can justify its intrusion into the personal and private life of the individual,"[4] the Court (in a majority opinion by Justice Kennedy, joined by Justices Breyer, Ginsberg, Souter, and Stevens) overruled its earlier decision in *Bowers* v. *Hardwick*,[5] which had held that the

---

[2] U.S. Const. amend. XIV, § 1, provides in pertinent part that "[n]o State shall make or enforce any law which shall abridge the privileges or immunities of citizens of the United States; nor shall any State deprive any person of life, liberty, or property, without due process of law; nor deny to any person within its jurisdiction the equal protection of the laws."

[3] 539 U.S. at 562.

[4] Ibid. at 578.

[5] 478 U.S. 186 (1986).

Constitution protects no "fundamental right" for "homosexuals to engage in sodomy,"[6] on the ground that "*Bowers* was not correct when it was decided, and it is not correct today."[7]

As Justice Kennedy told the story in *Lawrence*:

> Chief Justice Burger joined the opinion for the Court in *Bowers* and further explained his views as follows: "Decisions of individuals relating to homosexual conduct have been subject to state intervention throughout the history of Western civilization. Condemnation of those practices is firmly rooted in Judeao-Christian moral and ethical standards."[8]

Forgetting that "[t]he Fourteenth Amendment did not tear history up by the roots, and the regulation of [sexual practices such as sodomy] is one of the oldest and most untrammeled of legislative powers,"[9] Justice Kennedy rejected this reliance on "the history of Western civilization" over the centuries, with the airy assertion that:

> [W]e [i.e., the majority in *Lawrence*] think that our laws and traditions in the past half century are of most relevance here. These references show an emerging awareness that liberty gives substantial protection to adult persons in deciding how to conduct their private lives in matters pertaining to sex.

>   . . .

---

[6] Ibid. at 190.

[7] 539 U.S. at 578.

[8] Ibid. at 571.

[9] *Goesaert* v. *Cleary*, 335 U.S. 464, 465 (1948).

The sweeping references by Chief Justice Burger to the history of Western civilization and to Judeo-Christian moral and ethical standards did not take account of other authorities pointing in an opposite direction. *A committee advising the British Parliament* recommended in 1957 repeal of laws punishing homosexual conduct. . . .

Of even more importance, almost five years before *Bowers* was decided *the European Court of Human Rights* considered a case with parallels to *Bowers* and to today's case. An adult male in Northern Ireland alleged that he was a practicing homosexual who desired to engage in consensual homosexual conduct. The laws of Northern Ireland forbade him that right. . . . The court held that the laws proscribing the conduct were invalid under *the European Convention on Human Rights*. . . . Authoritative in *all countries that are members of the Council of Europe (21 nations then, 45 nations now)*, the decision is at odds with the premise in *Bowers* that the claim put forward was insubstantial in our Western civilization.

. . .

To the extent *Bowers* relied on values we share with a wider civilization, it should be noted that the reasoning and holding in *Bowers* have been rejected elsewhere. *The European Court of Human Rights* has followed not *Bowers* but its own decision. . . . *Other nations*, too, have taken action consistent with an affirmation of the protected right of homosexual adults to engage in intimate, consensual conduct. See Brief for Mary Robinson et al. as *Amici Curiae* 11-12. The right the petitioners seek in this case has been accepted as an integral part of human freedom in *many other countries*. There has been no showing that in this country the governmental interest in circumscribing personal choice is somehow more legitimate or urgent.[10]

Perhaps most telling in this passage was Justice Kennedy's explicit recognition—without explanation or excuse, let alone embarrassment—that these "other authorities" drawn from foreign law "point[ed] in an *opposite* direction" from "the history of Western civilization and ... Judeo-Christian moral and ethical standards."

Dissenting in *Lawrence*, Justice Scalia (joined by Chief Justice Rehnquist and Justice Thomas) acidly observed that:

> [C]onstitutional entitlements ... do not spring into existence, as the Court seems to believe, because *foreign nations* decriminalize conduct. The *Bowers* majority opinion *never* relied on "values we share with a wider civilization," ... but rather rejected the claimed right to sodomy on the ground that such a right was not "'deeply rooted in *this Nation's* history and tradition.'" ... *Bowers'* ... holding is likewise devoid of any reliance on the views of a "wider civilization." ... The Court's discussion of these foreign views (ignoring, of course, the many countries that have retained criminal prohibitions on sodomy) is therefore meaningless dicta. Dangerous dicta, however, since "this Court ... should not impose foreign moods, fads, or fashions on Americans."[11]

Pace Justice Scalia, though, disingenuous as it may be, the remarkable passage Justice Kennedy penned—and the principle it asserts—appear in a *majority* opinion of the

---

[10] 539 U.S. at 571-72, 572-73, 576-77 (emphasis supplied).

[11] Ibid. at 598 (separate opinion).

Supreme Court. So, rather than being "meaningless," they instead plainly import what Justice Kennedy and his brethren (and other jurists who think as they do) may—likely will—do in future "Cases" and "Controversies" they take up for decision.[12] As Justice Jackson presciently warned, dissenting in *Korematsu* v. *United States*,[13] once the Court has "validated" some principle:

> The principle then lies about like a loaded weapon ready for the hand of any authority that can bring forward a plausible claim of an urgent need. Every repetition imbeds the principle more deeply in our law and thinking and expands it to new purposes. All who observe the work of courts are familiar with . . . "the tendency of a principle to expand itself to the limit of its logic." . . . [I]f we review and approve, [a] passing incident becomes the doctrine of the Constitution. There it has a generative power of its own, and all that it creates will be in its own image.[14]

Four highly questionable principles lay at the heart of the majority's decision in *Lawrence*:

1. The first of these (albeit the least surprising) is the principle of "the living Constitution": the theory that, not just the application, but even the very *meaning* of constitutional provisions, phrases, and words will change (and in the nature of things in a progressively evolving world *must* change) with the needs of the times, as perceived by the Justices. This stands

---

[12] See U.S. Const. art. III, § 2, cls. 1-2.

[13] 323 U.S. 214 (1944).

[14] Ibid. at 246 (separate opinion).

out starkly in Justice Kennedy's rejection of "those practices
... firmly rooted in Judeao-Christian moral and ethical
standards," "throughout the history of Western civilization,"
on the ground that "we [i.e., Justices Kennedy, Breyer,
Ginsberg, Souter, and Stevens] think that our laws and
traditions of the past half century are of most relevance here.
These references show an emerging awareness that liberty
gives substantial protection to adult persons in deciding how
to conduct their private lives in matters pertaining to sex."[15]

Now, a not inaccurate assessment of what "liberty" has
always meant *in American constitutional law* can be gleaned
from how Congress and State legislatures have time and again
limited it, with the approval of WE THE PEOPLE[16] since the
Constitution was ratified. For, if "[n]o person shall ... be
deprived of life, liberty, or property, without due process of
law,"[17] "nor shall any State deprive any person of life, liberty,
or property, without due process of law,"[18] then "liberty"
includes no behavior that the government has traditionally
enjoyed the authority to curtail with "due process of law." So,
one may agree *arguendo* with Justice Kennedy that:

> [a]t the heart of liberty is the right to define one's own
> concept of existence, of meaning, of the universe, and of
> the mystery of human life. Beliefs about these matters could

---

[15] 539 U.S. at 571-72.

[16] U.S. Const. preamble.

[17] U.S. Const. amend. V.

[18] U.S. Const. amend. XIV, § 1.

not define the attributes of personhood were they formed under compulsion of the State.[19]

That is, one may agree as long as such agreement includes the qualification that, whereas freedom of *belief* is "absolute,"[20] freedom of *action*, even in the pursuit of "one's own concept of existence, of meaning, of the universe, and of the mystery of human life," is *not*, but may and often should be limited by "due process of law."

For a very long time prior to *Lawrence*, Americans considered "due process of law" compatible with the criminalization of sodomy, as evidenced by numerous statutes and court decisions (the last of them at the highest level being *Bowers*). Therefore, to claim that "liberty" in the American jurisprudential lexicon ever included the practice of sodomy is false. Legislatures might not always have chosen to criminalize sodomy in all its variants, or even at all, for *political* reasons; but, until *Lawrence*, they always had the *constitutional power* to do so, for any reason, not the least of which was the promotion of public morality.[21]

---

[19] 539 U.S. at 574, quoting from *Planned Parenthood* v. *Casey*, 505 U.S. 833, 851 (1992).

[20] *Cantwell* v. *Connecticut*, 310 U.S. 296, 303 (1940).

[21] Generally, legislators' personal motives for enacting (or not enacting) statutes, even if suspect, are not determinative of the legislature's constitutional authority in the premises—e.g., *United States* v. *O'Brien*, 391 U.S. 367, 382-85 (1968); *Communist Party of the United States* v. *SACB*, 367 U.S. 1, 84-86 (1961); *Watkins* v. *United States*, 354 U.S. 178, 199-200 (1957); *Weber* v. *Freed*, 239 U.S. 325, 330 (1915).

Moreover, even Justice Kennedy shrank from pretending that, from *Bowers* to *Lawrence*, Americans in vast numbers had radically changed their minds as to the social and political meaning of "liberty" so as to include sodomy (not that such a shift in public attitudes, if proven, would transform the specifically legal meaning of "liberty" in the Constitution in any event). Instead, he contended only for *"an emerging awareness"* that "liberty" now embraced the practice of sodomy. How far from an *actual* "awareness" this *"emerging* awareness" might be, Justice Kennedy did not say. Anyway, his invocation of a merely *"emerging* awareness" gives "the living Constitution" a life of an order entirely different than ever before because it derives, not from what the Court even claims to be the present, mature, and demonstrable conviction of WE THE PEOPLE, but from attitudes "we [i.e., the Justices] think" seem to be developing somewhere or other—but in fact may not now, and may never come to, represent WE THE PEOPLE'S considered and final view at all.

But the hubris of Justice Kennedy and others of his mind on this matter emerged most strikingly in his condescending conclusion that:

> Had those who drew and ratified the Due Process Clauses of the Fifth Amendment or of the Fourteenth Amendment known of the components of liberty in its manifold possibilities, they might have been more specific. They did not presume to have this insight. They knew times can blind us to certain truths and later generations can see that laws once thought necessary and proper in fact serve only to oppress. As the Constitution endures, persons

in every generation can invoke its principles in their own search for greater freedom.[22]

On its face, this is a disingenuous argument, because in constitutional law the phrase "necessary and proper" typically refers to legislative *discretion* (the choice to exercise a delegated power or not, depending on the legislators' assessment of what best serves the general welfare);[23] whereas, the majority in *Lawrence* was invoking a purported constitutional rule of total legislative *disability* (an absence of legal power as to that subject matter). Furthermore, it is also a defamatory argument, because it imputes to the Founding Fathers, the Civil War Congress, and WE THE PEOPLE in the late 1700s and 1860s a depth of ignorance and insouciance approaching political and moral negligence, if not depravity, in that they allegedly enacted (or at least interpreted) "due process of law" so as "in fact . . . only to oppress." In addition, it is a demeaning argument, because it presumes that, had the Founders and WE THE PEOPLE only been as intelligent, progressive, sensitive,

---

[22] 539 U.S. at 578-79.

[23] See, e.g., *McCulloch v. Maryland*, 17 U.S. (4 Wheat.) 316, 415-16 (1819) (construing the Necessary and Proper Clause of Article I, Section 8, Clause 18 of the Constitution): "It must have been the intention of those who gave these powers, to insure, as far as human prudence could insure, their beneficial execution. This could not be done by confiding the choice of means to such narrow limits as not to leave it in the power of Congress to adopt any which might be appropriate, and which were conducive to the end. . . . To have declared that the best means shall not be used, but those alone without which the power given would be nugatory, would have been to deprive the legislature of the capacity to avail itself of experience, to exercise its reason, and to accommodate its legislation to circumstances."

tolerant, and especially "insight[ful]" as Justices Kennedy, Breyer, Ginsberg, Souter, and Stevens, they would instead have included the practice of sodomy within the "liberty" that even "due process of law" cannot deny.[24] And *in fine*, it is a delusive argument, because "[t]he Constitution does not require legislatures to reflect [the latest] sociological insight."[25]

Yet, even assuming *arguendo* the innate intellectual and mayhap spiritual superiority of those Justices to the Founders and WE THE PEOPLE, one must nevertheless wonder why, if the *Lawrence* majority's conception of "the living Constitution" is correct, "[a]s the Constitution endures, persons in every generation can invoke its principles in their own search for *greater freedom*"? In the first place, why *"greater* freedom"? At any point in time, how can persons invoke the *Constitution's* "principles" in search of freedoms *beyond what the Constitution actually guarantees then are there*? From what legitimate, authoritative source can these enhanced freedoms possibly derive? Are the Constitution's "principles" of such protean stuff that they can bend so as to amend "the supreme Law of the

---

[24] Presumably, the Founders and WE THE PEOPLE would have realized with the majority in *Lawrence* that, "[w]hen homosexual conduct is made criminal . . . , that declaration in and of itself is an invitation to subject homosexual persons to discrimination both in the public and in the private spheres," 539 U.S. at 575. The majority left unexamined, however, whether, unlike contemporary jurists such as Justice Kennedy for whom "discrimination" in any form is inherently suspect, the Founders and WE THE PEOPLE might have considered discrimination against practitioners of sodomy to be legally proper and socially prudent.

[25] *Goesaert* v. *Cleary*, 335 U.S. 464, 466 (1948).

Land"[26]—including, presumably, those very "principles"
themselves? The answers to these questions must be found in
the realization that the matter is not one of constitutional law
at all, but of a civil war being waged in the guise of
constitutional interpretation.[27] Sudden and unprecedented
judicial discoveries of "greater freedom" are necessary to
promote one side in what Justice Scalia correctly identified as
an American "culture war,"[28] by attacking the limits on
antisocial conduct that the Founders left to legislatures to set
according to "due process of law." Indeed, most revealing is
how these discoveries so often burst upon the scene by
veritable saltations in the Court's constitutional jurisprudence,
just when they are needed and with perfect conformity to
political imperatives, rather than by gradual social evolution.[29]
Apparently, though, the Justices who ally the force of their
offices to one side in the "culture war" forget that, "if a people
be so situated, or have such different opinions that they cannot
agree in ascertaining and fixing [the nature and content of
individual rights], it is a very strong argument against their

---

[26] U.S. Const. art. VI, cl. 2.

[27] And not a bloodless war, either, by any stretch of the imagination. See,
e.g., *Roe* v. *Wade*, 410 U.S. 113 (1973).

[28] 539 U.S. at 602 (dissenting opinion). This matter is discussed post, at 37-
40.

[29] E.g., *Lawrence* (right to practice sodomy); *Everson* v. *Board of Education*,
380 U.S. 1, 16 (1947) ("wall of separation between Church and State"); *Roe* v.
Wade, 410 U.S. 113 (1973) (right to abortion).

attempting to form one entire society to live under one system of laws only."[30]

In the second place, why "greater *freedom*"? Why should "liberty" under the *Lawrence* majority's "living Constitution" expand in the direction only of conduct increasingly unrestricted by any laws? Once torn from their historical roots (and, even worse, from any considerations of transcendent morality, as discussed below), generalizations as to what constitutes "liberty" are not by intellectual necessity unidirectional in their application. Particularly in an era in which public officials and the media generate waves of mass hysteria in favor of waging a "war on drugs" and a "war on terrorism," as well as preemptive wars against any foreign nation or leader which or who might, someday, someway, be perceived to threaten the global hegemony of the United States, "liberty" may come to be viewed as a dangerous license and luxury that ought to be curtailed. Can anyone guarantee that the *Lawrence* majority's "living Constitution" will then not serve for that purpose? Surely, *Korematsu* provides a paradigm of such retrogression. For example, doubtlessly in this era, "the living Constitution" as applied by the present Court will not expand (or even preserve to its present extent) "the right of the people to keep and bear Arms"—notwithstanding that this right the Constitution expressly affirms is "necessary to the security of a free State."[31] Predictably, the "autonomy of self"

---

[30] R. Lee, *Letters from the Federal Farmer No. 2* (October 9, 1787).

[31] U.S. Const. amend. II.

which Justice Kennedy holds that "[l]iberty presumes" will not be found by any among the majority in *Lawrence* to guarantee the right of average Americans to arm themselves as a deterrent to usurpation and tyranny.[32] With the result, of course, that usurpation and tyranny will increase; and the Court, which owes its existence and authority solely to the "free State" the Constitution created and would be wholly illegitimate were it to serve any other type of state, will itself create the conditions of legalistic lawlessness that will ultimately engender its own, and with it the country's, destruction.

2. The second highly questionable principle enunciated in the majority's opinion in *Lawrence* is what may be styled "the *amoral* Constitution." In rejecting *Bowers*, Justice Kennedy adopted as "controlling" Justice Stevens's dissent in the latter case, in which Stevens had argued that simply because "'the governing majority in a State has traditionally viewed a particular practice as immoral is not a sufficient reason for upholding a law prohibiting the practice.'"[33]

This, of course, was anything but the opinion of the Supreme Court before *Lawrence*. The "police power" is the power of legislatures to enact laws to promote public health,

---

[32] Contrast 539 U.S. at 562.

[33] 539 U.S. at 577-78, quoting from *Bowers*, 478 U.S. at 216 (Stevens, J., dissenting).

safety, welfare, prosperity, good order, and morals.[34] The traditional view has always been that, in both Congress and the State legislatures, "the police power . . . may be put forth in aid of what is sanctioned by usage, or held by *the prevailing morality* or strong or preponderant opinion to be greatly and immediately necessary to the public welfare."[35] This is not to say that the exercise of the police power to promote morality is not subject to abuse, and has never been abused—only that it was never denied to constitute "due process of law." As the *Bowers* Court irrefutably pointed out, "[t]he law . . . is constantly based on notions of morality, and if all laws representing essentially moral choices are to be invalidated . . . the courts will be very busy indeed."[36]

Now, the majority in *Lawrence* could not have arrived at its conclusion rejecting *Bowers in reliance on these precedents*, on the suppositious ground that the present "prevailing morality" among Americans at large, or even among Texans, with respect to the practice of sodomy is actually amorality or

---

[34] See, e.g., *Black's Law Dictionary* (revised 4th ed., 1968), at 1317; *Atlantic Coast Line* v. *Goldsboro*, 232 U.S. 548, 558 (1914); *Liggett Co.* v. *Baldridge*, 278 U.S. 105, 111-12 (1928).

[35] *Noble State Bank* v. *Haskell*, 219 U.S. 104, 111 (1911) (emphasis supplied). *Accord*, e.g., *Heart of Atlanta Motel, Inc.* v. *United States*, 379 U.S. 241, 257 (1964); *Berman* v. *Parker*, 348 U.S. 26, 32 (1954); *Nebbia* v. *New York*, 291 U.S. 502, 526 (1934); *Brooks* v. *United States*, 267 U.S. 432, 436 (1925); *Thomas Cusack Co.* v. *City of Chicago*, 242 U.S. 526, 531 (1917); *Hoke* v. *United States*, 227 U.S. 308, 322 (1913); *Jacobson* v. *Massachusetts*, 197 U.S. 11, 31 (1905); *L'Hote* v. *City of New Orleans*, 177 U.S. 587, 596 (1900); *Barbier* v. *Connolly*, 113 U.S. 27, 31 (1885).

[36] 478 U.S. at 196.

immorality (in comparison to the "prevailing morality" of the past). For at issue in *Lawrence* was whether the Texas statute should be *upheld* (not overturned) by reference to "the prevailing morality"; the statute itself was the best evidence of what "the prevailing morality" was in that State; and, as Justice Scalia pointed out in his dissent:

> [There could be no] doubt [about] the "definitive [historical] conclusion" on which *Bowers* relied: that our Nation has a longstanding history of laws prohibiting *sodomy in general*—regardless of whether it was performed by same-sex or opposite-sex couples.... Whether homosexual sodomy was prohibited by a law targeted at same-sex sexual relations or by a more general law prohibiting both homosexual and heterosexual sodomy, the only relevant point is that it *was* criminalized—which suffices to establish that homosexual sodomy is not a right "deeply rooted in our Nation's history and tradition." The Court today agrees that homosexual sodomy was criminalized and thus does not dispute the facts on which *Bowers actually* relied.[37]

Thus, particularly revealing in Justice Stevens's dissent in *Bowers*, and even more so in Justice Kennedy's adoption of it as legally "controlling" in *Lawrence*, was Stevens's assumption that "a particular practice" is "immoral" solely because a "governing majority in a State has traditionally *viewed*" it as such—that is, that all morality is politically contingent and essentially arbitrary (a matter of "views," rather than of truth). Entirely disregarded by both Justices Stevens and Kennedy

---

[37] 539 U.S. at 596 (separate opinion).

(together with Justices Breyer, Ginsberg, and Souter; and Justice O'Connor in her separate concurring opinion) is whether, even if all morality is ultimately contingent and arbitrary, nevertheless a particular, historically conditioned morality in fact underlies the Constitution, such that it cannot be changed without amendment thereof,[38] and such that it can and should serve as a ground for legislation enacted with "due process of law" by both Congress and the States, and should be observed and respected by the courts. Even more importantly, entirely disregarded by those Justices is whether, notwithstanding anyone's "views," a singular morality exists upon which *all* rational law must be based—that is, a morality without which as a foundation purported governmental action is not properly to be accounted "law" at all, but merely the imposition of brute force.

That the Founding Fathers who wrote and WE THE PEOPLE who ratified the Constitution believed in a transcendent morality appears on the face of the Declaration of Independence:

> WHEN in the course of human events, it becomes necessary for one people to dissolve the political bands which have connected them with another, and to assume among the powers of the earth, the separate and equal station to which *the Laws of Nature and of Nature's God* entitle them, a decent respect to the opinion of mankind requires that they should declare the causes which impel them to the separation.—*We hold these truths to be self-*

---

[38] See U.S. Const. art. V.

evident, that all men are created equal, that *they are endowed by their Creator with certain unalienable Rights,* that among these are Life, Liberty, and the Pursuit of Happiness.—That *to secure these rights,* Governments are instituted among Men, deriving their *just powers* from the consent of the governed,—That whenever any Form of Government becomes destructive of *these ends,* it is the Right of the People to alter and abolish it. . . .[39]

And inasmuch as the Constitution could not be law at all were the Declaration of Independence not such, the Constitution must be informed by, incorporate, and operate according to the selfsame self-evident truths of politics, government, law, and morality that the Declaration identifies as its own foundational principles.

For that reason, both the Declaration of Independence explicitly and the Constitution implicitly reject the *Lawrence* majority's now-"controlling" notion that "the governing majority in a State" may not advance as "a sufficient reason for upholding a law prohibiting [a particular] practice" that the practice is immoral. Indeed, if a legislature may not invoke as a sanction for its acts "the Laws of Nature and of Nature's God," then on what rationally and historically valid footing stands the Constitution, or even the Declaration—and with them, for that matter, "[t]he judicial Power of the United States,"[40] which the majority in *Lawrence* employed to set up its new "controlling" principle of amorality at odds with both the

---

[39] Emphasis supplied.

[40] U.S. Const. art. III, § 1.

Constitution and the Declaration? If a legislature's embodiment in a statute of an appeal to and a reliance on the morality to be found in "the Laws of Nature and of Nature's God" is unconstitutional, because (in *Lawrence's* formulation) such a "statute furthers *no legitimate state interest* which can justify its intrusion into the personal and private life of the individual,"[41] then is not the Declaration of Independence itself no less suspect of inherent illegitimacy? And the Constitution, which depends on the Declaration? And the Supreme Court, which depends on the Constitution? How, then, without self-contradiction, could the majority in *Lawrence as a court under the Constitution* declare as not "due process of law" the very intellectual foundation of America's entire legal system? Indeed:

> Judicial power presupposes an established government capable of enacting laws and enforcing their execution, and of appointing judges to expound and administer them. The acceptance of the judicial office is a recognition of the authority of the government from which it is derived. And if the authority of that government is annulled and overthrown, the power of its courts and other officers is annulled with it. And if a ... court ... should come to the conclusion that the government under which it acted had been put aside and displaced by an opposing government, it would cease to be a court, and be incapable of pronouncing a judicial decision. . . .[42]

---

[41] 539 U.S. at 578 (emphasis supplied).

[42] *Luther* v. *Borden*, 48 U.S. (7 How.) 1, 40 (1849).

Moreover, how with intellectual rigor and propriety could the majority in *Lawrence* consign to the dustbin of history the self-evident truths of America's Founders, while at the same time invoking "certain truths" on the basis of which "later generations can see that laws once thought necessary and proper in fact serve only to oppress."[43] If the traditional morality that for hundreds (yea, thousands) of years justified the criminalization of sodomy consisted only of arbitrary "views," in what way is the new wisdom of the *Lawrence* majority that purported to decriminalize sodomy based upon "truths" no less arbitrary?[44] Apparently, Justices Kennedy, Breyer, Ginsberg, Souter, and Stevens expected this country to consider them—perforce of their offices, as they could never merit such deference perforce of their persons—uniquely situated to discern "certain truths" that transcend mere historical eras and outdated moral prejudices. And if with respect to sodomy, why not with respect to every other matter of moral concern?

Thus the incompleteness and weakness in Justice Scalia's warning that *Lawrence* will invalidate all legislation addressing specifically sexual morality:

> [T]he "societal reliance" on the principles confirmed in *Bowers* and discarded [in *Lawrence*] has been overwhelming. Countless judicial decisions and legislative enactments have relied on the ancient proposition that a governing majority's belief that certain sexual behavior is "immoral

---

[43] 539 U.S at 579.

[44] See ibid. at 577.

and unacceptable" constitutes a rational basis for regulation. . . . State laws against bigamy, same-sex marriage, adult incest, prostitution, masturbation, adultery, fornication, bestiality, and obscenity are likewise sustainable only in light of *Bowers'* validation of laws based on moral choices. Every single one of these laws is called into question by [*Lawrence*]; the Court makes no effort to cabin the scope of its decision to exclude them from its holding. . . . The impossibility of distinguishing homosexual from other traditional "morals" offenses is precisely why *Bowers* rejected the rational-basis challenge. . . .

. . .

I turn now to the ground on which the Court squarely rests its holding [in *Lawrence*]: the contention that there is no rational basis for the law here under attack. This proposition is so out of accord with our jurisprudence— indeed, with the jurisprudence of *any* society we know— that it requires little discussion.

The Texas statute undeniably seeks to further the belief of its citizens that certain forms of sexual behavior are "immoral and unacceptable" . . . —the same interest furthered by criminal laws against fornication, bigamy, adultery, adult incest, bestiality, and obscenity. *Bowers* held that this *was* a legitimate state interest. The Court [in *Lawrence*] reaches the opposite conclusion. The Texas statute, it says, "furthers *no legitimate state interest* which can justify its intrusion into the personal and private life of the individual". . . .The Court embraces instead Justice Stevens' declaration in his *Bowers* dissent, that "the fact that the governing majority in a State has traditionally viewed a particular practice as immoral is not a sufficient reason for upholding a law prohibiting the practice". . . .This effectively decrees the end of all morals legislation. If, as the Court asserts, the promotion of majoritarian sexual morality is not even a *legitimate* state interest, none of the above-mentioned laws can survive rational-basis review.[45]

But not just those laws. Rather, the majority opinion in *Lawrence* "effectively decrees the end of *all* . . . legislation" based on morals of *any* kind. For, if morality cannot be invoked as a legitimate basis for legislation in a sexual-morality case, how can it be invoked in any other? Surely the particular area of conduct to which WE THE PEOPLE address their moral judgments cannot determine the constitutional outcome. Thus, perforce of *Lawrence*, in the future to constitute "due process of law" as a basis for limiting "liberty," all legislation must be *amoral*—that is, all legislation must demonstrably serve some goal other than a concededly moral one. A "wall of separation" between morality and state must be thrown up and maintained.

In her concurring opinion, Justice O'Connor aligned herself with the majority in *Lawrence* solely on the question of whether the promotion of morality qualifies as a legitimate basis for legislation criminalizing the practice of sodomy. Justice O'Connor gave an appearance of straddling the fence. On the one hand, she noted that "I joined *Bowers*, and do not join the Court in overruling it." Nonetheless, on the other hand, she found herself "confident . . . that so long as the Equal Protection Clause requires a sodomy law to apply equally to the private consensual conduct of homosexuals and

---

[45] Ibid. at 589-90, 599 (dissenting opinion).

heterosexuals alike, such a law would not long stand in our democratic society."[46] The overall result being that she *did* join in reversing *Bowers* as a matter of practice. Her reasoning, however, was rather porous.

"Texas' sodomy law," she argued, "brands all homosexuals as criminals, thereby making it more difficult for homosexuals to be treated in the same manner as everyone else."[47] In fact, the statute obviously did not brand all "homosexuals" (i.e., individuals with homosexual tendencies) as criminals *per se*, but instead punished certain conduct in which any individuals might engage as the result of homosexual tendencies as well as for many other reasons.[48] On the other side, Justice O'Connor did not deny that homosexuality is a *voluntarily chosen* "lifestyle," and homosexual sodomy generally a *consensual* act—that is, she did not contend that every individual with homosexual tendencies is *innately and unchangeably* homosexual, or that every individual who engages in homosexual sodomy is thereby a homosexual. To the contrary, she referred to the Texas statute as being "applied to private, consensual conduct."[49] In addition, *pace* Justice O'Connor, that it is more difficult for individuals who voluntarily engage in criminal sexual acts to be treated thereafter in the same manner as individuals who do not

---

[46] Ibid. at 579, 584-85.

[47] Ibid. at 581.

[48] The homosexual activity rampant in prisons, for example, is not the result of most inmates' *being* homosexuals.

[49] 539 U.S. at 585.

engage in such acts is a consequence of the former individuals' manifestly antisocial behavior, not a reason for declaring that behavior acceptable and a constitutionally protected "liberty"—otherwise the discriminatory disabilities arising out of or attendant on conviction for any crime would invalidate the crime.

"Texas attempts to justify its law, and the effects of the law," Justice O'Connor continued,

> by arguing that the statute ... furthers the legitimate governmental interest of the promotion of morality. In *Bowers*, we held that a state law criminalizing sodomy as applied to homosexual couples did not violate substantive due process. . . .
>
> This case raises a different issue than *Bowers*: whether, under the Equal Protection Clause,[50] moral disapproval is a legitimate state interest to justify by itself a statute that bans homosexual sodomy, but not heterosexual sodomy. It is not. Moral disapproval of this group, like a bare desire to harm the group, is an interest that is insufficient. . . . Indeed, we have never held that moral disapproval, without any other asserted state interest, is a sufficient rationale under the Equal Protection Clause to justify a law that discriminates among groups of persons.
>
> . . .
>
> Texas argues, however, that the sodomy law does not discriminate against homosexual persons. Instead, the State maintains that the law discriminates only against

---

[50] The Equal Protection Clause provides that "[n]o State shall ... deny to any person within its jurisdiction the equal protection of the laws." U.S. Const. amend. XIV, § 1.

homosexual conduct. While it is true that the law applies
only to conduct, the conduct targeted ... is closely
correlated with being homosexual. Under such
circumstances, Texas' sodomy law is targeted at more than
conduct. It is instead directed toward gay persons as a
class. . . .

   . . .

   A State can of course assign certain consequences to a
violation of its criminal law. But the State cannot single out
one identifiable class of citizens for punishment that does
not apply to everyone else, with moral disapproval as the
only asserted state interest for the law.

   . . .

   That this law as applied to private, consensual conduct
is unconstitutional ... does not mean that other laws
distinguishing between heterosexuals and homosexuals
would similarly fail. . . . Texas cannot assert any legitimate
state interest here, such as national security or preserving
the traditional institution of marriage. Unlike the moral
disapproval of same-sex relations ... other reasons exist to
promote the institution of marriage beyond mere moral
disapproval of an excluded group.[51]

Justice O'Connor's emphasis on unconstitutional
"discrimination," however, had the smell of a red herring. For
in general:

   A law which affects the activities of some groups differently
   from the way in which it affects the activities of other
   groups is not necessarily banned by the Fourteenth
   Amendment. . . . Otherwise, effective regulation in the

---

[51] 539 U.S. at 582, 583, 584, 585.

public interest could not be provided, however essential
that regulation might be. For it is axiomatic that the
consequence of regulation by setting apart a classified
group is that those in it will be subject to some restrictions
. . . that do not apply to other groups or to all the public. . . .
This selective application of a regulation is discrimination
in the broad sense, but it may or may not deny equal
protection of the laws.[52]

And as Justice Scalia tellingly pointed out:

On its face [the Texas statute] applies equally to all persons.
Men and women, heterosexuals and homosexuals, are all
subject to its prohibition of deviate sexual intercourse with
someone of the same sex. To be sure, [the statute] does
distinguish between the sexes insofar as concerns the
partner with whom the sexual acts are performed: men can
violate the law only with other men, and women only with
other women. But this cannot itself be a denial of equal
protection, since it is precisely the same distinction
regarding partner that is drawn in state laws prohibiting
marriage with someone of the same sex while permitting
marriage with someone of the opposite sex.[53]

That is to say, inasmuch as (heterosexual) marriage has always
been encouraged and protected by statute, and "homosexual
marriage" always prohibited,[54] the admitted discrimination
between heterosexuals and homosexuals on that score cannot
possibly constitute a denial of equal protection of the laws.

---

[52] *Kotch* v. *Board of River Port Pilots Commissioners*, 330 U.S. 552, 556 (1947).

[53] 539 U.S. at 599-600 (dissenting opinion).

[54] Until the recent decision in Massachusetts. *See Goodridge* v. *Department of Public Health*, 440 Mass. 309 (2003).

Yet, even here, Justice Scalia seemed to forget the thrust of Justice O'Connor's opinion, that denying homosexuals the same "protection of the laws" available to heterosexuals, *for none other than a reason based on morality*, is unconstitutional. Therefore, according to O'Connor's logic, limiting marriage to heterosexuals is unconstitutional *if based solely upon moral principles*, no matter how traditional they may be; or, exclusive heterosexual marriage must now be justified, if at all, on *amoral* principles alone.[55]

Of course, Justice Scalia could also have explained that "[t]he Constitution does not require things which are different in fact or opinion to be treated in law as if they were the same";[56] that the measure of equal protection has always been whether "the distinctions drawn have some basis in practical experience";[57] and that "[i]t is by . . . practical considerations based on experience rather than by theoretical inconsistencies that the question of equal protection is to be answered."[58]

That the Texas statute criminalized only homosexual sodomy and not heterosexual sodomy is not dispositive of the constitutional issue. "It is no requirement of equal protection that all evils of the same genus be eradicated or none at all."[59] "[R]emedial legislation . . . need not . . . 'strike at all evils at the

---

[55] See, however, Justice Scalia's further comments, quoted post, at 35-36, 37-38.

[56] *Tigner* v. *Texas*, 310 U.S. 141, 147 (1940).

[57] *South Carolina* v. *Katzenbach*, 383 U.S. 301, 331 (1966).

[58] *Railway Express Agency, Inc.* v. *New York*, 336 U.S. 106, 110 (1949).

[59] Ibid., citing *Central Lumber Co.* v. *South Dakota*, 226 U.S. 157, 160 (1912).

same time.'"[60] The Supreme Court has "repeatedly recognized that 'reform may take one step at a time, addressing itself to the phase of the problem which seems most acute to the legislative mind.'"[61] This is because:

> Evils in the same field may be of different dimensions and proportions, requiring different remedies. Or so the legislature may think. . . . Or the reform may take place one step at a time, addressing itself to the phase of the problem which seems most acute to the legislative mind. . . . The legislature may select one phase of one field and apply a remedy there, neglecting the others.[62]

"If a class is deemed to present a conspicuous example of what the legislature seeks to prevent, the 14th Amendment allows it to be dealt with, although otherwise and merely logically not distinguishable from others not embraced in the law."[63] And, "[s]ince [homosexual sodomy] may, in the allowable legislative judgment, give rise to moral and social problems against which it may devise preventive measures, the legislature need not go to the full length of prohibition if it believes that as to [heterosexuals] other factors are operating which either eliminate or reduce the moral and social problems otherwise calling for prohibition."[64]

---

[60] *McDonald* v. *Board of Election Commissioners*, 394 U.S. 802, 811 (1969), quoting from *Semler* v. *Dental Examiners*, 294 U.S. 608, 610 (1935).

[61] *Morey* v. *Doud*, 354 U.S. 457, 465 (1957).

[62] *Williamson* v. *Lee Optical of Oklahoma, Inc.*, 348 U.S. 483, 489 (1955).

[63] *Central Lumber Co.* v. *South Dakota*, 226 U.S. 157, 160-61 (1912).

[64] *Goesaert* v. *Cleary*, 335 U.S. 464, 466 (1948).

Moreover, Texas was not required to prove that it had a reasonable basis for criminalizing homosexual sodomy. "Legislatures are presumed to have acted constitutionally even if source materials normally resorted to for ascertaining their grounds for action are otherwise silent, and their statutory classifications will be set aside only if no grounds can be conceived to justify them."[65]

> [Courts] cannot cross examine either actually or argumentatively the mind of [State] legislators nor question their motives. Since the line they have drawn is not without a basis in reason, [judges] cannot give ear to the suggestion that the real impulse behind [a particular piece of] legislation was [improper].[66]

"One who assails the classification in [the challenged] law must carry the burden of showing that it does not rest upon any reasonable basis, but is essentially arbitrary."[67]

Nonetheless, although every Justice in *Lawrence* agreed that the promotion of traditional sexual morality was the ground asserted for the statute by Texas, and although neither the challengers nor any Justice *proved* that traditional morality was "essentially arbitrary," why was the promotion of traditional morality not a reasonable and constitutional basis for the statute? Morality would not constitute such a basis *only if the Justices took the essentially arbitrary position that all morality*

---

[65] *McDonald* v. *Board of Election Commissioners*, 394 U.S. 802, 809 (1969).

[66] *Goesaert* v. *Cleary*, 335 U.S. 464, 466-67 (1948).

[67] *Lindsley* v. *Natural Carbonic Gas Co.*, 220 U.S. 61, 78-79 (1911), followed in *Morey* v. *Doud*, 354 U.S. 457, 464 (1957).

is self-evidently essentially arbitrary. Yet that, apparently, is what six of them did, adopting, in Justice O'Connor's words, the new rule that "moral disapproval, without any other asserted state interest, is [not] a sufficient rationale" for a statute that "discriminates";[68] or, in the *Lawrence* majority's words, that "'a State has traditionally viewed a particular practice as immoral is not a sufficient reason for upholding a law prohibiting that practice'".[69]

Why, though, did these Justices not follow, or even acknowledge, the long-standing rule that "[a] statutory discrimination will not be set aside if any state of facts reasonably may be conceived to justify it."[70] Could *no* facts "reasonably . . . be conceived to justify" the Texas statute? Justice O'Connor did argue that:

> Texas cannot assert any legitimate state interest here, such as national security or preserving the traditional institution of marriage. Unlike the moral disapproval of same-sex relations . . . other reasons exist to promote the institution of marriage beyond mere moral disapproval of an excluded group.[71]

Leaving aside that it was not Texas's burden to assert such an interest, but the challengers' burden to prove and the Court's burden to conclude that *no such interest could possibly be conceived by a reasonable person*, such interests abound:

---

[68] 539 U.S. at 582.

[69] Ibid. at 571.

[70] *McGowan v. Maryland*, 366 U.S 420, 426 (1961).

[71] 539 U.S. at 585.

First, connections between homosexuality and breaches of national security are notorious.[72]

Second, everyone who reads dispatches in the daily papers from what Justice Scalia called "the culture war"[73] knows that "the traditional institution of marriage" is under incessant attack by militant homosexuals and their allies. If homosexuality is a "lifestyle" that anyone may choose (rather than an innate, irradicable, psychosexual character found in, or a powerful emotional disorder that affects, only a small percentage of the population), then the more acceptable and widespread it becomes, the worse for traditional marriage. Especially in an era of massive propaganda promoting population control, rampant abortion, divorce, and marriages deliberately rendered sterile in order to cater to narcissistic hedonism and materialism—an era in which whole countries are steadily eroding through insufficient reproduction—and an era in which programs of social insurance throughout the Western World are threatened by a shrinking base of taxable workers, any legislature could reasonably believe that legitimization of homosexual sodomy can contribute only to

---

[72] See, e.g., J. Costello, *The Mask of Treachery* (1988). Although largely set in a foreign venue, this is the most widely reported and deplored case of espionage coupled with homosexuality in the twentieth century. If Justices Kennedy, Breyer, Ginsberg, Souter, Stevens, and O'Connor were not familiar with Anthony Blunt, Guy Burgess, Kim Philby, Donald McLean, and their like, the Justices could hardly pretend to greater "insight" than the Founding Fathers or WE THE PEOPLE. *Pace* 539 U.S. at 578-79.

[73] See post, at 37-40.

social degeneration and perhaps national collapse if not suicide.

Third, no one can doubt that homosexual sodomy (and other deviant behavior in which its practitioners routinely engage) are prime contributors to the spread of AIDS and other dangerous diseases.

Thus, in addition to the promotion of morality, criminalization of homosexual sodomy (in Texas or anywhere else) could reasonably be believed by anyone to subserve national security, social welfare, public health, and even continued national existence. Indeed, anyone could easily demonstrate a real and substantial relation in reason between that prohibition and those undeniably legitimate governmental goals.[74] How then was it that Justice O'Connor (and with her the majority in Lawrence) improperly chose to "shut out of view the fact, within the knowledge of all, that the public health, the public morals, and the public safety, may be endangered"?[75]

Whatever her reason, Justice O'Connor's ultimate principle of decision was no less defective than the result to which it led. As Justice Scalia pointed out:

> [Justice O'Connor's] reasoning leaves on pretty shaky
> grounds state laws limiting marriage to opposite-sex

---

[74] Compare *Railroad Retirement Board* v. *Alton R.R.*, 295 U.S. 330, 347-48 & n.5 (1935), and *Nebbia* v. *New York*, 291 U.S. 502, 525 (1934), with *Mayflower Farms, Inc.* v. *Ten Eyck*, 297 U.S. 266, 274 (1936). See also *Rinaldi* v. *Yeager*, 384 U.S. 305, 308-10 (1966).

[75] *Mugler* v. *Kansas*, 123 U.S. 623, 662 (1887).

couples. Justice O'Connor seeks to preserve them by the conclusory statement that "preserving the traditional institution of marriage" is a legitimate state interest. . . . Texas's interest in [the statute] could be recast in similarly euphemistic terms: "preserving the traditional sexual mores of our society." *In the jurisprudence Justice O'Connor has seemingly created, judges can validate laws by characterizing them as "preserving the traditions of society" (good); or invalidate them by characterizing them as "expressing moral disapproval" (bad).*[76]

That is, under "the jurisprudence Justice O'Connor has . . . created" (and the majority opinion in Lawrence implicitly adopted), constitutional law turns, not on objective facts and circumstances, authoritative legal principles, and intellectually rigorous reasoning, but instead on the mere labels lawyers and judges contrive to apply to a situation before them in order to rationalize a preconceived result—which double-talk, of course, the Court before Lawrence had always held unconstitutional.[77]

In short, Justice O'Connor's opinion provided additional evidence (were any more needed) for the conclusions that the *United States Reports* is the most extensive, intensive, and even subversive work of legal fiction ever written—and that anything can be "proven" by artful permutation and

---

[76] 539 U.S. at 601-02 (dissenting opinion, emphasis supplied).

[77] See, e.g., *Riley v. National Federation of the Blind of North Carolina, Inc.*, 487 U.S. 781, 795-96 (1988); *City of Madison Joint School District No. 8 v. WERC*, 429 U.S. 167, 173-74 & n.5 (1976); *Bigelow v. Virginia*, 421 U.S. 809, 826 (1975); *New York Times Co. v. Sullivan*, 376 U.S. 254, 268-69 (1964); *NAACP v. Button*, 371 U.S. 415, 429 (1963).

combination, or disregard, of the Court's precedents.[78] Nonetheless, notwithstanding the vapidity of her reasoning, Justice O'Connor did add a sixth vote for *absolutely delegitimizing the promotion of morality as a constitutional basis for legislation.*

3. The third highly questionable principle in *Lawrence* is only implicit in Justice Kennedy's and Justice O'Connor's opinions—but comes to the fore in Justice Scalia's dissent, in which he adverted to "[t]his proposition"—namely, "effectively [to] decree the end of all morals legislation"—as being "so out of accord with our jurisprudence—indeed, with the jurisprudence of *any* society we know." This principle is the Judiciary's aggressively partisan participation in "the culture war."

Justice Scalia explained:

[The majority's opinion in *Lawrence*] is the product of a Court, which is the product of a law-profession culture, that has largely signed on to the so-called homosexual agenda, ... the agenda promoted by some homosexual activists directed at eliminating the moral opprobrium that has traditionally attached to homosexual conduct.... [T]he American Association of Law Schools (to which any reputable law school *must* seek to belong) excludes from

---

[78] Inasmuch as the Court has, at one time or another, approved everything from *laissez-faire* to concentration camps, to indict its *corpus juris* as grounded upon rather elastic principles is to understate the matter. Compare, e.g., *Lockner* v. *New York*, 198 U.S. 45 (1905), with *Hirabayashi* v. *United States*, 320 U.S. 81 (1943), and *Korematsu* v. *United States*, 323 U.S. 214 (1944).

membership any school that refuses to ban from its job-interview facilities a law firm (no matter how small) that does not wish to hire as a prospective partner a person who openly engages in homosexual conduct. . . .

One of the most revealing statement's in [*Lawrence*] is the Court's grim warning that the criminalization of homosexual conduct is "an invitation to subject homosexual persons to discrimination both in the public and in the private spheres." . . . *It is clear from this that the Court has taken sides in the culture war, departing from its role of assuring, as neutral observer, that the democratic rules of engagement are observed.* Many Americans do not want persons who openly engage in homosexual conduct as partners in their business, as scoutmasters for their children, as teachers in their children's schools, or as boarders in their home. They view this as protecting themselves and their families from a lifestyle that they believe to be immoral and destructive. The Court views it as "discrimination" which it is the function of our judgments to deter. So imbued is the Court with the law profession's anti-anti-homosexual culture, that it is seemingly unaware that the attitudes of that culture are not obviously "mainstream". . . .[79]

Although as accurate as it was scathing, this condemnation of judicial elitism nonetheless left unanswered the question of what ultimate goal Justices Kennedy, Breyer, Ginsberg, Souter, and Stevens (and, in light of the result of her opinion, Justice O'Connor, too) sought to accomplish by so blatantly "tak[ing] sides in the culture war." To say (as Justice Scalia did) that they were only "*seemingly* unaware that the attitudes of [the anti-

---

[79] 539 U.S. at 602-03 (separate opinion) (emphasis supplied).

anti-homosexual] culture are not obviously 'mainstream'" woefully understates the matter. The Justices composing the majority in *Lawrence* could not possibly have been "unaware" of that fact to any degree. Indeed, by referring to an admittedly *only* "*emerging* awareness" that "liberty" includes the practice of homosexual sodomy, they tacitly admitted it.[80] Why then ally themselves with that "culture"? Surely their goal cannot have been simply to promote "the *homosexual* agenda." For the majority in *Lawrence* and the "law-profession culture" as a whole are not a cult of homosexuality. Neither do they likely give a rotten fig for "the homosexual agenda" for its own sake. Rather, the more probable answer to the question Justice Scalia failed to ask is that the majority in *Lawrence* and the "law-profession culture" as a whole truly intended the natural and inevitable consequence of Justice Kennedy's and Justice O'Connor's opinions: *the delegitimization, as a basis for legislation, of all traditional morality derived from "the Laws of Nature and of Nature's God"*—even though that required the responsible Justices to align themselves with the archtypical "crime against nature." (That this process would start with the delegitimization of *sexual* morality is hardly surprising, inasmuch as exciting and pandering to human beings' lowest appetites has historically proven a successful formula for inciting social and political *renversements*.) Furthermore, these Justices intended as well the consequence of which Justice Jackson warned in *Korematsu*, that "[t]he principle" of "the amoral Constitution" that they created in *Lawrence* will now

---

[80] Ibid. at 571-72.

"lie about like a loaded weapon ready for the hand of any authority that can bring forward a plausible claim of an urgent need."[81]

4. The fourth and final highly questionable principle enunciated by the majority in *Lawrence* (but not by Justice O'Connor) is the propriety of employing *foreign* law as an authoritative source for construing the Constitution. And not only authoritative, but possibly controlling. For, as the lengthy passage from *Lawrence* quoted above concluded:

> The right the petitioners seek in this case has been accepted as an integral part of human freedom in many other countries. *There has been no showing that in this country the governmental interest in circumscribing personal choice is somehow more legitimate or urgent.*[82]

When one realizes that "the governmental interest in circumscribing personal choice" is a proxy for *the constitutional power to legislate on that matter*, the significance of this passage explodes in ambit and audacity. For it imports no less than that the powers WE THE PEOPLE delegated to the States (or Congress, for that matter) can be nullified by adventitious majorities on the Supreme Court, if WE THE PEOPLE'S representatives cannot prove to the Justices' satisfaction that their "governmental interest" "is somehow *more* legitimate or urgent" than the parallel interest of the British Parliament, the European Court of Human Rights, "[o]ther nations," and "many other countries."

---

[81] 323 U.S. at 246 (dissenting opinion).

[82] 539 U.S. at 577 (emphasis supplied).

Given that every Justice who heard *Lawrence* agreed that the so-called "rational-basis test" of constitutionality applied to the case, and inasmuch as that test has always required the courts to "assume that, if a state of facts could exist that would justify such legislation, it actually did exist when the statute . . . was passed,"[83] that the majority in *Lawrence* shifted the burden of proof to Texas constituted a signal departure from traditional constitutional doctrine. Moreover, one is entitled to wonder exactly *how* Texas *could* have "show[n]" that its "governmental interest" in criminalizing homosexual sodomy was, in fact or law, "somehow more legitimate or urgent" than the contrary "governmental interest[s]" of all those "many other countries." Insofar as Texas, on the one hand, and those "many other countries," on the other, have different social systems; different political systems; different types of governments, with different powers and disabilities; and perhaps even radically different moral values in the ascendancy among their populations—adducing convincing proof that what Texans wanted was "somehow more legitimate or urgent" than what all these foreigners wanted appears problematic. After all, what common standards of comparison and judgment would apply? Moreover, what might constitute convincing proof to Justices such as Scalia, Rehnquist, and Thomas would doubtlessly be denigrated by Justices such as Kennedy, Breyer, Ginsberg, Souter, Stevens, and O'Connor—leaving the matter, once more, to the raw force of judicial democracy.

---

[83] *Munn v. Illinois*, 94 U.S. 113, 132 (1877).

To be sure, the majority in *Lawrence* did not explicitly rely exclusively upon foreign law to bolster its decision. It adverted to:

(i) the opinions of the American Law Institute[84]—a mouthpiece of the "law-profession culture" Justice Scalia identified as a powerful influence behind the Court;[85]

(ii) the facts that some States had repealed their sodomy laws, whereas in others the laws were not being enforced[86]—all of which was irrelevant to the question of whether the States nevertheless retained the constitutional power to enact and enforce such laws if they so chose;

(iii) the Court's earlier decisions in *Planned Parenthood* v. *Casey*[87] and *Romer* v. *Evans*[88]—which the majority in *Lawrence* described as "principal cases,"[89] begging the question of whether they were any better reasoned than *Lawrence* itself;[90]

---

[84] 539 U.S. at 572.

[85] Ibid. at 602 (dissenting opinion).

[86] Ibid. at 570-71, 572, 573.

[87] 505 U.S. 833 (1992).

[88] 517 U.S. 620 (1996).

[89] 539 U.S. at 573-74.

[90] "A case that cannot be tested by principle is not *law*." Ex parte *Bollman*, 8 U.S. (4 Cranch) 75, 104 (1807) (Johnson, J., dissenting). Moreover, the "ultimate touchstone" must be "the Constitution itself and not what [the courts] have said about it." *Graves* v. *New York ex rel.* O'Keefe, 306 U.S. 466, 491-92 (1939) (Frankfurter, J., concurring, footnote omitted).

(iv) the musings of certain noted members of the domestic legal *intelligentsia* who disagreed with *Bowers*[91]—again, uncritically accepted as meritorious;

(v) the fact that several State courts had interpreted their *State* constitutions contrary to *Bowers*[92]—a circumstance irrelevant to how the Constitution *of the United States* should be construed; and

(vi) foreign law.[93]

Yet, inasmuch as sources (ii) and (v) were legally irrelevant, and (i) and (iv) nothing but makeweights to impart intellectual *gravitas* to the majority's decision, the only *real* authorities (if authorities at all) were (iii) and (vi).

Casey and *Romer*, however, did not drive the majority's decision in *Lawrence*, but merely provided an excuse for allotting what amounted to decisive weight to foreign law. First, those two cases were not precedents for the majority's decision in *Lawrence*. *Casey* dealt, not with homosexual sodomy, but with abortion. Justice Kennedy cited it for his conclusion that "[p]ersons in a homosexual relationship may seek autonomy for the purposes [of the most intimate and personal choices], just as heterosexual persons do," because:

"At the heart of liberty is the right to define one's own concept of existence, of meaning, of the universe, and of the mystery of human life. Beliefs about these matters could

---

[91] 539 U.S. at 567-68, 576.

[92] Ibid. at 576.

[93] Ibid. at 572-73, 576-77.

not define the attributes of personhood were they formed under compulsion of the State."[94]

On its face, this equation of constitutional "liberty" with what Kennedy called "the autonomy of the person in making . . . choices"[95] is false, because it directly repudiates "the Laws of Nature and of Nature's God," which deny unfettered personal "autonomy" on the ground that only knowing and adhering to the truth can set men free. In any event, even if the constitutional right to hold "[b]eliefs about these matters"—or any other matters, for that matter—may be considered *absolute*,[96] the "liberty" to engage in conduct based on different beliefs is not. "Liberty" has always been subject to restraint in the interest of human welfare and social order. Yet no one's beliefs are "formed under compulsion of the State" just because his conduct based on those beliefs is proscribed. Surely, anyone can continue to believe that X is right, even though the State says that it is wrong. Moreover, were one's beliefs always "formed under compulsion of the State" when conduct based on those beliefs was proscribed, then essentially no conduct could ever be proscribed, because someone could always complain that his beliefs were thereby being unconstitutionally "formed under compulsion." After all, *every* kind of conduct—from the saintly nursing of Mother Teresa to the satanic murders of Charles Manson—can claim sanction in *someone's* "own concept of existence, of meaning, of the

---

[94] 539 U.S. at 574, quoting *Casey*, 505 U.S. at 851.

[95] Ibid. at 574.

[96] *Cantwell* v. *Connecticut*, 310 U.S. 296, 303 (1940).

universe, and of the mystery of human life." In short, on the point for which Justice Kennedy cited it, *Casey* was fundamentally nonsensical.

Romer, too, was beside the point in *Lawrence*, because it "struck down class-based legislation directed at homosexuals as a violation of the Equal Protection Clause," an issue the *Lawrence* majority did not decide (although it was the basis for Justice O'Connor's concurring opinion).[97] In addition, the statute *sub judice* in *Romer* was held to have been "born of animosity toward [homosexuals]" and to "ha[ve] no rational relation to a legitimate governmental purpose";[98] whereas, the statute challenged in *Lawrence* had been enacted to promote traditional morality, which prior to *Lawrence* had always been a legitimate governmental goal.

Second, the majority in *Lawrence* used the contention that "[t]he foundations of *Bowers* have sustained serious erosion from . . . *Casey* and *Romer*" to rationalize its conclusion that, "[w]hen our precedent has been thus weakened, *criticism from other sources is of greater significance.*"[99] Of these "sources," the critically important one was foreign law.[100] For the *Lawrence* majority followed its recitation of foreign opinions about "the protected right of homosexual adults" with the conclusion that Texas was required to but had not overcome this supposed

---

[97] 539 U.S. at 574.

[98] Ibid.

[99] Ibid. at 576 (emphasis supplied).

[100] The other two were the irrelevant authorities noted in paragraphs (ii) and (v), ante, at 42 and 43.

proof, because "[t]here has been no showing that in this country the governmental interest in circumscribing personal choice [in committing sodomy] is somehow more legitimate or urgent" than in foreign lands.[101]

In sum, foreign law not only was a very important component of the majority's decision in Lawrence, but also could be deemed the controlling component.

This should hardly be surprising, as the invasion of American law, and especially American constitutional law, by foreign law is a major front in "the culture war"—one of the ultimate goals of the cosmopolitan political and legal elite being to submerge in a New World Order "the separate and equal station [among the powers of the earth] to which the Laws of Nature and of Nature's God entitle" WE THE PEOPLE.

Indeed, it is possible to conclude even that foreign law was *doubly controlling* in *Lawrence*, inasmuch as Justice Kennedy's ruling—"[t]he rationale of *Bowers* [v. *Hardwick*] does not withstand careful analysis" because "'the fact that the governing majority in a State has traditionally viewed a particular practice as immoral is not a sufficient reason for upholding a law prohibiting the practice'"[102]—and Justice O'Connor's concurrence—"the State cannot single out one identifiable class of citizens for punishment that does not apply to everyone else, with moral disapproval as the only asserted

---

[101] 539 U.S. at 577.

[102] Ibid.

THE SUPREME COURT'S DECISION IN
LAWRENCE V. TEXAS

state interest for the law"[103]—both summarily struck from American law, *but not on the basis of American law*, a principle recognized therein since well before the Declaration's invocation of "the Laws of Nature and of Nature's God." This is evident from the reason Justice Kennedy offered in *Lawrence* for why "*Bowers* v. *Hardwick* should be and now is overruled": that, "[t]o the extent *Bowers* relied on values we share with a wider civilization, . . . the reasoning and holding of *Bowers* have been rejected elsewhere," in "[o]ther nations" and "in many other countries."[104] One may justifiably question whether the Kennedyesque principle that legislation must be amoral is a "value we share with a wider *civilization*," or exactly who is the "we" who share this value (besides the Justices, their clerks, and the "law-profession culture," together with those whose interests it advances)—but one cannot doubt that the principle is *foreign*, through and through. The historical source of Justice Kennedy's notions is open to debate. Surely, it long antedates the European Convention on Human Rights, the European Court of Human Rights, and such luminaries as Irish politician and *amicus curiae* Mary Robinson, upon whose ruminations and opinions he relied.[105] In the modern world, the amorality of law and politics is a fundamental dogma of Marxism-Leninism-Stalinism, which still permeates the thinking of Kennedy's "wider civilization" today. At length, it is traceable to the cynicism of Pontius

---

[103] Ibid. at 584 (separate opinion).

[104] Ibid. at 576-77. See ibid. at 572-73.

[105] Ibid. at 573, 576-77.

Pilate: "What is truth?" and to the boast of the Chief Priests: "We have no king but Caesar!"[106] In any event, *Lawrence* has now made it possible for illegal aliens to cross America's borders into her very laws, as well as into her physical territory.

What portends an especially ominous future, then, is the likely employment in other cases of *all* the noxious principles the majority in *Lawrence* simultaneously invoked: that is, the amalgamation of "the living Constitution," "the amoral Constitution," and foreign law that "point[s] in an opposite direction" from "Judeo-Christian moral and ethical standards,"[107] in prosecution of "the culture war." *Lawrence* having established the precedent:

> The principle then lies about like a loaded weapon ready for the hand of any authority that can bring forward a plausible claim of an urgent need. Every repetition imbeds the principle more deeply into our law and thinking and expands it to new purposes.... [This] passing incident becomes the doctrine of the Constitution. *There it has a generative power of its own, and all it creates will be in its own image.*[108]

What unconstitutional Frankenstein's monster *Lawrence's* principles may "create" in the future is difficult to predict with clarity, because their present "image" is fuzzy. Justice

---

[106] John 18:38, 19:15.

[107] 539 U.S. at 572.

[108] *Korematsu* v. *United States*, 323 U.S. 214, 246 (1944) (Jackson, J., dissenting) (footnote omitted, emphasis supplied).

Kennedy's opinion suggested, let alone established, *no intelligible standards* by which to determine such important matters as:

> ➤ With respect to what American constitutional issues is recourse to foreign law appropriate *vel non*?

> ➤ Which statutes, judicial decisions, administrative rulings, executive decrees, and so forth of what foreign nations or international organizations may the Supreme Court consult?

> ➤ Will the laws of some foreign nations or international organizations take precedence over others? Or will the laws of some foreign nations or organizations be excluded from consideration because of the natures of their political regimes, social or economic structures, or cultures? And,

> ➤ Whose interpretations of the foreign laws, decisions, rulings, and decrees that qualify for consideration will ultimately control—those of foreign authorities, or those of shifting majorities of Justices of the Supreme Court?

These and other uncertainties aside, Justices in future cases need not pour out *Lawrence's* toxic cocktail solely to declare statutes *un*constitutional. The same judicial pilpulism that can contract legislative or executive power on the basis of these principles can just as readily expand it to suit the interests of the "law-profession culture" and those whom it serves.

For one very likely example, the Justices could easily look to foreign lawmakers of political bents even more socialistic or fascistic than their American counterparts to discern an "emerging awareness" as to what sorts of legislation the "international community" considers appropriate to deal with supposed economic or social problems—and then translate these findings into an expansive definition of the means Congress may employ as "necessary and proper" in the exercise of its powers, as against individuals or the States.[109]

For an even more dangerous example, in *Knox* v. *Lee*,[110] the Supreme Court upheld on egregiously dubious grounds the constitutionality of legal-tender United States Notes.[111] In his opinion for the Court, Justice Strong contended that the General Government enjoys "the right to employ freely every means, not prohibited, necessary for its preservation," and that the selection of such means is "left to the discretion of Congress."[112] Concurring with a decisive fifth vote, Justice Bradley argued that the General Government "is invested with all those inherent and implied powers which, at the time of adopting the Constitution, were generally considered to belong to every government as such, and as being essential to its functions."[113] If, perforce of *Lawrence*, the practices of

---

[109] See U.S. Const. art. I, § 8, cl. 18.

[110] 79 U.S. (12 Wall.) 457 (1871).

[111] See E. Vieira, Jr., *Pieces of Eight: The Monetary Powers and Disabilities of the United States Constitution* (2d rev. ed. 2002), at 599-651.

[112] 79 U.S. (12 Wall.) at 533-34.

[113] Ibid. at 556 (separate opinion). See also *Juilliard* v. *Greenman*, 110 U.S. 421, 447 (1884). On the many errors in this decision, see generally, E. Vieira, Jr., *Pieces of Eight*, ante note 111, at 651-65.

foreign governments can establish what "inherent and implied powers" might be considered "essential to [the General Government's] functions" in ordinary times, let alone what powers might be deemed "necessary for its preservation" in periods of crisis, one must gape with wonder at what powers would *not* be allowable, save those the Constitution expressly prohibits. And probably not even those prohibited powers, either. For whenever politicians—in legislatures or courts— prate fulsomely about the "functions" *of government* and *"its* preservation," they typically mean the functions *they* desire to perform, and the preservation of *their* personal or party power. And nothing is a more corrosive solvent of constitutional limitations than the acid of political careerists' self-interest. Besides, in *Lawrence*, Justice Kennedy has already denigrated "those who drew and ratified . . . the Fifth Amendment or the Fourteenth Amendment" as lacking the "insight" of modern jurists.[114] If these Framers were "blind . . . to certain truths . . . that laws once thought necessary and proper in fact serve only to oppress," perhaps they were also blind to certain truths that laws once thought only oppressive are in fact necessary and proper. One can be sure, in any event, that "whenever a wrong principle of conduct, political or personal, is adopted on a plea of necessity, it will be afterwards followed on a plea of convenience."[115]

At a minimum, Americans can expect the courts, under the aegis of *Lawrence*, to employ "the living Constitution" and

---

[114] See 539 U.S. at 578-79.

[115] *Juilliard* v. *Greenman*, 110 U.S. 421, 458 (1884) (Field, J., dissenting).

foreign law steadily to inject into this country's *corpus juris* the thoroughgoing amorality of the rest of the contemporary world, until not only is legislation that promotes traditional morality held unconstitutional, but also legislation that prohibits supposedly "discriminatory" manifestations of that morality is held constitutional.

And at the maximum? No one can say what deep inroads the infusion of foreign law into the Constitution can make upon the rights, privileges, and immunities found within the Bill of Rights and protected under the rubrics "privileges and immunities," "life," "liberty," and "property" within Section 1 of the Fourteenth Amendment:

> ➤ Victims of governmentally sponsored euthanasia may be discovered to have no right to "life," because "an emerging awareness" in foreign lands informs the Justices that the true meaning of "life" focuses on its quality, not its bare existence.

> ➤ Through their special "insight," the Justices may discover that "[s]earches and seizures" characteristic of foreign police states are not "unreasonable" here.[116] Or that preventive detention without (or only with exorbitant) bail is permissible.[117]

> ➤ Some other judicial "insight" may rationalize suppression of political dissent against the "war on drugs," the "war on terrorism," or shooting wars, police

---

[116] Contrast U.S. Const. amend. IV.

[117] Contrast U.S. Const. amend. VIII.

actions, or bloody peace-keeping forays, because such criticisms give aid and comfort to some supposed enemy, and therefore are not properly within "freedom of speech" as that concept has come to be understood internationally.[118]

> Perhaps from the practices of countries with histories of serial atheistic gangster governments, such as Mexico,[119] the Justices will absorb an "emerging awareness" that the holding of public office by persons with strong religious convictions, or the participation in politics by institutions such as churches, their leaders, or even their members amounts to an unconstitutional "establishment of religion," even though "no religious Test shall ever be required as a Qualification to any Office or public Trust under the United States."[120] Or perhaps they will absorb it from domestic sources, inasmuch as such an equation of personal religious beliefs with improper "establishment" already has its exponents among cultural Bolsheviks in the Senate of the United States, where it appears (if so far in muted form) as a disqualifying "litmus test" applied to candidates for judicial appointment who oppose abortion to any degree out of religious conviction. And,

---

[118] Contrast U.S. Const. amend. I.

[119] See, e.g., F. Kelly, *Blood-Drenched Altars* (1935); M. Kenny, *No God Next Door* (1935); W. Parson, *Mexican Martyrdom* (1936).

[120] U.S. Const. art. VI, cl. 3.

➢ Notwithstanding that "[t]he right of the citizens to keep and bear arms has justly been considered as the palladium of the liberties of a republic,"[121] surely that right will be eviscerated, because "liberty" in most foreign countries does not encompass private individuals' possession of handguns or high-powered rifles, or even any kind of firearm.

But if *Lawrence's* use of foreign law to interpret the Constitution "lies about like a loaded weapon ready for the hand of any authority that can bring forward a plausible claim of an urgent need," what are the means for and likelihood of "gun control" in this instance? To answer that question requires reversion to fundamental principles.

---

[121] 2 J. Story, *Commentaries on the Constitution of the United States* (5th ed. 1891), § 1897, at 646, referring to U.S. Const. amend. II. Story's *Commentaries* are recognized as a standard work in constitutional law. E.g., *Field* v. *Clark*, 143 U.S. 649, 670-71 (1892).

CHAPTER 2

"Original Intent" as to the Use of Foreign Law in Constitutional Interpretation

A. What America's Founding Fathers denominated "the General Government" (and most people today mistakenly call "the Federal Government"[122]) derives its powers solely from the grant, or delegation, WE THE PEOPLE made, and continue to make, in the Constitution: "WE THE PEOPLE of the United States ... do ordain and establish this

---

[122] As the Constitution makes pellucid, "the Federal Government" actually consists of *five* parts: Congress—under Article I, § 1 ("[a]ll legislative Powers herein granted shall be vested in a Congress of the United States"); the President—under Article II, § 1 ("[t]he executive Power of the United States, shall be vested in a President of the United States of America"); the judiciary—under Article III, § 1 ("[t]he judicial Power of the United States, shall be vested in one supreme Court, and in such inferior Courts as the Congress shall from time to time ordain and establish"); the States—under the Tenth Amendment ("[t]he powers not delegated to the United States by the Constitution, nor prohibited by it to the States, are reserved to the States respectively, or to the people"); and WE THE PEOPLE—under the Preamble, the Tenth Amendment, and the Ninth Amendment ("[t]he enumeration in the Constitution, of certain rights, shall not be construed to deny or disparage others retained by the people").

Constitution for the United States of America."[123] The
Constitution expresses WE THE PEOPLE'S will in "authoritative
language."[124] It is the sole expression of that will. The verb "*do*
ordain*,*" in the present tense, not "have ordained," in the past
tense, implies the continuous nature of the delegation through
time, and with it the *permanent* assertion of WE THE PEOPLE'S
supreme temporal authority. The original, creative,
authoritative power is in WE THE PEOPLE, *not* in "we the
Judiciary" (or any other branch of the General Government),
which can exercise only derivative power. Moreover, the
Constitution was adopted by "WE THE PEOPLE *of the United
States,*" *not* "we the people" of any foreign nation or
international or supranational political entity. It is a
"Constitution *for the United States of America,*" not for any
foreign nation, or to be or serve as a vehicle for promoting the
interests of any foreign nation or international or supranational
political entity. And, ultimately, it is a Constitution for "WE
THE PEOPLE of the United States" *themselves* "to form a more
perfect Union, establish Justice, insure domestic Tranquility,
provide for the common defence, promote the general
Welfare, and secure the Blessings of Liberty"—all for "*ourselves
and our Posterity,*"[125] not for any foreign nation or international
or supranational political entity. Indeed, the "more perfect
Union" to which WE THE PEOPLE refer in the Constitution is
the "Union" derived from the Declaration of Independence,

---

[123] U.S. Const. preamble.

[124] E.g., *Cohens* v. *Virginia*, 19 U.S. (6 Wheat.) 264, 381 (1821).

[125] U.S. Const. preamble.

which "solemnly publish[ed] and declare[d], That the [thirteen] United Colonies are, and of Right ought to be FREE AND INDEPENDENT STATES," "to assume among the powers of the earth, the separate and equal station to which the Laws of Nature and of Nature's God entitle them."

The Supreme Court has never explicitly denied that, because "[t]he government of the United States was born of the Constitution,"[126] it "derives its authority wholly from powers delegated to it in the Constitution,"[127] and that "[t]he United States is entirely a creature of the Constitution. Its powers and authority have no other source. It can only act in accordance with . . . the Constitution."[128] Rather, the Court has consistently held that, outside of the Constitution, the General Government lacks all authority, power, and claim of right.[129] Specifically:

> ➤ "The government of the United States is one of delegated powers alone. Its authority is defined . . . by the Constitution."[130]

---

[126] *Downes* v. *Bidwell*, 182 U.S. 244, 288 (1901) (White, J., concurring).

[127] *Graves* v. *New York* ex rel. *O'Keefe*, 306 U.S. 466, 477 (1939).

[128] *Reid* v. *Covert*, 354 U.S. 1, 5-6 (1957) (opinion of Black, J.) (footnotes omitted).

[129] See, e.g., *Martin* v. *Hunter's Lessee*, 14 U.S. (1 Wheat.) 304, 326 (1816); *McCulloch* v. *Maryland*, 17 U.S. (4 Wheat.) 316, 405 (1819); *Scott* v. *Sandford*, 60 U.S. (19 How.) 393, 451 (1857); *United States* v. *Cruikshank*, 92 U.S. 542, 551 (1876).

[130] *United States* v. *Cruikshank*, 92 U.S. 542, 551 (1876).

➤ "[N]o department of the government of the United States—neither [the] President, nor Congress, nor the Courts—possesses any power not given by the Constitution."[131] And,

➤ "[T]he powers actually granted must be such as are expressly given, or given by necessary implication."[132]

B. *Delegated* powers are, in the nature of things, *limited* powers. For instance, a grant of "all legislative power" or "all judicial power" is limited to such power as is "legislative" or "judicial" in character. Even a grant of "all power" is limited to the power the grantor actually enjoys the privilege to delegate. For that reason, the very existence of the Constitution establishes that the powers of the General Government are not only delegated, but also definite, and limited by their very definition[133]—and can extend only to those powers WE THE PEOPLE have the competence to grant. For example, inasmuch as "tyranny" is a set of powers—including, for instance, the power to wantonly kill innocent human beings—that *no one* may claim a right to exercise, even WE THE PEOPLE could not delegate tyrannical powers to their government.[134] And the

---

[131] *Ex parte* Milligan, 71 U.S. (4 Wall.) 2, 136-37 (1866) (opinion of Chase, C.J.). Accord, *Ex parte* Quirin, 317 U.S. 1, 25 (1942).

[132] *Martin* v. *Hunter's Lessee*, 14 U.S. (1 Wheat.) 304, 326 (1816). Accord, *McCulloch* v. *Maryland*, 17 U.S. (4 Wheat.) 316, 405 (1819).

[133] See, e.g., *Marbury* v. *Madison*, 5 U.S. (1 Cranch) 137, 176-80 (1803); *Kansas* v. *Colorado*, 206 U.S. 46, 89-90 (1907); *Myers* v. *United States*, 272 U.S. 52, 230-31 (1926) (McReynolds, J., dissenting).

[134] See J. Locke, *An Essay Concerning the True Original, Extent, and End of Civil Government* (P. Laslett ed. 1960), § 199.

Supreme Court has recognized as much: "There are . . . rights in every free government beyond the control of the State. . . . There are limitations on [governmental power] which grow out of the essential nature of all free governments. Implied reservations of individual rights, without which the social compact could not exist. . . ."[135] Therefore, the Constitution contains no undefined and general powers, that "some theoretical government" might possess[136]—or *a fortiori* that some actual foreign governments happen to exercise. Neither could it contain any "independent and unmentioned power[s]"—for that would "conflict with the doctrine that this is a government of enumerated powers."[137] Instead, the General Government's every claim of power must find direct support in a constitutional grant, "in terms or by necessary implication."[138] And the "burden of establishing a delegation of power to the United States . . . is upon those making the claim."[139]

Even the Necessary and Proper Clause[140] is no exception to this rule. That Clause authorizes Congress "[t]o make all Laws which shall be necessary and proper for carrying into

---

[135] *Loan Association* v. *City of Topeka*, 87 U.S. (20 Wall.) 655, 663 (1875).

[136] *Kansas* v. *Colorado*, 206 U.S. 46, 81 (1907); *Myers* v. *United States*, 272 U.S. 52, 230 (1926) (McReynolds, J., dissenting).

[137] *Kansas* v. *Colorado*, 206 U.S. 46, 88, 89 (1907).

[138] Ibid. at 83-84; *Downes* v. *Bidwell*, 182 U.S. 244, 288 (1901) (White, J., concurring).

[139] *Bute* v. *Illinois*, 333 U.S. 640, 653 (1948).

[140] U.S. Const. art. I, § 8, cl. 18.

Execution . . . all . . . Powers vested by this Constitution in the Government of the United States." Thus, on its face it is "not the delegation of a new and independent power, but simply provision for making effective [the enumerated constitutional] powers"[141]—and thereby depends upon and can operate only within the ambit of those powers. The Necessary and Proper Clause cannot inflate any other "Power vested by th[e] Constitution" beyond that power's otherwise legitimate scope within the letter and spirit of the Constitution[142]—because the "Laws" it sanctions must be "necessary *and proper for carrying into Execution*" such other power *as it exists*, not as a specious reading of the Necessary and Proper Clause might *extend* it. Therefore, the Necessary and Proper Clause does not license— but, properly construed, prohibits—the limitless implication of new powers "by conjecture, supposition, or mere reasoning on the meaning or intention of the writing" in the Constitution.[143] As the Supreme Court ruled long ago, "[l]et the end be legitimate, let it be within the scope of the constitution, and all means which are appropriate, which are plainly adapted to that end, which are not prohibited, but consist with letter and spirit of the constitution, are constitutional."[144] That is, "Laws which shall be necessary and proper" depend upon "the scope of the [C]onstitution," its "prohibit[ions]," and its "letter and spirit"

---

[141] *Kansas* v. *Colorado*, 206 U.S. 46, 88 (1907). Accord, *Kinsella* v. *United States* ex rel. *Singleton*, 361 U.S. 234, 247 (1960).

[142] *Reid* v. *Covert*, 354 U.S. 1, 20-22 (1957) (opinion of Black, J.).

[143] *Rhode Island* v. *Massachusetts*, 37 U.S. (12 Pet.) 657, 723 (1838).

[144] *McCulloch* v. *Maryland*, 17 U.S. (4 Wheat.) 316, 421 (1819).

outside and independent of the Necessary and Proper Clause itself. All this, of course, is in keeping with what the Tenth Amendment makes strikingly clear, that the *only* powers the General Government may exercise are those "delegated . . . by the Constitution." And because "[t]h[e General G]overnment is . . . one of *enumerated powers,*"[145] *there necessarily can be no "inherent" governmental authority of any kind*: "[P]owers not granted are prohibited."[146]

C. Nothing is better settled than that, as to what the Supreme Court curiously calls "fundamental rights":[147]

> The very purpose of [the] Bill of Rights was to withdraw certain subjects from the vicissitudes of political controversy, to place them beyond the reach of majorities and officials and to establish them as legal principles to be applied by the courts. One's right to life, liberty, and property, to free speech, a free press, freedom of worship and assembly, and other fundamental rights may not be

---

[145] Ibid. at 405 (emphasis supplied).

[146] *United States* v. *Butler,* 297 U.S. 1, 68 (1936).

[147] One would think that *all* constitutional rights are fundamental rights, by virtue of their recognition in "the supreme Law of the Land." U.S. Const. art. VI, cl. 2. But the Supreme Court's reasoning is apparently more subtle. In any event, *United States* v. *Carolene Products Co.,* 304 U.S. 144, 152 & n.4 (1938), appears to be the origin for the Court's specious dichotomy between "economic" and "social" rights, which supposedly are entitled to only a minimum of constitutional protection, and "fundamental rights," which are entitled to "more exacting judicial scrutiny." See generally, Vieira, "Rights and the United States Constitution: The Declension From Natural Law to Legal Positivism," 13 *Georgia Law Review* 1447 (1979). And see *Lynch* v. *Household Finance Corp.,* 405 U.S. 538, 542-52 (1972).

submitted to vote; they depend on the outcome of no elections.[148]

This principle of political inviolability—of withdrawal of "the supreme Law of the Land"[149] from the naked control of representative institutions, let alone simple majoritarian democracy, while subject to the extraordinary power of amendment[150]—logically applies, however, to *every* provision of the Constitution, be it classified as a right, power, privilege, or immunity. For the Bill of Rights explicitly defines but a small part of "the Blessings of Liberty,"[151] to "secure" which WE THE PEOPLE "do ordain and establish this Constitution" as a whole (even before the Bill of Rights was ratified).[152] *No* election means just that: Neither votes for Representatives, Senators, or the President; nor votes in Congress; nor votes among the Justices of the Supreme Court can change the Constitution. The powers WE THE PEOPLE have delegated to the General Government are not to be either increased or decreased; the rights, powers, privileges, and immunities WE THE PEOPLE have secured, retained, and reserved for themselves are not to be infringed; and the overarching purposes of the Constitution are not to be defeated, diminished, or disregarded by the actions of that government or any branch thereof. "[I]t is impossible to conceive that

---

[148] *West Virginia State Board of Education* v. *Barnette*, 319 U.S. 624, 638 (1943).

[149] U.S. Const. art. VI, cl. 2.

[150] U.S. Const. art. V.

[151] See U.S. Const. amend. IX. See also U.S. Const. amend. XIII.

[152] U.S. Const. preamble.

where conditions are brought about to which any particular provision of the Constitution applies, its controlling influence may be frustrated by the action of any or all of the departments of the government."[153]

Moreover, if constitutional principles "may not be submitted to vote" and "depend on the outcome of no elections" *domestically*, they cannot possibly be held hostage or interpreted and applied according to the outcome of *foreign* elections or other forms of political decision-making. After all, *every* invasion, injection, or even insinuation of foreign law into America's constitutional *corpus juris*, for whatever purpose and to whatever degree, necessarily contradicts, subverts, and destroys *pro tanto* the "separate and equal station" "among the powers of the earth"[154] of the "more perfect Union" for which WE THE PEOPLE "do ordain and establish this Constitution."[155] And, as Justice Jackson warned, every such invasion, injection, or insinuation will have "a generative power of its own, and all that it creates will be in its own image."[156]

D. Inasmuch as the Constitution cannot be changed other than through formal amendments, it cannot be changed through the rhetorical thimblerigging of specious "construction" or "interpretation." The Constitution, however, contains no provision explicitly setting out a rule for

---

[153] *Downes* v. *Bidwell*, 182 U.S. 244, 289 (1901) (White, J., concurring).

[154] Declaration of Independence.

[155] U.S. Const. preamble. It is not for nothing that "to form a more perfect Union" is set *first* among the Preamble's goals.

[156] *Korematsu* v. *United States*, 323 U.S. 214, 246 (1944) (dissenting opinion).

its own construction and interpretation. This raises two questions: First, who decides what rule of construction and interpretation is proper in constitutional law? Second, what is that rule?

1. Contrary to the present-day fetish among the legal *intelligentsia*, "judicial supremacy" through "judicial review"— the notion that courts, and particularly the Supreme Court of the United States, are the ultimate and unreviewable interpreters of the Constitution—is a delusion. The undeniable historical and legal realities are that WE THE PEOPLE, not "we the judges," enacted the Constitution, and that "[t]he power to enact carries with it final authority to declare the meaning of the legislation."[157] At the time the Constitution was ratified, Blackstone's *Commentaries on the Laws of England*[158] "had been published about twenty years, and it has been said that more copies of the work had been sold in this country than in England, so that undoubtedly the framers of the Constitution were familiar with it."[159] Blackstone taught that *"the law,* and the *opinion of the judge* are not always convertible terms, or one and the same thing; since it sometimes may happen that the judge may *mistake* the law"—and that, "whenever a question arises between the society at large and any magistrate vested with powers originally delegated by that society, it must be decided by the voice of the society itself: there is not upon

---

[157] *Propper* v. *Clark*, 337 U.S. 472, 484 (1949).

[158] W. Blackstone, *Commentaries on the Laws of England* (Amer. ed., 4 Vols. & App., 1771-1773).

[159] *Schick* v. *United States*, 195 U.S. 65, 69 (1904).

earth any other tribunal to resort to."[160] This gives no credence, let alone comfort, to the idea that WE THE PEOPLE in the late 1700s could have believed on any plausible legal ground that Justices of the Supreme Court would be infallible expositors of constitutional law, or that their pronouncements, no matter how erroneous or even fraudulent, would bind WE THE PEOPLE themselves, and be capable of being overridden only by amendment of the Constitution. And the actual history of "judicial review" (or perhaps more accurately put, the *absence* of any such history) in America during that era proves the point beyond cavil.[161]

2. The rule of legal construction that WE THE PEOPLE employed in the late 1700s (and must, absent amendment of the Constitution, continue to use today) is "original intent" or "original meaning." "Original intent" does not attempt to draw from the personal, perhaps idiosyncratic, beliefs of the individual Framers who participated in the Federal Convention of 1787 the meaning of constitutional provisions. Because, as with any legislation, "it is impossible to determine with certainty what construction" the Framers as a whole put upon—or, more importantly, *should* have put upon—the Constitution, simply "by resorting to the speeches of individual[s],"[162] those being "so often influenced by personal

---

[160] 1 *Commentaries* at 71, 212.

[161] See, e.g., 2 W. Crosskey, *Politics and the Constitution in the History of the United States* (1953), ch. XXVII.

[162] *United States* v. *Trans-Missouri Freight Association*, 166 U.S. 290, 318 (1897). Accord, *United States* v. *Wong Kim Ark*, 169 U.S. 649, 699 (1898).

or political considerations, or by the assumed necessities of the situation."[163] Besides, the Framers themselves constituted a decided minority among the delegates to the State conventions that ratified the Constitution, let alone among WE THE PEOPLE by whom those conventions were chosen and influenced, and for whom they spoke. So "original intent" poses the question: What would the Constitution have meant to a typical, educated American conversant with Anglo-American law in the late 1700s?

To answer this question, "original intent" turns to the only *objective* evidence WE THE PEOPLE have today—indeed, the only objective evidence WE THE PEOPLE had then: namely, the actual language of the Constitution, then-contemporary definitions and usages of words and phrases, *pre*-constitutional legal precedents, then-current legal and political theory, and Anglo-American history. As Blackstone taught:

> THE fairest and most rational method to interpret the will of the legislator, is by exploring his intentions at the time when the law was made, by *signs* the most natural and probable. And these signs are either the words, the context, the subject matter, the effects and consequence, or the spirit and reason of the law.[164]

Thus, as Blackstone evidences, this approach is not anachronistic. Indeed, at the founding of the Republic the doctrine of "original intent" was already hundreds of years

---

[163] *Downes* v. *Bidwell*, 182 U.S. 244, 254 (1901).

[164] 1 *Commentaries*, ante note 158, at 59.

old.[165] And out of necessity, as well as familiarity, "original intent" became the interpretive method of the Framers who drafted the Constitution, of WE THE PEOPLE who ratified it, and of the first national governments that applied it. For what rule of construction could Americans have employed to interpret the newly ratified Constitution other than to ask what it meant to them at that time, by reading its words in their then-current linguistic, legal, political, and historical contexts? No judicial, legislative, or executive precedents under the Constitution existed upon which WE THE PEOPLE could draw. No legal sophists had yet popularized the fantasy that the Constitution, as a supposedly "living" document, was capable of protean meanings that would "evolve" over time in response to different political, economic, and social circumstances—and, if they had, their imaginings would have been irrelevant to the issue of what the Constitution meant then and there, before any supposed "evolution" took place. To serve its purpose, then, the Constitution had to be interpreted and applied at that moment according to some generally knowable and fixed meaning—a meaning that every legally literate individual in the United States doubtlessly presumed to exist in, and to be capable of elucidation from, the Constitution's text itself, read in the context of the times.

Therefore, (i) inasmuch as Americans of that era were thoroughly familiar with "original intent," the Framers must have employed "original intent" when they composed the

---

[165] See, e.g., Berger, "Original Intention in Historical Perspective," 54 *George Washington Law Review* 101 (1986).

HOW TO DETHRONE THE IMPERIAL JUDICIARY

Constitution, and WE THE PEOPLE must have utilized "original intent" when they ratified it, because otherwise no one could have known with any semblance of surety what the Constitution meant; and (ii) inasmuch as "original intent" could have supplied a construction of all the Constitution's provisions, as everyone at that time must have presumed— then "original intent," by practical necessity and historical and legal absence of any alternative, must be the *exclusive* means of interpreting the Constitution, not just for the late 1700s and early 1800s, but *for all time.*

E. "Original intent" starts with *the Constitution's* "intent," which must be derived from *its words.*

1. "Why not assume that the framers of the Constitution, and the people who voted it into existence, meant exactly what it says?"[166] Rehearsing this exhortation would be trivial, were it not that Justices of the Supreme Court, again and again in their opinions, have substituted for the Constitution's *actual* verbiage their "own verbal formula[s]" in order "to reshape the Constitution in accordance with predilections of what is deemed desirable."[167]

---

[166] *Lake County Commissioners* v. *Rollins*, 130 U.S. 662, 670 (1889).

[167] *Coleman* v. *Alabama*, 399 U.S. 1, 23 (1970) (Burger, J., dissenting). See, e.g., Ex parte *Wells*, 59 U.S. (18 How.) 307, 314 (1856): "It not infrequently happens in discussions upon the Constitution, that an involuntary change is made in the words of it, or in their order, from which, as they are used, there may be a logical conclusion, though it be different from what the Constitution is in fact. And even though the change may appear to be equivalent, it will be found upon reflection not to convey the full meaning of the words used in the Constitution."

Thus, the Supreme Court has traditionally recognized—and, perhaps surprisingly, has never denied—that the Framers of the Constitution, writing for WE THE PEOPLE, employed words in "their natural sense";[168] in their "natural and obvious sense";[169] in their "natural signification";[170] with their "natural meaning";[171] with their "normal and ordinary . . . meaning";[172] with the meaning they had "in common use,"[173] in the "common parlance of the times,"[174] or in "ordinary acceptation";[175] according to "ordinary and common usage";[176] in a "sense most obvious to . . . common understanding";[177]

---

[168] *Gibbons* v. *Ogden*, 22 U.S. (9 Wheat.) 1, 188 (1824); *McPherson* v. *Blacker*, 146 U.S. 1, 27 (1892); *South Carolina* v. *United States*, 199 U.S. 437, 449 (1905).

[169] *The Pocket Veto Case*, 279 U.S. 655, 679 (1929).

[170] *Lake County Commissioners* v. *Rollins*, 130 U.S. 662, 670 (1889).

[171] *Wright* v. *United States*, 302 U.S. 583, 588 (1938).

[172] *United States* v. *Sprague*, 282 U.S. 716, 731 (1931); *Green* v. *United States*, 356 U.S. 165, 210 (1958) (Black, J., dissenting).

[173] *Tennessee* v. *Whitworth*, 117 U.S. 129, 147 (1886); *The Pocket Veto Case*, 279 U.S. 655, 679 (1929).

[174] *United States* v. *South-Eastern Underwriters Association*, 322 U.S. 533, 539 (1944).

[175] *Briscoe* v. *Bank of Kentucky*, 36 U.S. (11 Pet.) 257, 328c (1837) (Baldwin, J., concurring).

[176] *The Pocket Veto Case*, 279 U.S. 655, 679 (1929).

[177] *Eisner* v. *Macomber*, 252 U.S. 189, 219-20 (1920) (Holmes, J., dissenting). Accord, *Ohio* ex rel. *Popovici* v. *Agler*, 280 U.S. 379, 383-84 (1930).

and, generally, in their common sense[178] and "plain meaning."[179]

2. "[N]atural signification," "ordinary and common usage," and "plain meaning" refer, of course, to what the words import in the language in which they are written. Thus, on its face the Constitution prescribes the official national language of the United States to be English.[180]

3. "[N]atural signification," "ordinary and common usage," and "plain meaning" also necessarily imply that the words have some ascertainable, generally accepted meanings. That is, there can lurk within the Constitution no ineradicable vagueness. Indeed, if there did, the Constitution would be *pro tanto* no "law" at all. For a statute written "in terms so vague that men of common intelligence must necessarily guess at its meaning and differ as to its application, violates the first essential of due process of law."[181] But history attests that "the framers of the Constitution were ... practical men, ... prescribing in language clear and intelligible the powers the government was to take."[182]

---

[178] See 1 J. Story, *Commentaries*, ante note 121, § 451, at 345.

[179] *Bronson* v. *Kinzie*, 42 U.S. (1 How.) 311, 318 (1843).

[180] This would hardly require mention, except that with huge influxes of foreigners who neither speak nor apparently desire to learn English, a political issue has arisen over whether an official national language exists. How anyone could deny that the language in which "the supreme Law of the Land" is written is not thereby the official national language escapes understanding.

[181] *Connally* v. *General Construction Co.*, 269 U.S. 385, 391 (1926).

[182] *South Carolina* v. *United States*, 199 U.S. 437, 449 (1905).

"[C]lear and intelligible" *to whom?* To WE THE PEOPLE *of the late 1700s.* Neither the Framers who composed, nor WE THE PEOPLE who read and ratified the Constitution could predict whether or how the particular words and phrases they used and approved—because they understood them in particular senses—might change (or be claimed to have changed) in meaning in the dim and distant future. Indeed, operating on the basis of "original intent," they must have presumed that the Constitution's words and phrases, no matter how much their denotations and connotations might change in other contexts and for other purposes, would nevertheless always remain the same for the purpose of interpreting and applying the Constitution—that is, they would display a *legal fixity* of meaning. For that reason, proper construction of the Constitution—as the Supreme Court has traditionally held—must determine "[w]hat . . . those who framed and adopted it understood [its] terms to designate and include"[183]—"that sense in which [the words were] generally used by those for whom the instrument was intended,"[184] the common understanding "when the Constitution was adopted,"[185] "the common parlance of the times in which the Constitution was written,"[186] "according to their accepted

---

[183] *Pollock* v. *Farmers' Loan & Trust Co.*, 157 U.S. 429, 558 (1895).

[184] *Ogden* v. *Saunders*, 25 U.S. (12 Wheat.) 213, 332 (1827) (Marshall, C.J., dissenting).

[185] *Ohio* ex rel. *Popovici* v. *Agler*, 280 U.S. 379, 383 (1930); *Eisner* v. *Macomber*, 252 U.S. 189, 219-20 (1920) (Holmes, J., dissenting).

[186] *United States* v. *South-Eastern Underwriters Association*, 322 U.S. 533, 539 (1944). Accord, *Gibbons* v. *Ogden*, 22 U.S. (9 Wheat.) 1, 190 (1824).

meaning in that day,"[187] and "in 'a sense most obvious to the common understanding at the time.'"[188] Note the emphasis here on *"common"* parlance and understanding—not the gnosis or intuition of a narrow political, judicial, academic, intellectual, or other elite.

Because the Constitution's words and phrases must be understood "according to their accepted meaning in that day," that certain of them may have developed different meanings over time is inadmissible as an argument for construing the Constitution. For this procedure would amount, not to *re*interpretation, but to *mis*interpretation. To be sure, "in the course of time, as is often the case with language, the meaning of words or terms is changed"; but, even so, the meaning of the Constitution does not change *pari passu.*[189] The *"meaning* [of constitutional provisions] is changeless; . . . only their *application* . . . is extensible."[190] "What [the Constitution] meant when adopted it still means for the purpose of interpretation,"[191] notwithstanding swings in public opinion at

---

[187] *Scott* v. *Sandford*, 60 U.S. (19 How.) 393, 418 (1857).

[188] *Eisner* v. *Macomber*, 252 U.S. 189, 219-20 (1920) (Holmes, J., dissenting). For an example of proper constitutional analysis on this score, see *Knowlton* v. *Moore*, 178 U.S. 41, 96-106 (1900).

[189] See N. Chipman, *Principles of Government: A Treatise on Free Institutions* (1833), at 254.

[190] *Home Building & Loan Association* v. *Blaisdell*, 290 U.S. 398, 451 (1934) (Sutherland, J., dissenting).

[191] *Smiley* v. *Holm*, 285 U.S. 355, 365 (1932). Accord, *South Carolina* v. *United States*, 199 U.S. 437, 448-49 (1905).

home or abroad,[192] changes in "the ebb and flow of economic events,"[193] or shifts in public policy.[194] Therefore:

> [W]hile [the Constitution] remains unaltered, it must be construed now as it was understood at the time of its adoption. It is not only the same in words, but the same in meaning, and delegates the same powers to the government, and reserves and secures the same rights and privileges to the citizen; and as long as it continues to exist in its present form, it speaks not only in the same words, but with the same meaning and intent with which it spoke when it came from the hands of its framers, and was voted on and adopted by the people of the United States. And any other rule of construction would abrogate the judicial character of [the Supreme Court], and make it the mere reflex of the popular opinion or passion of the day.[195]

For, "[i]f . . . we are at liberty to give old words new meanings . . . there is no power which may not . . . be conferred on the general government"[196]—or, as *Lawrence* shows, no power that may not be taken from (or, in another context, given to) either the General Government or the States.

---

[192] *Scott v. Sandford*, 60 U.S. (19 How.) 383, 426 (1857).

[193] *West Coast Hotel Co. v. Parrish*, 300 U.S. 379, 402 (1937) (Sutherland, J., dissenting).

[194] *Patton v. United States*, 281 U.S. 276, 306 (1930). For "'[p]olicy and humanity' are dangerous guides in the discussion of a legal proposition. He who follows them far is apt to bring back the means of error and delusion." *Edwards v. Kearzey*, 96 U.S. 595, 604 (1878).

[195] *Scott v. Sandford*, 60 U.S. (19 How.) 383, 426 (1857).

[196] Passenger Cases, 48 U.S. (7 How.) 283, 478 (1849).

4. That the Constitution "speaks not only in the same words, but with the same meaning and intent with which it spoke when it came from the hands of its framers" applies to the specifically *legal* meaning its words and phrases had in that day. "We are bound to interpret the Constitution in the light of the law as it existed at the time it was adopted."[197] "The law as expounded for centuries cannot be set aside or disregarded because some of the judges are now of a different opinion from those who, [two] centur[ies] ago, followed it in framing our Constitution."[198]

It is sometimes said that "[t]he Constitution was written to be understood by the voters; its words and phrases were used in their normal and ordinary as distinguished from technical meaning."[199] This view, however, is somewhat misleading. For the Constitution must be interpreted "in such a manner as, consistently with the words, shall fully and completely effectuate the whole objects of it. . . . No court of justice can be authorized so to construe any clause of the constitution as to defeat its obvious ends, when another construction, equally accordant with the words and sense thereof, will enforce and protect them."[200] And to construe the Constitution to "enforce and protect" its "obvious ends," one must often distinguish between the *technical* meanings of its words and phrases, and

---

[197] *Mattox* v. *United States*, 156 U.S. 237, 243 (1895).

[198] *Pollock* v. *Farmers' Loan & Trust Co.*, 157 U.S. 429, 591 (1895) (separate opinion of Field, J., referring to antient English common law).

[199] *United States* v. *Sprague*, 282 U.S. 716, 731 (1931).

[200] *Prigg* v. *Pennsylvania*, 41 U.S. (16 Pet.) 539, 612 (1842).

their *full dictionary* meanings, and employ the former to the
exclusion of the latter.

The "technical" meaning of a word or phrase is the
meaning the law gives to it, which often may be narrower, and
almost always is more precise, than the meaning given to it by
persons generally. When the issue is the interpretation of a
specifically legal document—and no document could be more
specifically legal than "the supreme Law of the Land" itself[201]—
the technical meanings of its words and phrases constitute
their common meanings, because: (i) it is the commonality of
their legal meanings within the legal profession that qualifies
those meanings as their technical meanings; and (ii) the law
presumes that every man (lawyer or not) knows the law,
particularly if he is among WE THE PEOPLE who originally did,
and then continually "do ordain and establish this Constitution
for the United States of America."[202] In the late 1700s, WE THE
PEOPLE drew these technical meanings from the law of
England, the Colonies, and the independent States.[203] Later
Amendments drew their technical meanings from the law as it
had developed until then.

Prescinding from the technical meanings of its words and
phrases would render much of the Constitution unintelligible
or so plastic as to be a "law" in name only. For examples: The

---

[201] U.S. Const. art. VI, cl. 2.

[202] U.S. Const. preamble.

[203] See, e.g., *United States* v. *Palmer*, 16 U.S. (3 Wheat.) 610, 630 (1818).

word "dollars" in the Constitution[204] refers, not to anything that politicians or judges might fancifully call a "dollar," but uniquely to the Spanish milled dollar adopted as America's monetary unit by the Continental Congress before the Constitution was drafted.[205] The power of the President to "pardon"[206] takes in many of the prerogatives of the English King in that regard.[207] "The freedom of speech" in the First Amendment[208] does not protect defamation or obscenity—not because they cannot be forms of "speech" (as by dictionary definitions they surely can), but because common law always held them legally actionable, and therefore not part of "[t]he *freedom* of speech." The words "jury" in the Sixth Amendment[209] and "trial by jury" in the Seventh[210] "were placed in the Constitution . . . with reference to the meaning affixed to them in the law as it was in this country and in England at the adoption of the Constitution."[211] And the words

---

[204] U.S. Const. art. I, § 9, cl. 1 ("a Tax or duty may be imposed . . . not exceeding ten dollars"); amend. VII ("where the value in controversy shall exceed twenty dollars").

[205] See E. Vieira, Jr., *Pieces of Eight*, ante note 111, at 134-41, 183-99.

[206] U.S. Const. art. II, § 2, cl. 1 (the President "shall have Power to grant Reprieves and Pardons for Offenses against the United States, except in Cases of Impeachment").

[207] See Ex parte *Wells*, 59 U.S. (18 How.) 307, 309-11 (1856).

[208] U.S. Const. amend. I ("Congress shall make no law . . . abridging the freedom of speech").

[209] U.S. Const. amend. VI ("the accused shall enjoy the right to a speedy and public trial, by an impartial jury").

[210] U.S. Const. amend. VII ("the right of trial by jury shall be preserved").

[211] *Thompson* v. *Utah*, 170 U.S. 343, 344 (1898).

"privileges and immunities" were included in Section 1 of the
Fourteenth Amendment to reverse the Supreme Court's
earlier erroneous decisions in *Barron* v. *Baltimore*[212] and *Scott* v.
Sandford[213] (among other reasons).[214] Thus, to understand these
terms—and many others, such as "Bill of Attainder,"[215] "Bills of
Credit,"[216] "Militia,"[217] and "religious Test"[218]—any American
in the late 1700s, or thereafter, would have had (and now has)
to read the Constitution's verbiage in its technical sense.
Indeed, focusing on the technical meanings of its words and
phrases is the only way in which to interpret the Constitution
with objectivity, accuracy, and anything approaching certainty.

F. English common law of the *pre*-constitutional period is
the sole ostensible foreign law that has a definite role to play in
construction of the Constitution.[219]

---

[212] 32 U.S. (7 Pet.) 243 (1833).

[213] 60 U.S. (19 How.) 393 (1857).

[214] See 2 W. Crosskey, *Politics and the Constitution*, ante note 161, chs. XXX
and XXXI.

[215] U.S. Const. art. I, § 9, cl. 2, and § 10, cl. 1.

[216] U.S. Const. art. I, § 10, cl. 1.

[217] U.S. Const. art. I, § 8, cls. 15-16, and amend. II.

[218] U.S. Const. art. VI, cl. 3.

[219] For the purposes of what follows, *pre*-constitutional English common
law is taken *arguendo* to constitute "foreign" law, although the Colonies,
prior to the Declaration of Independence, were constituent parts of the
British Empire. Were English common law treated as the Colonies'
domestic law until the Declaration (and thereafter insofar as the States had
adopted it as part of their laws), then, as explained below, *no* foreign law
whatsoever would qualify as a source of American constitutional law, except
in the limited cases in which the Constitution expressly requires otherwise.

1. In general, English common law of the *pre-constitutional* period is one of the most important legal-historical sources of the meaning (and specifically the technical meaning) of many constitutional provisions.[220] English "common law throws light on the meaning and scope of the Constitution,"[221] because the common law "is the system from which our judicial ideas and legal definitions are derived."[222] "The interpretation of the Constitution . . . is necessarily influenced by the fact that its provisions are framed in the language of the English common law, and are to be read in the light of its history."[223] Indeed:

> The language of the Constitution cannot be interpreted safely except by reference to the common law . . . when the instrument was framed and adopted. The statesmen and lawyers . . . who submitted it to the ratification of the . . . States, were born and brought up in the atmosphere of the common law, and thought and spoke in its vocabulary. . . . [W]hen they came to put their conclusions into the form of fundamental law in a compact draft, they expressed them in

---

[220] E.g., *Moore* v. *United States*, 91 U.S. 270, 274 (1876); *Ex parte Bain*, 121 U.S. 1, 10-12 (1887); *Smith* v. *Alabama*, 124 U.S. 465, 478-79 (1888); *Pollock* v. *Farmers' Loan & Trust Co.*, 157 U.S. 429, 572 (1895); *United States* v. *Wong Kim Ark*, 169 U.S. 649, 654-56 (1898); *Schick* v. *United States*, 195 U.S. 65, 68-70 (1904); *South Carolina* v. *United States*, 199 U.S. 437, 449-50 (1905); *Kansas* v. *Colorado*, 206 U.S. 46, 94-95 (1907); *Patton* v. *United States*, 281 U.S. 276, 287-90 (1930); *Dimick* v. *Schiedt*, 293 U.S. 474, 476-82, 487 (1935); *United States* v. *Wood*, 299 U.S. 123, 133-39 (1936). See, e.g., 2 J. Story, *Commentaries*, ante note 121, §§ 1338-41, at 212-14.

[221] *Kansas* v. *Colorado*, 206 U.S. 46, 94 (1907).

[222] *Moore* v. *United States*, 91 U.S. 270, 274 (1876).

[223] *Smith* v. *Alabama*, 124 U.S. 465, 478 (1888).

terms of the common law, confident that they could be shortly and easily understood.[224]

2. Nonetheless, in determining what a provision of the Constitution means, WE THE PEOPLE "must look to those settled usages and modes of proceeding existing in the common ... law of England before the emigration of our ancestors, which were shown not to have been unsuited to their civil and political condition by having been acted on by them after the settlement of this country."[225] So, if there was "no settled practice under the English law," that law "cannot ... be treated as embedded in the [Constitution]."[226] And "every rule of the common law and every statute of England obtaining in the Colonies, in derogation of the principles on which the new government [of the United States] was founded, was abrogated."[227] In such cases, not English

---

[224] Ex parte *Grossman*, 267 U.S. 87, 108-09 (1925). Accord, e.g., *United States* v. *Wong Kim Ark*, 169 U.S. 649, 654 (1898); *South Carolina* v. *United States*, 199 U.S. 437, 449-50 (1905); *Dimick* v. *Schiedt*, 293 U.S. 474, 476 (1935).

[225] *Tumey* v. *Ohio*, 273 U.S. 510, 523 (1927).

[226] *United States* v. *Wood*, 229 U.S. 123, 137 (1936), citing *Callan* v. *Wilson*, 127 U.S. 540, 549 (1888); *Thompson* v. *Utah*, 170 U.S. 343, 350 (1898); *Patton* v. *United States*, 281 U.S. 276, 288 (1930), *Dimick* v. *Schiedt*, 293 U.S. 474, 476 (1935); *Continental Bank* v. *Chicago, R.I. & P. Ry.*, 294 U.S. 648, 699 (1935).

[227] *United States* v. *Wong Kim Ark*, 169 U.S. 649, 709 (1898) (Fuller, C.J., dissenting). E.g., *Grosjean* v. *American Press Co.*, 297 U.S. 233, 248-29 (1936) (freedom of the press not limited to antient common-law freedom from prior restraint); *Powell* v. *Alabama*, 287 U.S. 45, 60-65 (1932) (traditional English common-law denial of counsel to individuals prosecuted for felonies not acceptable in America).

common law, but "[o]ur own Constitution and form of government must be our only guide."[228]

G. The admonition that "[o]ur own Constitution and form of government must be our *only* guide" applies to all other foreign law—which generally is completely irrelevant to, and totally excluded as an acceptable source for, interpretation and application of the Constitution.

1. With the three very specific exceptions of Congress's power "[t]o define and punish . . . Offenses against the Law of Nations";[229] of the disability of every "Person holding any Office of Profit or Trust under [the United States]" to "accept . . . any . . . Emolument, Office, or Title, of any kind whatever, from any King, Prince, or foreign State";[230] and of the power of the President, "by and with the Advice and Consent of the Senate, to make Treaties"[231] which become part of "the supreme Law of the Land"[232] and to which "[t]he judicial Power shall extend";[233] the Constitution itself provides no basis for the notion that foreign law may promiscuously be

---

[228] *Fleming* v. *Page*, 50 U.S. (9 How.) 603, 618 (1850) (power of conquest over foreign lands not within the President's "executive Power" in Article II, Section 1, Clause 1, because such a power is incompatible with a republican form of government).

[229] U.S. Const. art. I, § 8, cl. 10.

[230] U.S. Const. art. I, § 9, cl. 8.

[231] U.S. Const. art. II, § 2, cl. 2.

[232] U.S. Const. art. VI, § 2. See, e.g., *Ware* v. *Hylton*, 3 U.S. (3 Dall.) 199, 236-37 (1796).

[233] U.S. Const. art. III, § 2, cl. 1.

consulted in order to construe its provisions. In the first instance, foreign law ("the Law of Nations") becomes the predicate for Congress's action, which must reasonably relate a defined "Offense" to that "Law."[234] In the second instance, specific foreign laws must be consulted to determine whether particular "Office[s], or Title[s]" fall within the prohibited class. In the third instance, it may be necessary to consult foreign law to determine what a treaty means, or how to apply it. Overall, perforce of the legal doctrine *inclusio unius exclusio alterius*, these three particularized situations that may call for the employment of foreign law in constitutional exegesis compel the conclusion that nowhere else is such use permissible.

As explained above, other than the Declaration of Independence, which sets out the broad principles of separate and independent national sovereignty derived from "the Laws of Nature and of Nature's God," and the existence of "certain unalienable Rights" with which "all men . . . are endowed by their Creator," the Constitution is the sole "authoritative language" that expresses WE THE PEOPLE'S will.[235] Necessarily, then, the General Government—or any branch or "Officer[ ] of the United States," including "Judges of the supreme Court"[236]—lacks all powers save those WE THE PEOPLE have delegated to it, in definite and thereby limited terms, in the

---

[234] See, e.g., *United States v. Smith*, 18 U.S. (5 Wheat.) 153, 160-62 (1820); Ex parte Quirin, 317 U.S. 1, 27 (1942).

[235] E.g., *Cohens v. Virginia*, 19 U.S. (6 Wheat.) 264, 381 (1821).

[236] U.S. Const. art. II, § 2.

Constitution.[237] "The government of the United States was born of the Constitution";[238] and "[i]ts power and authority have *no other* source."[239]

"In this respect we differ radically from nations where all . . . power, without restriction or limitation, is vested in a . . . body subject to . . . the discretion of its members."[240] And for this reason, with the special exceptions noted above, constitutional analysis has no need—and no right—to refer to "all the powers which usually belong to the sovereignty of a nation";[241] to any "implied attribute of sovereignty possessed by all nations";[242] to "the laws of nations" in general,[243] to the "laws or usages of other nations" in particular,[244] or to "the law

---

[237] *Martin* v. *Hunter's Lessee*, 14 U.S. (1 Wheat.) 304, 326 (1816); *McCulloch* v. *Maryland*, 17 U.S. (4 Wheat.) 316, 405 (1819); *Scott* v. *Sandford*, 60 U.S. (19 How.) 393, 451 (1857); *United States* v. *Cruikshank*, 92 U.S. 542, 551 (1876); Ex parte *Quirin*, 317 U.S. 1, 25 (1942); Ex parte *Milligan*, 71 U.S. (4 Wall.) 2, 136-37 (1866) (opinion of Chase, C.J.).

[238] *Downes* v. *Bidwell*, 182 U.S. 244, 288 (1901) (White, J., concurring).

[239] *Reid* v. *Covert*, 354 U.S. 1, 5-6 (1957) (opinion of Black, J.) (emphasis supplied).

[240] *United States* v. *Butler*, 297 U.S. 1, 63 (1936).

[241] *Scott* v. *Sandford*, 60 U.S. (19 How.) 393, 401 (1857).

[242] *Afroyim* v. *Rusk*, 387 U.S. 253, 257 (1967).

[243] *Fleming* v. *Page*, 50 U.S. (9 How.) 603, 617 (1850).

[244] *Scott* v. *Sandford*, 60 U.S. (19 How.) 393, 451 (1857). Accord, *Chisholm* v. *Georgia*, 2 U.S. (2 Dall.) 419, 466 (1793) (opinion of Cushing, J.) ("point [of constitutional law] turns not . . . upon the law of any other country whatever").

of any other country whatever";[245] or to "decisions . . . by the
Courts of any other country."[246] For "no laws or usages of
other nations . . . can enlarge the powers of the government,
to take from the citizens the rights they have reserved."[247] The
Constitution (interpreted, of course, in the light of the
Declaration of Independence) is America's one and only
"supreme Law of the Land."

Insofar as the "powers actually granted [in the
Constitution to the General Government] must be such as are
expressly given, or given by necessary implication,"[248] and
inasmuch as "[t]he burden of establishing a delegation of
power to the United States . . . is upon those making the
claim,"[249] one may ask: Except in the specific instances noted
above, *exactly where* did WE THE PEOPLE delegate to any
component part of the General Government a power to
interpret and apply the Constitution according or by reference
to foreign law? Plainly, WE THE PEOPLE explicitly delegated no
authority to construe the Constitution with reference to
foreign law in Article III, wherein resides "[t]he judicial Power
of the United States."[250] Admittedly, the three specific

---

[245] *Chisholm* v. *Georgia*, 2 U.S. (2 Dall.) 419, 466 (1793) (opinion of Cushing,
J.).

[246] *Osborn* v. *Bank of the United States*, 22 U.S. (9 Wheat.) 738, 851 (1824).

[247] *Scott* v. *Sandford*, 60 U.S. (19 How.) 393, 451 (1857). See also *Afroyim* v.
Rusk, 387 U.S. 253, 257 (1967).

[248] *Martin* v. *Hunter's Lessee*, 14 U.S. (1 Wheat.) 304, 326 (1816). Accord,
McCulloch v. *Maryland*, 17 U.S. (4 Wheat.) 316, 405 (1819).

[249] *Bute* v. *Illinois*, 333 U.S. 640, 653 (1948).

[250] U.S. Const. art. III, § 1.

provisions of the Constitution to which foreign law could be material (noted above) might generate "Cases . . . arising under this Constitution" or "Treaties made, or which shall be made, under the[ ] Authority [of the United States],"[251] to which "[t]he judicial Power" would properly attach. But because these provisions constitute explicit exceptions to a general dearth of justification for consulting foreign law on constitutional questions, they exclude any plausible ground for implying the propriety of applying foreign law in other areas, let alone of a general judicial license to seize upon such law as a tool of constitutional construction across the board. Any other conclusion would enable the Judiciary, through the rhetorical juggling trick of "interpreting" the Constitution, to amend it *ad libitum*, in violation of both WE THE PEOPLE'S contrary command,[252] and the Supreme Court's own admission that the *"courts, as well as other departments* [of the General Government] are bound by th[e Constitution]."[253] "Judicial power, as contradistinguished from the power of the laws"—and "the supreme Law of the Land" first and foremost—"has no existence. Courts are the mere instruments of the law, and can will nothing."[254]

2. a. Even more fundamentally, foreign law in general (other than *pre*-constitutional English common law) *must* be irrelevant to interpretation and application of the Constitution

---

[251] U.S. Const. art. III, § 2, cl. 1.

[252] See U.S. Const. art. V.

[253] *Marbury* v. *Madison*, 5 U.S. (1 Cranch) 137, 180 (1803).

[254] *Osborn* v. *Bank of the United States*, 22 U.S. (9 Wheat.) 738, 866 (1824).

because, *without first repealing the Declaration of Independence*,
even WE THE PEOPLE could not delegate to the General
Government, or to any of its branches or officers, any power
to subject the United States, the States, or Americans generally
to such law. On its face, though, each of the three
constitutional exceptions to which specific foreign laws could
be material—that is, "Offenses against the Law of Nations";[255]
the prohibition of any foreign "Emolument, Office; and
Title";[256] and "Treaties"[257]—is obviously perfectly consistent
with the Declaration of Independence. An extended
comparison and contrast of "Treaties" with decisions of the
Supreme Court, as to their real or purported effects on the
Constitution, is warranted, however.

"Treaties" presume that the United States enjoys what the
Declaration of Independence called "the separate and equal
status" "among the powers of the earth" "to which the Laws of
Nature and of Nature's God" entitled the thirteen original
States, and continue to entitle this country. For "[a] treaty is, in
its nature, a contract between two nations"[258] or "primarily a
compact between independent nations."[259]

In addition, for a President, "with the Advice and Consent
of the Senate, to make [a] Treat[y]"[260] which becomes "the

---

[255] U.S. Const. art. I, § 8, cl. 10.

[256] U.S. Const. art I, § 9, cl. 8, and § 10, cl. 1.

[257] U.S. Const. art. II, § 2, cl. 2.

[258] *Foster* v. *Neilson*, 27 U.S. (2 Pet.) 253, 314 (1829).

[259] Head Money Cases, 112 U.S. 580, 598 (1884).

[260] U.S. Const. art. II, § 2, cl. 2.

supreme Law of the Land," with "the Judges in every State [to] be bound thereby, any Thing in the Constitution or Laws of any State to the Contrary notwithstanding,"[261] and through which foreign law may to some degree enter into and become part of that "supreme Law," is a constitutional world apart from a decision of an evanescent majority of the Supreme Court that some foreign law can be consulted in order to define a provision or principle of the Constitution. First, pursuant to WE THE PEOPLE'S mandate, a "Treat[y]" is passed upon by representative, and therefore politically responsible, bodies: the President and the Senate. And if the "Treat[y]" is not self-executing, it requires further action by the entire Congress and the President.[262] Whereas, a judicial decision such as *Lawrence* is "the product of a Court, which is the product of a law-profession culture"[263]—and perhaps not even the original product of the Justices themselves, but of their clerks, who come wet behind the ears from the intellectual hothouses of that "law-profession culture," infected with the latest communicable viruses of "good thinking" in "the culture war."[264]

Second, contrary to uninformed belief in some quarters, "a treaty cannot change the Constitution or be held valid if it be in violation of the Constitution. This results from the nature

---

[261] U.S. Const. art. VI, cl. 2.

[262] See, e.g., *Foster* v. *Neilson*, 27 U.S. (2 Pet.) 253, 314-15 (1829).

[263] 539 U.S. at 602 (Scalia, J., dissenting).

[264] See, e.g., E. Lazarus, *Closed Chambers: The First Eyewitness Account of the Epic Struggles Inside the Supreme Court* (1998).

and fundamental principles of our government."[265] "It would
not be contended that [the Treaty Power] extends as far as to
authorize what the Constitution forbids, or a change in the
character of the government or in that of one of the
States. . . ."[266] "[T]reaties made by the President and Senate . . .
must yield to the paramount and supreme law of the
Constitution."[267] And "the courts of justice have no right to
annul or disregard any of [a treaty's] provisions, unless they
violate the Constitution of the United States."[268] Whereas,
according to the mythology of "judicial supremacy" that "the
federal judiciary is supreme in the exposition of the law of the
Constitution," a decision of the Supreme Court supposedly
defines the Constitution thereafter, such that *the interpretation*
of the [Constitution] enunciated by th[e Supreme Court] . . . *is*
the supreme law of the land" as against everyone else in the
world.[269] (This, in the face of the self-evident proposition that
"no amount of repetition of . . . errors in judicial opinions can
make the errors true,"[270] and of the Court's own admission that

---

[265] The Cherokee Tobacco, 78 U.S. (11 Wall.) 616, 620-21 (1871).

[266] *Geofroy* v. *Riggs*, 133 U.S. 258, 267 (1890). Accord, *Asakura* v. *City of Seattle*, 265 U.S. 332, 341 (1924).

[267] *United States* v. *Wong Kim Ark*, 169 U.S. 649, 701 (1898). Accord, *Doe* v. *Braden*, 57 U.S. (16 How.) 635, 656 (1863); *Holden* v. *Joy*, 84 U.S. (17 Wall.) 211, 243 (1872); *United States* v. *Minnesota*, 270 U.S. 181, 208 (1926); *Reid* v. *Covert*, 354 U.S. 1, 16-18 (1957) (Black, J., announcing the judgment of the Court).

[268] *Doe* v. *Braden*, 57 U.S. (16 How.) 635, 657 (1853).

[269] *Cooper* v. *Aaron*, 358 U.S. 1, 18 (1958) (emphasis supplied).

[270] *Wallace* v. *Jaffree*, 472 U.S. 38, 107 (1985) (Rehnquist, C.J., dissenting).

its constitutional precedents are entitled to the least force of *stare decisis*.[271])

Third, no "Treat[y]" can operate to cede any part of the territory of a State to some foreign nation without that State's consent.[272] Whereas, by stripping a State's legislature of power to enact certain laws, through insinuation of foreign law into the Constitution, as the majority in *Lawrence* did to Texas, the Supreme Court subjects the State's entire territory to foreign jurisdiction *pro tanto*. And,

Fourth, "Congress by legislation, and so far as the people and authorities of the United States are concerned, c[an] abrogate a treaty made between this country and another country which ha[s] been negotiated by the President and approved by the Senate."[273] If such "abrogat[ion]" violates an international contract, "[i]ts infraction becomes the subject of international negotiations and reclamations, so far as the injured party chooses to seek redress, which may in the end be enforced by actual war. . . . [W]*ith all this the judicial courts have nothing to do and can give no redress.*"[274] Whereas, according to the naïve popular mythology of "judicial supremacy," WE THE

---

[271] See, e.g., *Mitchell v. W.T. Grant Co.*, 416 U.S. 600, 627-28 (1974) (Powell, J., concurring).

[272] *Geofroy v. Riggs*, 133 U.S. 258, 267 (1890).

[273] *La Abra Silver Mining Co.* v. *United States*, 175 U.S. 423, 460 (1899). Accord, *The Cherokee Tobacco*, 78 U.S. (11 Wall.) 616, 621 (1871); *Botiller* v. *Dominguez*, 130 U.S. 238, 247 (1889); *Chae Chan Ping* v. *United States,* 130 U.S. 581, 600-03 (1889); *Fong Yue Ting* v. *United States*, 149 U.S. 698, 720-21 (1893)

[274] *Head Money Cases*, 112 U.S. 580, 598-99 (1884) (emphasis supplied).

PEOPLE cannot override one of the Supreme Court's unilateral pronouncements on the Constitution except through a constitutional amendment—but the Court can always overrule any of its previous opinions.[275]

b. *A fortiori*, if WE THE PEOPLE are powerless, in the face of the Declaration of Independence, to delegate an all-embracing power to the General Government to subordinate the Constitution to foreign law, then that government's officials—and particularly its judges, who are nothing more than "the mere instruments of the law"—cannot possibly even claim, let alone exercise, such a power. Moreover, on this score no crack of equivocation exists in the Constitution through which such a claim could slither in.

"If, from the imperfection of human language, there should be serious doubts respecting the extent of any given power, . . . the objects for which it was given, especially, when those objects are expressed in the instrument itself, should have great influence in the construction."[276] One of WE THE PEOPLE'S overarching goals for the Constitution is "to form a more perfect Union"[277]—in reference, undoubtedly, to the original "Union" the Declaration of Independence made

---

[275] See, e.g., *Gideon* v. *Wainright*, 372 U.S. 335, 346 (1963) (opinion of Douglas, J.) ("all constitutional questions are always open"), and *Mitchell* v. *W.T. Grant Co.*, 416 U.S. 600, 627-28 (1974) (Powell, J., concurring) ("especially with respect to matters of constitutional interpretation . . . if the precedent or its rationale is of doubtful validity, then it should not stand").

[276] *Gibbons* v. *Ogden*, 22 U.S. (9 Wheat.) 1, 188-89 (1824).

[277] U.S. Const. preamble.

possible. Another of WE THE PEOPLE'S paramount goals is "to
. . . secure the Blessings of Liberty to ourselves and our
Posterity"[278]—which derives from the Declaration's assertion
of the "self-evident" "truth[ ]" "that all men . . . are endowed
by their Creator with certain unalienable Rights," rights of
which no government can deprive them by any exercise of
power consistent with "the Laws of Nature and of Nature's
God," and which WE THE PEOPLE retained and reserved for
themselves in the Bill of Rights.[279] As to the "more perfect
Union," WE THE PEOPLE never intended to refer to any
international organization, such as the European Court of
Human Rights (or the forty-five nations in which its decisions
are "[a]uthoritative"), the opinions of which the majority in
Lawrence considered of "importance."[280] As to "Liberty," WE
THE PEOPLE referred to that concept as it was understood in
the late 1700s (with respect to the Bill of Rights) or in the late
1860s (with respect to the Fourteenth Amendment)—not as
the *Lawrence* majority redefined it on the basis of an "emerging
awareness" in 2003.[281] And as to "due process of law," WE THE
PEOPLE in those eras never doubted that their State legislatures

---

[278] U.S. Const. preamble.

[279] In particular, see U.S. Const. amends. IX ("[t]he enumeration in the
Constitution, of certain rights, shall not be construed to deny or disparage
others retained by the people") and X ("[t]he powers not delegated to the
United States by the Constitution, nor prohibited by it to the States, are
reserved to the States respectively, or to the people"). See also U.S. Const.
amend. XIII.

[280] 539 U.S. at 573, 576.

[281] Ibid. at 572.

could reasonably limit "liberty" in order to promote morality—rather than, as the *Lawrence* majority concluded, that "'view[ing] a particular practice as immoral is not a sufficient reason for upholding a law prohibiting the practice'."[282] Thus, the *Lawrence* majority's reliance on foreign law is illegitimate, on grounds that derive, not only from the Constitution's text, but also from the Constitution's purpose to effectuate the fundamental principles of the Declaration of Independence.

Moreover, the repudiation by Justices Kennedy, Breyer, Ginsberg, Souter, Stevens, and O'Connor of morality as a basis for legislation affronts the Declaration's "appeal[ ] to the Supreme Judge of the world for the rectitude of our intentions." "Rectitude" means "moral integrity."[283] Plainly, the *Lawrence* majority's conclusion in 2003 that morality consists of nothing more than arbitrary human "view[s]" that are "not a sufficient reason for upholding a law" is at war with Americans' conviction in 1776 that the morality *vel non* of human behavior is an *objective* quality that "the Supreme Judge of the world" will always recognize. If Americans asserted as much in 1776 as the political-*cum*-legal basis for "assum[ing] among the powers of the earth, the separate and equal station to which the Laws of Nature and of Nature's God entitle them"—*and thereby as the basis for claiming the right and power thereafter to legislate for themselves, under their State constitutions and then under the Constitution of the United States as well*—how

---

[282] Ibid. at 577.

[283] E.g., *Webster's New Collegiate Dictionary* (1977), at 967.

could the majority in *Lawrence*, on the basis of any other
beliefs, deny any contemporary Americans that same right and
power simply because they chose to legislate specifically for
the purpose of promoting "rectitude"?

Central to the entire system of American constitutionalism
is that, as even the Supreme Court acknowledges:

> *The first official action of this nation declared the foundation of
> government* in these words: "We hold these truths to be self-
> evident, that all men are created equal, that they are
> endowed by their Creator with certain unalienable rights,
> that among these are life, liberty, and the pursuit of
> happiness." While such declaration of principles may not
> have the force of organic law, or be made the basis of
> judicial decision as to the limits of right and duty, and while
> in all cases reference must be had to the organic law of the
> nation for such limits, yet the latter is but the body and the
> letter of which the former is the thought and the spirit, and
> *it is always safe to read the letter of the constitution in the spirit
> of the Declaration of Independence.* No duty rests more
> imperatively upon the courts that the enforcement of those
> constitutional provisions intended to secure that equality of
> rights which is the foundation of free government.[284]

Judicial pettifogging aside, the Declaration of Independence
must perpetually "have the force of organic law" and "be . . . the
basis of judicial decision as to the limits of right and duty"
embodied in the Constitution—because, if the Colonies had
failed in securing their independence, and the authority of the

---

[284] *Gulf, Colorado & Santa Fe Ry.* v. *Ellis*, 165 U.S. 150, 159-60 (1897)
(emphasis supplied).

King had been re-established in this country—if "[t]he first official action of this nation" had failed—no one would contend that the States' acts against the Crown, or its loyal subjects, could have been upheld as resting upon any legal foundation.[285] That is, *the Constitution is properly law only because of the Declaration's efficacy—and, therefore, only in conformity with what the Declaration identified as the "self-evident" "truths" of political life.* Namely:

➢ "that all men are created equal, [in] that they are endowed by their creator with certain unalienable Rights";

➢ "[t]hat to secure these rights, Governments are instituted among Men, deriving their just powers from the consent of the governed";

➢ "[t]hat whenever any Form of Government becomes destructive of these ends, it is the Right of the People to alter or abolish it, and to institute new Government, laying its foundation on such principles and organizing its powers in such form, as to them shall seem most likely to effect their Safety and Happiness"; and

➢ that "when a long train of abuses and usurpations, pursuing invariably the same Object evinces a design to reduce them under absolute Despotism, it is their right, it is their duty, to throw off such Government, and to provide new Guards for their future security."

---

[285] *Williams v. Bruffy*, 96 U.S. 176, 186 (1878).

In such wise, the Declaration of Independence repudiated the false and vicious dogmas of legal positivism that government is the source and supreme judge of law; that government is anterior and superior to the people; and that abuses and usurpations—or worse yet, outright tyranny—cannot deprive government of its legitimacy, or public officials of their positions. Surely, too, if the Declaration sanctioned as "self-evident" "the Right of the People to alter or abolish" "any Form of Government" *in toto*, it also recognized their lesser included right to condemn and set aside the mere statutes, judicial opinions, and other purported public acts of tyrants or usurpers—and to condemn and set aside the tyrants and usurpers themselves—without "alter[ing] or abolish[ing]" the basic institutions of government. Furthermore, the Declaration recognized that WE THE PEOPLE'S need to exercise their "Right . . . to alter or abolish" could likely arise not just from statutes, judicial opinions, or other public acts that amounted to mere errors on the part of public officials, but from actual political conspiracies directed against their liberties: "long train[s] of abuses and usurpations, pursuing invariably the same Object [that] evince[ ] a design to reduce them under absolute Despotism."

To what extent such a "long train of abuses and usurpations" has been coupled together out of cases preceding *Lawrence*, and which *Lawrence* as the engine will now pull forward at increasing speed, must be investigated next.

CHAPTER 3

The Insinuation of Foreign Law into Constitutional Jurisprudence, from *Trop* v. *Dulles* to *Lawrence* v. *Texas*

If a concern for "original intent" was not the reason for the employment of foreign law as a primary *ratio decidendi* in *Lawrence*, what was? The motivation in that case was, as it had been in many cases theretofore, *judicial opportunism*.

The history of the problem is traceable at least to the late 1800s. The majorities in *Knox* v. *Lee*[286] and *Juilliard* v. *Greenman*[287] needed to concoct some colorable argument to sustain the constitutionality of legal-tender United States Notes—which every Justice knew could not be found in Constitution. As Justice Field observed in *Juilliard*, "[i]f there be anything in the history of the Constitution which can be established with moral certainty, it is that the framers . . .

---

[286] 79 U.S. (12 Wall.) 457 (1871).

[287] 110 U.S. 421 (1884).

intended to prohibit the issue of legal tender notes both by the general government and by the States."[288] So the renegade Justices turned to foreign law to provide an intellectual prop.[289] This reliance, however, was essentially *de minimis*, and ended with these decisions, because thereafter the Court refused to hear any other case that challenged the constitutionality of legal-tender paper currency.

However, in later cases (discussed below) primarily involving the issue of whether some punishment was "cruel and unusual" under the Eighth Amendment,[290] several Justices relied on foreign law for the same reason that drove *Knox* and *Juilliard*: They could find in no traditional source of constitutional interpretation the validation they needed. None of these Justices, however, explained why the use of foreign law was permissible in Eighth-Amendment jurisprudence in particular or in constitutional law in general—just as no Justice in *Lawrence* explained why the use of foreign law was allowable in construing the Fourteenth Amendment. Nonetheless, because the issue of "cruel and unusual punishments" arose again and again in a divided Court, the Justices' adverting to foreign law became a familiar theme.

A. At issue in *Trop* v. *Dulles*[291] was whether a native-born American could constitutionally be stripped of his citizenship

---

[288] Ibid. at 451 (dissenting opinion).

[289] See *Knox*, 79 U.S. (12 Wall.) at 533-34 (opinion of Strong, J., for the Court), 556 (Bradley, J., concurring); *Juilliard*, 110 U.S. at 447.

[290] U.S. Const. amend. VIII ("nor cruel and unusual punishments inflicted").

[291] 356 U.S. 86 (1958).

because of his conviction by court-martial for desertion during wartime. In an opinion announcing the judgment of the Court, Chief Justice Warren opined that:

> [U]se of denationalization as a punishment is barred by the Eighth Amendment. . . .
>
> This punishment is offensive to cardinal principles for which the Constitution stands. It subjects the individual to a fate of ever-increasing fear and distress. . . . He is stateless, *a condition deplored in the international community of democracies.* . . .
>
> *The civilized nations of the world are in virtual unanimity that statelessness is not to be imposed as punishment for crime.* It is true that several countries prescribe expatriation in the event that their nationals engage in conduct in derogation of native allegiance. . . . But use of denationalization as punishment for crime is an entirely different matter. The United Nations' survey of the nationality laws of 84 nations of the world reveals that only two countries, the Philippines and Turkey, impose denationalization as a penalty for desertion. In this country the Eighth Amendment forbids this to be done.[292]

Why what "the international community of democracies" "deplored" or as to what "[t]he civilized nations of the world [were] in virtual unanimity" was material Chief Justice Warren did not explain—doubtlessly because he had nothing cogent to say.[293] For if, construed without reference to foreign law, the

---

[292] Ibid. at 101-03 & nn.35, 37-38 (opinion of Warren, C.J., joined by Black, Douglas, and Whittaker, JJ.) (footnotes omitted; emphasis supplied).

[293] As Chief Justice Rehnquist observed many years later, "if it is evidence of a *national* consensus for which we are looking, then the viewpoints of other

Eight Amendment forbids denationalization, then foreign law is supererogatory. Conversely, if, construed without reference to foreign law, the Eight Amendment permits denationalization, that conclusion can be overridden only if foreign law, under some circumstances, controls constitutional construction—such as if contemporary international legal opinion carries more weight than the common law and the beliefs of Americans in the late 1700s, or even the beliefs of Americans today as evidenced in the practices of their own government. Perhaps, though, in 1958 this was too much for Chief Justice Warren to expect the country to accept.

B. *Gregg* v. *Georgia*[294] dealt with whether imposition of the death penalty under State law violated the Eighth Amendment. Although *Gregg* did not explicitly inject foreign law into American constitutional law, it did erect an analytical framework which Justices in later cases employed to rationalize their reliance on foreign law.

In an opinion announcing the judgment of the Court, Justice Stewart (joined by Justices Powell and Stevens) explained that:

> [T]he Court has not confined the prohibition embodied in the Eighth Amendment to "barbarous" methods that were generally outlawed in the 18th century. Instead, the

---

countries simply are not relevant. . . . [T]he *Trop* plurality—representing the view of only a minority of the Court—offered no explanation for its . . . citation [of international laws]". *Atkins* v. *Virginia*, 536 U.S. 304, 325 (2002) (dissenting opinion).

[294] 428 U.S. 153 (1976).

Amendment has been interpreted in a flexible and dynamic
manner. The Court early recognized that "a principle to be
vital must be capable of wider application than the mischief
which gave it birth." . . . Thus the Clause forbidding "cruel
and unusual" punishments *"is not fastened to the obsolete but
may acquire meaning as public opinion becomes enlightened by a
humane justice."* [295]

Thus, *an assessment of contemporary values* concerning
the infliction of a challenged sanction is relevant to the
application of the Eighth Amendment. . . . [T]his
assessment does not call for a subjective judgment. It
requires, rather, that we look to *objective indicia that reflect
the public attitude* toward a given sanction.

But our cases also make clear that *public perceptions of
standards of decency with respect to criminal sanctions are not
conclusive. A penalty also must accord with "the dignity of man,"*
which is the "basic concept underlying the Eighth
Amendment." [296]

Although constitutional "interpret[ation] in a flexible and
dynamic manner" is typically a code-phrase for "the living
Constitution" (and probably was employed as such by Justice
Stewart), the Eighth Amendment may be one of the narrow
arenas in which that doctrine could find a legitimate
application. For a not implausible construction of the
Amendment is that it refers to "punishments" deemed "cruel
and unusual," not just according to the standards of the late

---

[295] Ibid. at 171 (emphasis supplied).

[296] Ibid. at 173 (emphasis supplied).

1700s, but also in light of the perhaps different standards of the times in which they are inflicted.

Even if so, however, the constitutional problem nevertheless remains: *Who* is to say what constitutes "humane justice" or "the dignity of man," and on *what* basis? A further issue is whether the test of "cruel and unusual punishments" is unidirectional—that is, whether "punishments" that are not unconstitutionally "cruel and unusual" for the times in which they are inflicted are nonetheless repugnant to the Eighth Amendment because they are no less or even more "cruel and unusual" than "punishments" prohibited in the late 1700s.[297] For example, in a society under siege by organized "terrorists," capital punishment might hardly appear "cruel" even for acts of "terrorism" that resulted in no fatalities—indeed, it might be deemed a necessary means of self-defense to protect "the dignity of man" for members of that society. Yet for Justice Stewart, although an "assessment of contemporary values" based on "objective indicia that reflect the public attitude" was "relevant," mere "public perceptions of standards of decency" would be disregarded, unless "[a] penalty also . . . accord[ed] with "the dignity of man"'" *as the Justices perceived it.*

With this as their premise, Justices in later cases would naturally seize on foreign law as a valuable source of colorable arguments against capital punishment. By referring to supposedly "objective indicia that reflected the public attitude"

---

[297] Although statistics may allow determinations of whether "punishments" in one era were more or less "unusual" than in another era, how one can evaluate comparative "cruel[ty]" is problematic.

in foreign countries against capital punishment, and then expatiating on "the dignity of man" as foreigners conceived of it, the Justices could jury-rig a basis for denouncing such punishment as "cruel and unusual," *even when the "public attitude" in a State or the United States as a whole strongly favored it.* Of course, recourse to foreign law or public opinion is neither constitutionally "objective," nor even relevant, unless the Constitution actually allows consideration of such matters. And nowhere from *Trop* to *Lawrence* would any Justice ever prove that it does. Nevertheless, "the principle [would lay] about like a loaded weapon ready for the hand of any authority that could bring forward a plausible claim of an urgent need."[298]

In *Gregg*, Justice Stewart touched obliquely upon another reason for using foreign law and like devices to "interpret[the Constitution] in a flexible and dynamic manner," when he repeated the myth of "judicial supremacy" that "[a] decision [of the Supreme Court] that a given punishment is impermissible under the Eighth Amendment *cannot be reversed short of a constitutional amendment.*"[299] Now, this statement is not true, even on its own terms. For, unless drafted explicitly as an *ex post facto* law or bill of attainder, a constitutional amendment will not reverse the Court's decision (in the sense of commanding the execution of the prisoner whose sentence of death was set aside), but only the faulty constitutional principle enunciated in the case, and that just for future cases.

---

[298] Korematsu, 323 U.S. at 246 (Jackson, J., dissenting).

[299] 428 U.S. at 176 (emphasis supplied).

Moreover, a later Court, or for that matter the selfsame Court, can reverse the faulty constitutional principle in a subsequent case without a constitutional amendment—and can even overturn the original erroneous decision directly—for example, if it had been obtained by fraud.[300] In addition, were the erroneous decision in favor of the death penalty, it could be effectively nullified altogether if the President (or the Governor of the State) pardoned the convicted individual.[301]

Yet, for the Supreme Court to maintain its institutional "supremacy" against everyone and everything except a constitutional amendment—while at the same time remaining able to reach the often different results the justices desire in situations that would, on any principled legal basis, demand identical outcomes—the Court must retain the flexibility surreptitiously to change the Constitution as it goes along from case to case, so that it never finds itself confined, let alone bound, by its own prior decisions, or even by the reasoning in those decisions. That is, *judicial imperialism demands judicial opportunism. Judicial opportunism requires the justices to go outside the actual law of the Constitution as circumstances dictate. And the*

---

[300] See *Hazel-Atlas Glass Co.* v. *Hartford-Empire Co.*, 322 U.S. 238, 244-50 (1944).

[301] See U.S. Const. art. II, § 2, cl. 1 (the President "shall have Power to grant Reprieves and Pardons for Offenses against the United States, except in Cases of Impeachment"). See Ex parte *Garland*, 71 U.S. (4 Wall.) 333, 380 (1867) (a pardon "releases the punishment and blots out of existence the guilt, so that in the eye of the law the offender is as innocent as if he had never committed the offence").

*justices can hardly go farther outside the actual law of the
Constitution than to resort to foreign law.*

C. In *Coker* v. *Georgia*,[302] the Court decided that a sentence
of death for the crime of raping an adult woman violated the
Eighth Amendment, either because "death is ... a
disproportionate penalty for [that] crime,"[303] or because "the
death penalty is in all circumstances cruel and unusual
punishment."[304] In noting that "Georgia [among all the States]
is the sole jurisdiction in the United States at the present time
that authorizes a sentence of death when the rape victim is an
adult woman,"[305] Justice White's plurality opinion also recalled
that in *Trop* v. *Dulles*:[306]

> [T]he plurality took pains to note the climate of
> international opinion concerning the acceptability of a
> particular punishment. It is thus not irrelevant here that out
> of 60 major nations in the world surveyed in 1965, only
> three retained the death penalty for rape where death did
> not ensue. United Nations Department of Economic and
> Social Affairs, Capital punishment 40, 86 (1986).[307]

Justice White went on to observe that:

---

[302] 433 U.S. 584 (1977).

[303] Ibid. at 597 (White, J., announcing the opinion of the Court, joined by
Stewart, Blackmun, and Stevens, JJ.).

[304] Ibid. at 600 (Brennan, J., concurring in the judgment), 600-01 (Marshall,
J., concurring in the judgment).

[305] Ibid. at 595-96.

[306] 356 U.S. 86, 102 (1958), discussed ante, at 96-98.

[307] 433 U.S. at 596 n.10.

> [R]ecent events evidencing the attitude of state legislatures
> and sentencing juries do not wholly determine this
> controversy, for the Constitution contemplates that in the
> end *our own judgment* will be brought to bear on the
> question of the acceptability of the death penalty under the
> Eighth Amendment.[308]

If this meant that the Justices must pass in each case on the
sufficiency of the evidence adduced for or against "the
acceptability of the death penalty"—and be bound in their
determination by the record, the rules of evidence, standards
of proof, and legal logic conscientiously applied—the assertion
cannot be faulted. But the ruling in *Coker* as well as subsequent
cases made clear that Justice White meant *"our own* judgment"
with exactly that emphasis—namely, that the Justices'
subjective views of "acceptability" would ultimately control: «Le
loi, c'est moi.»

Justice White never tried to explain, however, where in
the Constitution a warrant for such a result can be found. How
could he have? His assertion exceeded in gall even the familiar
judicial flippancy that "the Constitution is what the judges say
it is." For that boast at least plays lip service to "the supreme
Law of the Land"[309] by implicitly representing that the Justices
are actually interpreting it, not simply substituting their "own
judgment" for WE THE PEOPLE'S mandate. Justice White's
declaration amounted to the quite different claim that the
Constitution actually *abdicates* in favor of *the Justices'* "own

---

[308] Ibid. at 597 (emphasis supplied).

[309] U.S. Const. art. VI, cl. 2.

judgment." No longer are the Justices even pretending to say what the Constitution *itself* is; now, they are arrantly announcing that *they* are the Constitution. Of course, if that is the situation, the Justices can incorporate foreign law—or even intergalactic legal principles drawn from episodes of *Star Trek*—into the Constitution, because the sources of their inspirations are ultimately beside the point, the inspirations themselves becoming the "law" of each case simply perforce of their enunciations. The sources are cited solely to brush legalistic coloration, and thereby political camouflage, onto what is fundamentally an absolutist regime: the pretense, a "court" in the judicial sense; the reality, a "court" in the monarchical sense.

D. *Enmund* v. *Florida*[310] held that imposition of the death penalty on a person who merely aids and abets the commission of a felony in the course of which others commit a murder violates the Eighth Amendment. Per Justice White, the Court observed that, in reaching its conclusion in *Coker*, the plurality opinion there had:

> stressed that our judgment "should be informed by objective factors to the maximum possible extent." . . . Accordingly, the Court looked to the historical development of the punishment at issue, legislative judgments, *international opinion*, and the sentencing decisions juries have made *before bringing its own judgment to bear on the matter*.[311]

---

[310] 458 U.S. 782 (1982).

[311] Ibid. at 788-89 (emphasis supplied), citing 433 U.S. at 592.

The Court further observed that "the doctrine of felony murder has been abolished in England and India, severely restricted in Canada and a number of other Commonwealth countries, and is unknown in continental Europe."[312] The Court apparently was little concerned that "the doctrine of felony murder" had been unquestioned in *pre*-constitutional English common law (howsoever England and "other Commonwealth countries" treated it later on), and that the doctrine "is unknown in continental Europe" because European law derived, not from Anglo-American common law, but from the quite different *corpus* of Roman law.

Justice White then stressed once again that, "[a]lthough the judgments of legislatures, juries, and prosecutors weigh heavily in the balance, *it is for us ultimately to judge* whether the Eighth Amendment permits imposition of the death penalty."[313] Which made clear that *the Justices could strike every consideration other than foreign law and opinion* if they so chose (or, for that matter, could consult nothing but their own personal views). One wonders where in the Constitution this license lies. Surely not in WE THE PEOPLE'S delegation of "[t]he judicial Power"[314]—for "[j]udicial power, as contradistinguished from the power of the laws, has no existence. Courts are the mere instruments of the law, and can will nothing."[315] "In the ordinary use of language it will hardly

---

[312] 458 U.S. at 796 n.22.

[313] Ibid. at 797 (emphasis supplied).

[314] U.S. Const. art. III, § 1.

[315] *Osborn* v. *Bank of the United States*, 22 U.S. (9 Wheat.) 738, 866 (1824).

be contended that the decisions of Courts constitute laws.
They are, at most, only evidence of what the laws are; and are
not of themselves laws. They are often re-examined, reversed,
and qualified by the Courts themselves, whenever they are
found to be either defective, or ill-founded, or otherwise
incorrect."[316] The authority Justice White arrogated to the
Court in both *Coker* and *Enmund* could have derived only from
WE THE PEOPLE'S delegation to the Justices of a true
"constitutive Power": namely, not just the power to opine on
what the law is as made by others, but the power themselves
to make the law from the whole cloth of their own
imaginations. Merely to state this hypothesis is to draw into
serious question the good sense or the good faith of the people
who advance it.

E. *Thompson* v. *Oklahoma*[317] held that the death penalty
applied to a fifteen-year-old murderer constitutes "cruel and
unusual punishment[ ]." In an opinion announcing the
judgment of the Court, Justice Stevens contended that "Eighth
Amendment jurisprudence must reflect 'evolving standards of
decency'"[318]—with the extent of the evolution to be judged, *à
la* Darwin, by travels to far-away lands.

> The conclusion that it would offend civilized standards
> of decency to execute a person who was less than 16 years
> old at the time of his . . . offense is consistent with the views

---

[316] *Swift* v. *Tyson*, 41 U.S. (16 Pet.) 1, 18 (1842).

[317] 487 U.S. 815 (1988).

[318] 487 U.S. at 820 n.4 (opinion of Stevens, J., in which Brennan, Marshall,
and Blackmun, JJ., joined).

that have been expressed . . . by the leading members of the Western European community. . . . Although the death penalty has not been entirely abolished in the United Kingdom or New Zealand (it has been abolished in Australia, except in the State of New South Wales . . .), in neither of these countries may a juvenile be executed. The death penalty has been abolished in West Germany, France, Portugal, The Netherlands, and all of the Scandinavian countries, and is available only for exceptional crimes such as treason in Canada, Italy, Spain, and Switzerland. Juvenile executions are also prohibited in the Soviet Union.[319]

Typically, too, Justice Stevens's theory assumed without argument, let alone proof, that human "decency" always "evolv[es]," in the sense of following an unidirectional course toward "progress." Yet the principle of decision he applied could not logically preclude future courts from "reflect[ing d]evolving standards." Indeed, without some overarching and always controlling standard of "rectitude" by which to judge, what constitutes "decency" (and its progress or retrogression) is a matter merely of personal taste raised to the level of social convention or political power. In that event, depending on circumstances, Stalinism could be read into the Constitution with as much justification as Stevensism.

Justice Stevens then went on to observe that "three major human rights treaties explicitly prohibit juvenile death

---

[319] Ibid. at 830-31 (footnotes omitted), citing *Trop* v. *Dulles*, 356 U.S. 86, 102 (1958); *Coker* v. *Georgia*, 433 U.S. 584, 596 (1977); and *Enmund* v. *Florida*, 458 U.S. 782, 796-97 & n.22 (1982).

penalties."[320] (If anything, though, this reference was wholly
irrelevant, inasmuch as two of these treaties were signed but
not ratified by the United States; and although the third was
ratified, it did not apply to the case, because it addressed the
protection of civilians only in time of war.)

Dissenting, Justice Scalia acidly commented:

> When the Federal Government, and almost 40% of the
> States . . . , allow for the imposition of the death penalty on
> any juvenile who has been tried as an adult, . . . it is
> obviously impossible for the plurality to rely upon any
> evolved societal consensus discernible in legislation—or at
> least discernible in legislation of *this* society, which is
> assuredly all that is relevant.
>
> . . . The plurality's reliance upon Amnesty
> International's account of what it pronounces to be
> civilized standards of decency in other countries [487 U.S. at
> 830-31 & n.34] . . . is totally inappropriate as a means of
> establishing the fundamental beliefs of this Nation. That
> 40% of our States do not rule out capital punishment for 15-
> year-old felons is determinative of the question before us
> here, even if that position contradicts the uniform view of
> the rest of the world. We must never forget that it is a
> Constitution for the United States of America that we are
> expounding. The practices of other nations, particularly
> other democracies, can be relevant to determining whether
> a practice uniform among our people is not merely an
> historical accident, but rather so "implicit in the concept of
> ordered liberty" that it occupies a place not merely in our
> mores but, text permitting, in our Constitution as well. See

---

[320] 487 U.S. at 831 n.34.

Palko v. Connecticut, 302 U.S. 319, 325 (1937) (Cardozo, J.).
But where there is not first a settled consensus among our
own people, the views of other nations, however
enlightened the justices of this Court may think them to be,
cannot be imposed upon Americans through the
Constitution. In the present case, therefore, the fact that a
majority of foreign nations would not impose capital
punishment upon persons under 16 at the time of the crime
is of no more relevance than the fact that a majority of
them would not impose capital punishment at all, or have
standards of due process quite different from our own.[321]

Now, *Lawrence* would prove prescient Justice Scalia's
concern that other Justices might someday decide a
constitutional question based on the fact that foreign nations
"have standards of due process quite different from our own."
But in some other particulars he was wrong. For one, even if
American "liberty" were (in Justice Scalia's deprecatory phrase)
"merely an historical accident," to the same degree would the
Constitution as a whole be such an "accident"—which, even if
true, would neither decrease its character and binding
authority as "law" in America, nor license its misconstruction
by reference to foreign laws that are no less "historical
accident[s]."

For another, "the concept of ordered liberty" refers to
"liberty" in the specifically American experience, not "liberty"

---

[321] Ibid. at 868 & n.4 (separate opinion, in which Rehnquist, C.J., and
White, J., joined). In joining this opinion, Justice White appeared to
repudiate his former reliance on "international opinion" in *Enmund*.

in the abstract. *Palko* v. *Connecticut*[322] was what lawyers' style
an "incorporation" case, holding that the Due Process Clause
of the Fourteenth Amendment could impose upon the States
"immunities that are valid as against the federal government
by force of specific pledges of particular amendments [in the
Bill of Rights that] have been found to be implicit in the
concept of ordered liberty, and thus ... become valid as
against the states."[323] *Palko* was inaccurate as to the legal
foundation for its holding, in that the Fourteenth Amendment
applies the Bill of Rights to the States through the
Amendment's Privileges and Immunities Clause, not its Due
Process Clause.[324] In any event, though, no one ever imagined
in *Palko* (or before) that "liberty" in the Fourteenth
Amendment should or even could be construed with reference
to how other countries or civilizations might understand
"liberty" in their laws or dictionaries. As the Court held in
Meyer v. *Nebraska*,[325] the Fourteenth Amendment protects
"those privileges *long recognized at common law* as essential to
the orderly pursuit of happiness by free men."[326] Of course,
Justice Scalia may also have been thinking of "the concept of

---

[322] 302 U.S. 319 (1937).

[323] Ibid. at 324-25.

[324] See 2 W. Crosskey, *Politics and the Constitution*, ante note 161, chs. XXX-
XXXI. The Supreme Court adopted the "incorporation" doctrine so as
partially to reverse, without having actually to repudiate, its earlier blunder
in *The Slaughter-House Cases*, 83 U.S. (16 Wall.) 36 (1873). See Crosskey, ch.
XXXII.

[325] 262 U.S. 390 (1923).

[326] Ibid. at 399 (emphasis supplied).

ordered liberty" in the sense of "the Laws of Nature and of Nature's God," which undergird and inform the Constitution through the Declaration of Independence.[327] In that case, however, not the laws of particular foreign nations, but the overarching principles of "rectitude" that control all laws (and absent compliance with which mere acts of government are not "laws" at all), are uniquely relevant.

Its demerits aside, Justice Scalia's dissent did correctly recognize the danger of, and rightly denounce as unconstitutional, other Justices' reliance on foreign law for constitutional exegesis. Moreover, Scalia savaged the notion that the Justices' own opinions *are* the Constitution:

> Having avoided any attempt to justify its holding on the basis of the original understanding of what was "cruel and unusual punishment," and having utterly failed in justifying its holding on the basis of "evolving standards of decency" evidenced by "the work product of state legislatures and sentencing juries," . . . the plurality proceeds . . . to set forth its views regarding the desirability of ever imposing capital punishment for a murder committed by a 15-year-old. . . .
>
> This is in accord with the proposition set out at the beginning of the plurality's discussion . . . , that "'[a]lthough the judgments of legislatures, juries, and prosecutors weigh heavily in the balance, it is for us ultimately to judge whether the Eighth Amendment permits imposition of the death penalty.'" . . . I reject that proposition in the sense intended here. It is assuredly "for us ultimately to judge"

---

[327] See U.S. Const. amends. IX and X.

what the Eighth Amendment permits, but that means it is
for us to judge whether certain punishments are forbidden
because, despite what society thinks, they were forbidden
under the original understanding of "cruel and unusual,"
. . . or because they come within current understanding of
what is "cruel and unusual," because of the "evolving
standards of decency" *of our national society*; but not because
they are out of accord with the perceptions of decency, or
of penology, or of mercy, entertained—or strongly
entertained, or even held as an "abiding conviction"—by a
majority of the small and unrepresentative segment of our
society that sits on this Court.[328]

F. Justice Scalia's admonition bore fruit (albeit only
temporarily) in *Stanford* v. *Kentucky*,[329] which held that
imposition of the death penalty on 16- and 17-year-old
murderers does not violate the Eighth Amendment. In an
opinion announcing the judgment of the Court, Scalia
observed:

> [The] petitioners are left to argue that their punishment is
> contrary to the "evolving standards of decency that mark
> the progress of a maturing society" . . . . They are correct in
> asserting that this Court has "not confined the prohibition
> embodied in the Eight Amendment to 'barbarous' methods
> that were generally outlawed in the 18th century," but
> instead has interpreted the Amendment "in a flexible and
> dynamic manner." . . . In determining what standards have
> "evolved," however, we have looked not to our own

---

[328] 487 U.S. at 872-73. Again, by joining in this dissent, apparently Justice
White abjured his former contrary view in *Enmund*.

[329] 492 U.S. 361 (1989).

conceptions of decency, but to those of modern American society as a whole.

. . .

We emphasize that it is *American* conceptions of decency that are dispositive, rejecting the contentions of petitioners and their various amici (accepted by the dissent . . .) that the sentencing practices of other countries are relevant.[330]

The punishment is either "cruel *and* unusual" (i.e., society has set its face against it) or it is not. The audience for these arguments . . . is not this Court but the citizenry of the United States. It is they, not we, who must be persuaded. For . . . our job is to *identify* the "evolving standards of decency"; to determine, not what they *should* be, but what they *are*. We have no power under the Eighth Amendment to substitute our belief. . . .

We reject the dissent's contention that our approach, by "largely return[ing] the task of defining the contours of the Eighth Amendment protection to political majorities," leaves "'[c]onstitutional doctrine [to] be formulated by . . . those institutions which the Constitution is supposed to limit'" . . . . When this Court cast loose from the historical moorings consisting of the original application of the Eighth Amendment, it did not embark rudderless upon a wide-open sea. Rather, it limited the Amendment's extension to those practices contrary to the "evolving *standards* of decency that mark the progress of a maturing *society*." Trop v Dulles, 356 US, at 101 . . . (plurality opinion) (emphasis added). It has never been thought that this was a

---

[330] Ibid. at 369 & n.1 (separate opinion, in which Rehnquist, C.J., and White and Kennedy, JJ., joined).

shorthand reference to the preferences of a majority of this Court. By reaching a decision supported neither by constitutional text nor by the demonstrable current standards of our citizens, the dissent displays a failure to appreciate that "those institutions which the Constitution is supposed to limit" include the Court itself. To say, as the dissent says that "'it is for *us* ultimately to judge whether the Eighth Amendment permits imposition of the death penalty,'" . . . and to mean that as the dissent means it, i.e., that it is for *us* to judge, not on the basis of what we perceive the Eighth Amendment originally prohibited, or on the basis of what we perceive the society through its democratic processes now overwhelmingly disapproves, but on the basis of what we think "proportionate" and "measurably contributory to acceptable goals of punishment"—to say and mean that, is to replace judges of the law with a committee of philosopher-kings.[331]

The plain lesson Justice Scalia taught, however, was lost on Justices Brennan, Blackmun, Marshall, and Stevens, who joined in Brennan's dissenting opinion, wherein he argued:

> Our cases recognize that objective indicators of contemporary standards of decency in the form of legislation in other countries are also of relevance to Eighth Amendment analysis. . . . Many countries . . . have formally abolished the death penalty, or have limited its use to exceptional crimes such as treason. . . . Twenty-seven others do not in practice impose the penalty. . . . Of the nations that retain capital punishment, a majority . . . prohibits the execution of juveniles. . . . In addition to national laws, three leading human rights treaties ratified or

---

[331] Ibid. at 378-79.

signed by the United States explicitly prohibit juvenile death penalties. Within the world community, the imposition of the death penalty for juvenile crimes appears to be overwhelmingly disapproved.[332]

Of no little significance was Justice Brennan's invocation of "[o]ur cases"—that is, other musings by the Supreme Court, rather than the terms of the Constitution—as his authority. Then he asserted that the "rejection [of the death penalty] generally throughout the world"—along with its "rejection . . . by a majority of the States, the rarity of the sentence for juveniles . . . , [and] the decisions of respected organizations in relevant fields that this punishment is unacceptable"— "provide to my mind a strong grounding for the view that it is not constitutionally tolerable that certain States persist in authorizing the execution of adolescent offenders."[333]

Again, when Justice Brennan's irrelevant authorities are stripped away, the centrality of foreign law comes to the fore. That "a majority of the States" has "reject[ed]" the death penalty, and that "the sentence for juveniles" is "rar[e]," are *political data*, not *constitutional proofs*, in that "rejection" and "rarity" of the death penalty are perfectly consistent with continued existence of the legal power to impose it. So Brennan's argument reduced to the "overwhelming[ ] disapprov[al]" of the death penalty "[w]ithin the world

---

[332] Ibid. at 389-90 (footnotes omitted) (separate opinion).

[333] Ibid.

community," coupled with "decisions of respected organizations in relevant fields."[334]

G. *Printz v. United States*[335] shifted the Court's focus from the death penalty to so-called "gun control."[336] The Court (per Justice Scalia) held unconstitutional the provision of the Brady Act that required local chief law enforcement officers to conduct background checks on proposed handgun transferees.[337]

Dissenting, Justice Breyer (joined by Justice Stevens) argued:

> At least some other countries, facing the same basic problem, have found that local control is better maintained through application of a principle that is the direct opposite of the principle the majority derives from the silence of our Constitution. The federal systems of Switzerland, Germany, and the European Union, for example, all provide that constituent states, not federal bureaucracies, will themselves implement many of the laws, rules, regulations, or decrees enacted by the central "federal" body. . . . They do so in part because they believe that such a system interferes less, not more, with the independent

---

[334] Justice Brennan's reference to these "respected organizations" appears to have been a judicial oar dipped into the waters of constitutional exegesis in favor of the NGOs ("nongovernmental organizations"), now so active in the UN and elsewhere.

[335] 521 U.S. 898 (1997).

[336] "Gun control" is to the Second Amendment as "occupational control" would be to the Thirteenth: a euphemism for doing precisely what the Amendment prohibits.

[337] 18 U.S.C. § 922(s)(2).

authority of the "state," member nation, or other subsidiary government, and helps to safeguard individual liberty as well. . . .

Of course, we are interpreting our own Constitution, not those of other nations, and there may be relevant political and structural differences between their systems and our own. . . . But their experience may nonetheless cast an empirical light on the consequences of different solutions to a common legal problem—in this case the problem of reconciling central authority with the need to preserve the liberty-enhancing autonomy of a smaller constituent governmental entity. . . .

As comparative experience suggests, there is no need to interpret the Constitution as containing an absolute principle—forbidding the assignment of virtually any federal duty to any state official.[338]

Although Justice Breyer made formal obeisance to the fact that "we are interpreting our own Constitution, not those of other nations," he did not suffer that fact to thwart his practical reliance on those nations' "experience" as a means of determining as a matter of American law that "there is no need to interpret the Constitution" in one way as opposed to another. Precisely why "comparative experience" of foreign nations is a proper source for what may be "need[ed]" in constitutional interpretation, Justice Breyer did not adequately explain, however. That, according to him, "the[ ] experience [of foreign nations] may . . . cast an empirical light on the consequences of different solutions to a common legal

---

[338] 521 U.S. at 976-77 (separate opinion).

THE INSINUATION OF FOREIGN LAW INTO CONSTITUTIONAL
JURISPRUDENCE

problem" simply begged the question, because the "legal problem" cannot be "common" where "the supreme Law *of the Land*"[339] being interpreted is *unique to the United States*. The "comparative experience[s]" of foreign nations might by themselves provide *political data* useful to a body charged with amending the Constitution, but not *legal principles* usable by a court concerned only with construing it.

H. The Court denied a petition for a writ of certiorari in *Knight v. Florida*,[340] another death-penalty case. Although this intimated nothing about the merits of the litigation,[341] Justice Breyer dissented, contending:

> A growing number of courts outside the United States . . . have held that lengthy delay in administering a *lawful* death penalty renders ultimate execution inhuman, degrading, or unusually cruel.
>
> . . .
>
> Obviously this foreign authority does not bind us. After all, we are interpreting a "Constitution for the United States of America" . . . .
>
> Nonetheless, . . . this Court has long considered as relevant and informative the way in which foreign courts have applied standards roughly comparable to our own constitutional standards in roughly comparable circumstances. . . .

---

[339] U.S. Const. art. VI, cl. 2 (emphasis supplied).

[340] 528 U.S. 990 (1999).

[341] See, e.g., *Barber v. Tennessee*, 513 U.S. 1184, 1184 (1995).

> In these cases, the foreign courts ... have considered roughly comparable questions under roughly comparable legal standards. . . . Consequently, I believe their views are useful even though not binding.[342]

Inasmuch as the Supreme Court treats even its own constitutional precedents as not binding upon it, for Justice Breyer to concede—as he had to—that the decisions of "foreign courts" are "not binding" upon the Court, and that foreign "standards" are only "*roughly* comparable to our own constitutional standards in *roughly* comparable circumstances," was far less important than his conclusion that those decisions were nonetheless "relevant," "informative," and "useful" for deciding the constitutional issue *sub judice*. Because, if decisions of foreign courts are *at all* "useful" for deciding a constitutional issue, in some circumstances they could become the *determinative* factor, and thus could *control* the outcome of the case, even if they were not treated as formally "binding" at the onset. Moreover, as a matter of the received doctrine of *stare decisis*, through the Supreme Court's opinion adopting them, these decisions of foreign courts would thereafter bind all lower American courts.[343]

---

[342] 528 U.S. at 995-98.

[343] See *Hutto* v. *Davis*, 454 U.S. 370, 375 (1982) (lower courts must follow the Supreme Court's precedent "no matter how misguided the judges of those courts may think it to be"). That this rule of robotic response may require judges of lower courts to perjure themselves as to their oaths of office apparently has not dawned on the Supreme Court. See U.S. Const. art. VI, cl. 3 ("all . . . judicial Officers, both of the United States and of the several States, shall be bound by Oath or Affirmation, to support this Constitution"). Inasmuch as the Supreme Court's precedents are not "this Constitution,"

Of course, one might presume that foreign legal "standards" only *roughly* comparable to our own constitutional standards in *roughly* comparable circumstances" would rarely prove even marginally "useful" to precise legal minds. Indeed, especially in constitutional litigation, rough comparisons even among wholly American statutes and court decisions ought to be excluded as substandard grist for the judicial mill. One *might* presume as much, that is, until one realized that the roughness of the comparisons are inconsequential, because the comparisons themselves are nothing more than rhetorical props for the Justices' own personal judgments—and, for that very reason, the roughness of the comparisons might even maximize their "useful[ness]" by providing greater leeway for amending the Constitution under the cloak of construing it.

I. In *Atkins* v. *Virginia*,[344] the Court held that the execution of a mentally retarded individual constitutes "cruel and unusual punishment[ ]" because it is excessive or disproportionate. Writing the majority opinion, Justice Stevens (joined by Justices Breyer, Ginsberg, Kennedy, O'Connor, and Souter) explained that review under "'the evolving standards of decency that mark the progress of a maturing society'" "should be informed by "'objective factors to the maximum extent possible','" and that the "'clearest and

---

compelling judges of lower courts slavishly to follow them forces those judges to violate their "Oath[s] or Affirmation[s]" of office whenever in good conscience they disagree with the Supreme Court on a constitutional issue.

[344] 536 U.S. 304 (2002).

most reliable objective evidence of contemporary values is the legislation enacted by the country's legislatures.'"[345] Nonetheless, he added, "the objective evidence, though of great importance, d[oes] not 'wholly determine' the controversy, 'for the Constitution contemplates that in the end our own judgment will be brought to bear on the question of the acceptability of the death penalty.'"[346] Exactly *where* the Constitution contemplates anything of the kind, Justice Stevens did not say, however. Yet, once again, the subjective factor of "our own judgment" was held to be capable of overriding the "clearest and most reliable objective evidence."

On the merits, Justice Stevens found:

> [T]he large number of States prohibiting the execution of mentally retarded persons . . . provides powerful evidence that today our society views mentally retarded offenders as categorically less culpable than the average criminal. . . . The practice, therefore, has become truly unusual, and it is fair to say that a national consensus has developed against it.[347]

Moreover, he held that "[o]ur independent evaluation of the issue reveals no reason to disagree with the judgment of 'the legislatures that have recently addressed the matter' and concluded that death is not a suitable punishment for a mentally retarded criminal."[348]

---

[345] Ibid. at 311-12.

[346] Ibid. at 312.

[347] Ibid. at 315-16 (footnote omitted).

[348] Ibid. at 321.

Yet, although both the objective and the subjective indicia
coincided, Justice Stevens went further:

> Additional evidence makes it clear that th[e] legislative
> judgment reflects a much broader social and professional
> consensus. . . . [R]epresentatives of widely diverse religious
> communities in the United States, reflecting Christian,
> Jewish, Muslim, and Buddhist traditions, have filed an
> *amicus curiae* brief explaining that even though their views
> about the death penalty differ, they all "share a conviction
> that the execution of persons with mental retardation
> cannot be morally justified." . . . Moreover, within the
> world community, the imposition of the death penalty for
> crimes committed my mentally retarded offenders is
> overwhelmingly disapproved. . . . Finally, polling data
> shows a widespread consensus among Americans, even
> those who support the death penalty, that executing the
> mentally retarded is wrong. . . . Although these factors are
> by no means dispositive, their consistency with the
> legislative evidence lends further support to our conclusion
> that there is a consensus among those who have addressed
> the issue.[349]

In light of "the legislative evidence," and the Court's
having "no reason to disagree with [it]," this "[a]dditional
evidence" was pure—and, as the dissent rightly argued,
controversial—surplusage. So the majority in *Atkins* must have
included it, not because those Justices needed it in that case,
but because they *wanted* it to be available in other cases. By
including the "[a]dditional evidence," even unnecessarily, the
majority in *Atkins* created another precedent for future use of

---

[349] Ibid. at 316-317 n.21 (emphasis supplied).

similar material. To be sure, Justice Stevens conceded (as he had to) that "these factors [were] by no means dispositive." Nevertheless, as admissible "evidence" they could influence the outcome of a case. And perhaps even *control* it, because the "additional evidence" as to what "the world community ... overwhelmingly disapproved" the majority in *Atkins* considered as part and parcel of "[o]ur [that is, the Justices'] independent evaluation," which "in the end" could trump every other card in every other case. Indeed, if (as Justice Stevens said), what "the world community ... overwhelmingly disapproved" was capable of "lend[ing] *further* support to our conclusion," under some circumstances in other cases it could form the *entire basis of* "support" for "our conclusion."

Dissenting in *Atkins*, Chief Justice Rehnquist (joined by Justices Scalia and Thomas)

> call[ed] attention to the defects in the Court's decision to place weight on foreign laws, the views of professional and religious organizations, and opinion polls in reaching its conclusion. . . . The Court's suggestion that these sources are relevant to the constitutional question finds little support in our precedents and ... is antithetical to considerations of federalism, which instruct that any "permanent prohibition upon all units of democratic government must [be apparent] in the operative acts (laws and the application of laws) that the people have approved."[350]

---

[350] Ibid. at 322.

I fail to see . . . how the views of other countries regarding
the punishment of their citizens provide any support for the
Court's ultimate determination. While it is true that some
of our prior opinions have looked to "the climate of
international opinion," . . . to reinforce a conclusion
regarding evolving standards of decency, . . . we have since
explicitly rejected the idea that the sentencing practices of
other countries could "serve to establish the first Eighth
Amendment prerequisite, that [a] practice is accepted
among our people." *Stanford* [v. *Kentucky*, 492 U.S. 361, 369
(1989).[351]] . . .

Stanford's reasoning makes perfectly good sense, and
the Court offers no basis to question it. For if it is evidence
of a *national* consensus for which we are looking, then the
viewpoints of other countries simply are not relevant. And
nothing in *Thompson*,[352] *Enmund*,[353] *Coker*,[354] or *Trop*[355]
suggests otherwise. *Thompson, Enmund,* and *Coker* rely only
on the bare citation of international laws by the *Trop*
plurality as authority to deem other countries' sentencing
choices germane. But the *Trop* plurality—representing . . .
only a minority of the Court—offered no explanation for its
own citation . . . .[356]

Unfortunately, Chief Justice Rehnquist undercut his own
argument when he conceded that "some of our prior opinions

---

[351] Discussed ante, at 113-17.

[352] *Thompson* v. *Oklahoma*, 487 U.S. 815 (1988), discussed ante, at 107-13.

[353] *Enmund* v. *Florida*, 458 U.S. 782 (1982), discussed ante, at 105-07.

[354] *Coker* v. *Georgia*, 433 U.S. 584 (1977), discussed ante, at 103-05.

[355] *Trop* v. *Dulles*, 356 U.S. 86 (1958), discussed ante, at 96-98.

[356] 536 U.S. at 324-25.

have looked to 'the climate of international opinion,' . . . to reinforce a conclusion regarding evolving standards of decency." For if such evidence be admissible to "*reinforce* a conclusion," it must be no less admissible to *force* that "conclusion" in the first instance, in the absence of other evidence—particularly inasmuch as the Justices have arrogated to themselves the power to impose "our own judgment" on the constitutional question, based upon whatever evidence they find, or pretend to find, convincing.

Chief Justice Rehnquist identified the following critical issue:

> *Thompson, Enmund,* and *Coker* rel[ied] only on the bare citation of international laws by the *Trop* plurality as authority to deem other countries' sentencing choices germane. But the *Trop* plurality—representing the view of only a minority of the Court—*offered no explanation for its own citation . . . .*

Neither, later on, did Justice Breyer's dissent in *Foster* v. *Florida,*[357] nor the majority opinion in *Lawrence.* That is, no one has ever explained why or how foreign law may be used in— and perhaps even control—construction of the Constitution, or provided any reason why such an explanation is not mandatory, and why its absence alone does not constitute sufficient grounds for rejecting such use of foreign law out of hand.[358]

---

[357] 537 U.S. 990 (2002), discussed post.

[358] As a loyal member of the Court, Rehnquist avoided extrapolating from this data to the conclusion that "judicial supremacy" through "judicial

The reason no Justice has ever explained why or how
foreign law may be used to construe the Constitution is that
the Justices' use of such law is not a matter of *reason*, but of
raw *force*. As Justice Scalia charged, dissenting in *Atkins*:

> Beyond the empty talk of a "national consensus," the
> Court gives us a brief glimpse of what really underlies
> today's decision: pretension to a power confined *neither* by
> the moral sentiments originally enshrined in the Eighth
> Amendment (its original meaning), *nor even* by the current
> moral sentiments of the American people. "'[T]he
> Constitution,'" the Court says, "contemplates that in the
> end our own *judgment* will be brought to bear on the
> question of the acceptability of the death penalty under the
> Eighth Amendment'" . . . . The arrogance of this
> assumption of power takes one's breath away. And it
> explains, of course, why the Court can be so cavalier about
> the evidence of consensus. It is just a game, after all. "[I]n
> the end," it is the *feelings* and *intuition* of a majority of the
> Justices that count . . . .[359]

This also explains why it was futile for Chief Justice Rehnquist
to "take issue with the blind-faith credence [the majority in
Atkins] accord[ed] the opinion polls brought to [the Court's]
attention."[360] The majority put no "blind faith *credence*" in

---

review" is basically a snare and a delusion, if adventitious majorities of
Justices can impose on the country novel schemes of constitutional
interpretation without adducing convincing reasons, and if dissenting
Justices do not thoroughly expose the usurpation by conducting the sort of
detailed inquiry the present study undertakes.

[359] 536 U.S. at 348 (separate opinion, joined by Rehnquist, C.J., and
Thomas, J.).

[360] Ibid. at 326 (dissenting opinion).

opinion polls or anything else. Its purported reliance on polls was not a matter of "credence," but of convenience and camouflage: The Justices used whatever was at hand that would cloak their "own judgment" in the mantle of legitimate constitutional analysis.

More importantly, this may "explain[ ] . . . why the Court can be so cavalier about" foreign law: "It is just a game, after all."[361] But (as will be seen) perhaps more than that, too.

J. *Foster* v. *Florida*[362] was another death-penalty case in which the Court denied a petition for a writ of certiorari. Dissenting, Justice Breyer argued:

> Courts of other nations have found that delays . . . can render capital punishment degrading, shocking, or cruel. . . . Just as "attention to the judgment of other nations" can help Congress determine "the justice and propriety of [America's] measures," . . . so it can help guide this Court when it decides whether a particular punishment violates the Eighth Amendment.[363]

Pace Breyer, however, the analogy between Congress and the Court collapses with its own statement, because "[a]ll *legislative* Powers herein granted shall be vested in a Congress,"[364] whereas only "[t]he *judicial* Power of the United States, shall be vested in one supreme Court"[365]—and the

---

[361] Ibid. at 348 (Scalia, J., dissenting).

[362] 537 U.S. 990 (2002).

[363] Ibid. at 992-93 (separate opinion).

[364] U.S. Const. art. I, § 1 (emphasis supplied).

[365] U.S. Const. art. III, § 1 (emphasis supplied).

plainly legislature power to amend the Constitution has not
been vested even in Congress alone, and to no degree
whatsoever in the Court, but instead in Congress and
"Convention[s]" the proposals of which must be "ratified by
the Legislatures of three fourths of the several States, or by
Conventions in three fourths thereof."[366] Thus rather tepid was
Justice Thomas's critique of Justice Breyer, that "[w]hile
Congress, as a *legislature*, may wish to consider the actions of
other nations on any issue it likes, this Court's Eighth
Amendment jurisprudence should not impose foreign moods,
fads, or fashions on Americans."[367] First, the question is not one
of "impos[ing] foreign *moods, fads, or fashions*," but foreign
laws. Second, the issue is not what the Court *"should not"*
impose, but what it *cannot possibly impose*, under the Eighth
Amendment or any other provision of the Constitution, and
consistently with the Declaration of Independence.

K. Finally, the Court decided *Lawrence*, with the results
described above. As of this writing, *Lawrence* marks the second
majority decision within about a year in which the same line-
up of six Justices has supported the use of foreign law in
constitutional exegesis: *Atkins*—Justice Stevens, joined by
justices Breyer, Ginsberg, Kennedy, O'Connor, and Souter;
Lawrence—Justice Kennedy, joined by justices Breyer,
Ginsberg, Souter, and Stevens, with Justice O'Connor
concurring separately. And the same minority of three Justices

---

[366] U.S. Const. art. V.

[367] 537 U.S. at 990 n.* (separate opinion concurring in the denial of
certiorari).

has opposed such use in both cases: Chief Justice Rehnquist and justices Scalia and Thomas.

Justice Scalia's explanation in *Atkins* of "why the Court can be so cavalier about" foreign law may apply in *Lawrence*, too: "It is just a game, after all."[368] Nothing but what Chief Justice Rehnquist denounced in *Atkins* as "a *post hoc* rationalization for the majority's subjectively preferred result,"[369] yet perhaps these are merely appearances. Perhaps there is another, more disquieting explanation. The consistent use of foreign law by Justices Breyer, Ginsberg, Kennedy, O'Connor, Souter, and Stevens may not be a mere "game" or "rationalization" after all, but instead a conscious, long-term strategy: *gradually to infiltrate foreign law into constitutional interpretation, systematically to subvert the Constitution with principles of globalism, and ultimately to subordinate the Constitution (and all American law dependent upon it) to a new system of one-world jurisprudence—the recondite, but real meaning of the "emerging awareness" to which Justice Kennedy referred in* Lawrence.[370] Certainly the course of events affords WE THE PEOPLE ample cause to wonder whether this majority's actions amount merely to a series of disconnected "*post hoc* rationalizations," or add up to what the Declaration of Independence denounced as "a long train of abuses and usurpations, pursuing invariably the same Object" which "evinces a design to reduce [Americans] under absolute Despotism"—among which "long train" in

---

[368] 536 U.S. at 348 (dissenting opinion).

[369] Ibid. at 322 (dissenting opinion).

[370] 539 U.S. at 572.

1776 was that the King "ha[d] combined with others to subject us to a jurisdiction foreign to our constitution, and unacknowledged by our laws; giving his Assent to their Acts of pretended Legislation." What, one may ask, has changed since then, except the identity of the malefactors?

In any event, whether the Justices' embrace of a globalistic jurisprudence finds its source in the simple-minded opportunism of *"post hoc* rationalization[s]" deemed convenient for deciding particular cases, in an idiosyncratic favoritism for a New World Order the justices have absorbed from the fever swamps of Washingtonian "good thinking," or in the importunity of clerks whose supposed brilliance reflects only the thoroughness of the brainwashing they have received at leading law schools, the fatal danger to America is the same. If foreign law may legitimately be employed to construe the Eighth Amendment, and then the Fourteenth Amendment, who knows how much more of the Constitution can *and soon will* be subjected to—and radically changed by—it? "The principle . . . lies about like a loaded weapon ready for the hand of any authority that can bring forth a plausible claim of an urgent need"[371]—or that can muster five votes in the Supreme Court in the name of "judicial supremacy."

---

[371] *Korematsu* v. *United States*, 323 U.S. 214, 246 (1944) (Jackson, J., dissenting).

CHAPTER 4

The Plain Illegality
of the Promiscuous Use
of Foreign Law in
Constitutional Interpretation

A. Except in those limited instances the Constitution explicitly sanctions,[372] the promiscuous use of foreign law for the purpose of interpreting the Constitution is *never* necessary or proper.

On the one hand, if the interpretation of the Constitution without reference to foreign law is the same as the interpretation with reference to it, then foreign law is supererogatory—as lawyers say, merely "cumulative" evidence—and therefore inadmissible. On the other hand, if the interpretation of the Constitution without reference to foreign law is different from the interpretation with reference to it, then, unless foreign law is already binding on the Supreme Court perforce of the Constitution, its incorporation therein under the cloak of "construction" amounts to an

---

[372] See U.S. Const. art. I, § 8, cl. 10; art. I, § 9, cl. 8 and § 10, cl. 1; and art. II, § 2, cl. 2.

amendment of "the supreme Law of the Land."[373] Amending the Constitution, however, is not within "[t]he *judicial* Power of the United States,"[374] because WE THE PEOPLE have explicitly committed that power to *political* branches of government: to wit, Congress, the State Legislatures, and State Conventions.[375] Yet no one, including its most consistent proponents, openly denies that foreign law is *not* binding in constitutional exegesis. As even Justice Breyer conceded in *Knight* v. *Florida*,[376] "[o]bviously . . . foreign authority does not bind us. After all, we are interpreting a 'Constitution for the United States of America'."[377] And if not binding, foreign law cannot be controlling, either—because whatever evidence or legal principles control the decision of a "Case[ ]" or "Controvers[y]"[378] are, by hypothesis, binding, inasmuch as a court must always accept that evidence and follow that law. Therefore, *the promiscuous use of foreign law to interpret the Constitution is always either an irrelevance or an usurpation—or a species of tyranny, if the foreign law is to any degree inimical to American institutions or to "the Laws of Nature and of Nature's God" that the Declaration of Independence invoked and incorporated as the legal basis for the independence of the original thirteen States, and therefore as the legal basis for the Constitution they ratified.*

---

[373] U.S. Const. art. VI, cl. 2.

[374] U.S. Const. art. III, § 1 (emphasis supplied).

[375] U.S. Const. art. V.

[376] 528 U.S. 990 (1999), discussed ante, at 119-21.

[377] 528 U.S. at 996.

[378] U.S. Const. art. III, § 2, cls. 1-2.

B. Because the promiscuous use of foreign law for interpretation of the Constitution is never necessary or proper, such use violates the long-standing rule that the Supreme Court will not address a constitutional question unless it is "strict[ly] necess[ary]" to decide a "Case[ ]" or "Controvers[y]."[379] For any such use of a particular foreign law itself inevitably and unavoidably raises at least two constitutional issues: namely, the relevance and the effect of that law in the litigation *sub judice*.

C. The promiscuous use of foreign law to interpret the Constitution by Justices who must be presumed to understand the foregoing principles is plainly *knowing, intentional*, and *willful*. Even so, could it nevertheless be a matter of mere error? Could these Justices not defend their actions on the ground that, in employing foreign law to interpret the Constitution, they are relying on the doctrine of "the living Constitution," and that, even if "the living Constitution" could be proven false in comparison to "original intent," nonetheless it *is* the method of constitutional exegesis the contemporary Judiciary, legal profession, and legal *intelligentsia* generally accept? The only possible answer to this special pleading is *No*, as to whatever version of "the living Constitution" may be examined.

---

[379] *Rescue Army* v. *Municipal Court*, 331 U.S. 549, 568-75 (1947). *Accord, e.g., Carter* v. *Carter Coal Co.*, 298 U.S. 238, 325 (1936); *Spector Motor Service* v. *McLaughlin*, 323 U.S. 101, 105 (1944); *Coffman* v. *Breeze Corp.*, 323 U.S. 316, 324-25 (1945); *Alma Motor* v. *Timkin Co.*, 329 U.S. 129, 136-37 (1946).

1. Some hierophants of "the living Constitution" argue that no one today can reliably determine what certain words or phrases in the Constitution actually meant to Americans of the late 1700s; and, therefore, that to impart any legal effect to this obscure verbiage contemporary courts must impute to the words modern meanings—which in practice reduces to meanings congenial to particular judges' legal, political, economic, or other ideological or cultural points of view, presuppositions, or prejudices. Unfortunately for these special pleaders, however, no one can gainsay that a statute couched "in terms so vague that men of common intelligence must necessarily guess at its meaning and differ as to its application violates the first essential of due process of law."[380] Therefore, although these supposedly mysterious passages may have been law when WE THE PEOPLE understood what they meant, today they must be deemed unconstitutional (as the lawyers' jargon has it, "void for vagueness"), because no one really *knows* what they import, or it would not be necessary for judges to impart new meanings to them (that is, to "guess at [their] meaning[s]").

Contemporary judicial *substitution* of new words for old—for the process cannot qualify as "interpretation" when the old words are purportedly unintelligible—cannot cure vagueness in the Constitution, though, any more than in a statute, because just as judges lack power to rewrite statutes (the Constitution having "vested" "[a]ll legislative Powers . . . in . . . Congress" in Article I, Section 1), so too are they powerless to

---

[380] *Connally* v. *General Construction Co.*, 269 U.S. 385, 391 (1926).

amend the Constitution by verbal interpolations or otherwise, WE THE PEOPLE having reserved the full authority as to that matter for themselves in Article V.

2. Other exegetes of "the living Constitution" argue that, although certain words and phrases may be understandable today, even as they were in the late 1700s, nonetheless they now ought to be reinterpreted in order to comport with new political, economic, social, and cultural realities and necessities. Reinterpreted, that is, exclusively by the Judiciary, and ultimately by the Supreme Court—which rightly denies Congress such an interpretive license.[381]

This approach to "the living Constitution" neither obviates nor mitigates the problem of vagueness, but merely redirects its focus. Instead of being importuned to believe that judges *must*, as a practical matter, substitute modern verbiage for the original constitutional words and phrases of now unknown meaning, WE THE PEOPLE are simply told that judges *ought*, as a matter of policy, to reinterpret words and phrases of always known and once accepted meanings in order to make them gibe with novel, complex, and controversial concepts that not only lie entirely outside of the Constitution *but also themselves require interpretation and thereby invite endless dispute*. The latter consequence of this approach to "the living Constitution" opens up the matter of construction to such a degree that *everyone*—not only men of "common intelligence," but even men of extraordinary intelligence who concoct and

---

[381] See, e.g., *Eisner* v. *Macomber*, 252 U.S. 189, 206 (1920).

dispute these theories—"must necessarily guess at [the Constitution's] meaning and differ as to its application," because that "meaning" and "application" become simply matters of protean political, economic, and social policy. That the vagueness in this approach is extrinsic, rather than intrinsic, to the Constitution exacerbates its illegitimacy.

3. There is, however, a plausibly acceptable version of "the living Constitution": namely, that some words or phrases in "the supreme Law of the Land"[382] WE THE PEOPLE originally did intend to be taken in their *contemporary* meanings, *as those meanings might change from era to era.* For example, what constitutes an *"unreasonable* search and seizure,"[383] or *"cruel and unusual* punishments,"[384] or the *"Arms"* "the people" enjoy "the right . . . to keep and bear."[385] In the clearest of these cases, the particular "Arms" that WE THE PEOPLE had in mind in the late 1700s were the "Arms" of a then-contemporary member of the "Militia." For example, Congress early provided that "every citizen" enrolled in the Militia "shall . . . provide himself with a good musket or firelock . . . or with a good rifle."[386] WE THE PEOPLE could never have rationally intended, however, that *only the particular "Arms" with which individuals could supply themselves in the late 1700s* would come within, and thereby forevermore uniquely define and delimit, "the right of the

---

[382] U.S. Const. art. VI, cl. 2.

[383] U.S. Const. amend. IV (emphasis supplied).

[384] U.S. Const. amend. VIII (emphasis supplied).

[385] U.S. Const. amend. II (emphasis supplied).

[386] Act of 8 May 1792, ch. 33, § 1, 1 Stat. 271, 271.

people to keep and bear Arms," no matter what improvements in individual weaponry developed over the years. "Arms" must be construed, then, in a generic—and therefore "living," or expanding—sense. The "Arms" Congress specified in 1792 were, first, the "Arms" typically used by a light infantryman, irregular, guerrilla, or *franc tireur* of that era (because the Militia employed all of those tactics, depending on circumstances); and, second, the "Arms" available to individuals in the marketplace that would serve such purposes—from which one can deduce that the Constitution (as understood by Members of Congress closest to the founding) intended such *types and source* of "Arms" to be within "the right of the people to keep and bear." So, today, "Arms" within the Second Amendment would not be limited to flintlocks (with which WE THE PEOPLE were familiar in the late 1700s), but would embrace any form of long gun or hand gun that might serve a light infantryman, irregular, guerrilla, or *franc tireur* of the present era, including the ubiquitous semiautomatic (or even burst-fire) rifle in a military caliber, equipped with a detachable magazine, pistol grip, flash suppressor, and bayonet lug (with all of which WE THE PEOPLE are familiar today).

Most revealing of modern times, though, is that the Clinton administration and Congress used precisely those features which define a modern firearm suitable for the Militia to create a class of so-called "assault weapons" for prohibition[387]—in plain violation of Congress's constitutional

---

[387] 18 U.S.C. § 922(v, w).

trust and duty "[t]o provide *for* . . . *arming* . . . the Militia,"[388]
not disarming WE THE PEOPLE who form it. "Whatever
functions Congress are, by the Constitution, authorized to
perform, they are, when the public good requires it, bound to
perform."[389] If Congress chooses itself not to "arm[ ] . . . the
Militia," at least it should take no action to prevent the
members of the Militia from arming themselves. At present,
"the unorganized militia" consists of "all able-bodied males of
at least 17 years of age and . . . under 45 years of age who are,
or who have made a declaration of intention to become,
citizens of the United States" and "who are not members of
the National Guard or the Naval Militia."[390] The so-called
"assault-weapons ban" thus denied these people access to the
very weapons best suited for the Militia. Ergo, the ban was a
plainly intentional violation of both Congress's explicit
constitutional duty "[t]o provide *for* . . . *arming* . . . the Militia"
and the Second Amendment.

4. Yet, in all of these instances involving either the
illegitimate or the plausible "living Constitution," the
fundamental question of construction remains: "Reasonable"
or "cruel and unusual" to *whom*? "Arms" for *whom*? The only
possible answer being: to or for *Americans*, not foreigners. As
the Preamble to the Constitution states, "WE THE PEOPLE *of
the United States*, in Order to form a more perfect *Union*,
establish Justice, insure *domestic* Tranquility, provide for the

---

[388] U.S. Const. art. I, § 8, cl. 16 (emphasis supplied).

[389] *United States* v. *Marigold*, 50 U.S. (9 How.) 560, 567 (1850).

[390] 10 U.S.C. § 311.

common defence, promote the *general* Welfare, and secure the Blessings of Liberty *to ourselves and our Posterity*, do ordain and establish this Constitution *for the United States of America.*"[391] Therefore, even "the living Constitution" provides no excuse for promiscuously interpolating foreign law into constitutional interpretation—unless the Preamble can now be read as a mandate "to form a more perfect Union *with foreigners*, insure [*international or global*] Tranquility, provide for the common defence [*of a New World Order*], promote the general Welfare [*of people throughout the world*] and secure the Blessings of Liberty to [*a global community, according to foreigners' ideas of what constitutes Liberty*]." Inasmuch as this new dispensation is constitutionally absurd, use of foreign law in constitutional construction must be, not only knowing, intentional, and willful, but also *malicious*, in the sense of an act performed with knowledge of, or with willful blindness to or reckless disregard of, its wrongfulness.

D. Thus, the employment by certain Justices of foreign law in cases such as *Lawrence* constitutes a clear-cut violation of their "Oath[s] or Affirmation[s], to support this Constitution."[392] For "support" implies, after all, that *something* is already there, which the Justices' duty is to *maintain* in its original form—not to supply, supplement, supplant, subvert, or suppress. A violation of the Justices' "Oath[s] or Affirmation[s]" constitutes the crime of perjury or false

---

[391] Emphasis supplied.

[392] U.S. Const. art. VI, cl. 3.

swearing.[393] It is also a criminal abridgment of the civil rights of all Americans who may be affected by the justices' perfidious decisions.[394] And, therefore, it is both a lack of that "good Behaviour" required of all "Judges" of the General Government as a condition of "hold[ing] their Offices,"[395] and a "high Crime[ ] and Misdemeanor[ ]" which justifies their "removal from Office on Impeachment . . . and Conviction."[396]

---

[393] See 18 U.S.C. §§ 1001(a)(2) (false statements), 1621(1) (perjury).

[394] See 18 U.S.C. §§ 241-42.

[395] U.S. Const. art. III, § 1.

[396] U.S. Const. art. II, § 4.

Part II

Remedies for Certain Justices' Promiscuous Use of Foreign Law in Constitutional Interpretation

Introduction

Identifying and proving the Justices' dereliction of duty is not enough, however. An effective remedy must be specified. And remedy there must be.

> No man in this country is so high that he is above the law. No officer of the law may set that law at defiance with impunity. All the officers of the government, from the highest to the lowest, are creatures of the law, and are bound to obey it.

> It is the only supreme power in our system of government, and every man who by accepting office participates in its functions is only the more strongly bound to submit to that supremacy, and to observe the limitations which it imposes upon the exercise of the authority which it gives.[397]

"The Judges ... of the supreme ... Court[ ]" exercise "[t]he judicial Power of the United States" not in their own right, but as delegates of WE THE PEOPLE.[398] They are the mere creatures of the law; and, as such, lack any authority to transform the

---

[397] *United States* v. *Lee*, 106 U.S. 196, 220 (1882).

[398] Compare U.S. Const. art. III, § 1 with U.S. Const. preamble ("to ... establish Justice").

law into their creature. To be sure, the Court does claim that "the federal judiciary is supreme in the exposition of the law of the Constitution" and that "the interpretation of the [Constitution] enunciated by th[e Supreme] Court . . . is the supreme law of the land."[399] But notwithstanding—or even because of—this hyperbole, a mechanism must exist *under the law* by which even the self-styled "exposit[ors]" of the law can be compelled to conform their behavior to the law, under circumstances in which they are not allowed to misinterpret the law so as to immunize themselves from control or punishment for violation of their "Oath[s] or Affirmation[s]" of office. Otherwise, they may do what is impossible in a true government of laws: "set th[e supreme] law at defiance with impunity."

Now, many possible remedies for certain Justices' promiscuous use of foreign law for purposes of constitutional misinterpretation can be imagined. None of them, however, is either facile or foolproof.

---

[399] *Cooper v. Aaron*, 358 U.S. 1, 18 (1958).

CHAPTER 5

Interposition
by the States

1. In a case such as *Lawrence*, which stripped a State of a
• portion of her reserved sovereignty[400] by prohibiting her
use of her police power to promote public morality through
punishment of homosexual sodomy, Texas as the aggrieved
party could simply refuse to acquiesce in and to apply the
majority's decision. In *Lawrence*, the majority reversed the
decision of a Texas court, and "remanded [the case] for further
proceedings not inconsistent with th[e majority's] opinion."[401]
If the Texas courts—supported by the State's Governor and
Legislature—defied *Lawrence's* mandate, the complainants in
Lawrence might appeal again from another order of those
courts,[402] might seek an extraordinary writ (mandamus or
prohibition) from the Court compelling compliance with

---

[400] See U.S. Const. amend. X: "The powers not delegated to the United
States by the Constitution, nor prohibited by it to the States, are reserved to
the States respectively, or to the people."

[401] 539 U.S. 579.

[402] As happened in *Martin v. Hunter's Lessee*, 14 U.S. (1 Wheat.) 304 (1816).

HOW TO DETHRONE THE IMPERIAL JUDICIARY

Lawrence,[403] or might ask that State officials be held in contempt of court.[404] The issue in every instance would be whether Texas was constitutionally justified in denying effect to *Lawrence*.

There can be no question that "[a]n unconstitutional act is not a law; it confers no rights; it imposes no duties . . . ; it is, in legal contemplation, as inoperative as though it had never been passed."[405] If this be true of an actual statute, it must also (indeed, even more) be true of an unconstitutional judicial decision:

> In the ordinary use of language it will hardly be contended that the decisions of Courts constitute laws. They are, at most, only evidence of what the laws are; and are not of themselves laws. They are often re-examined, reversed, and qualified by the Courts themselves, whenever they are found to be either defective, or ill-founded, or otherwise incorrect.[406]

Because judicial decisions do not rise to the level of "laws" at all, they cannot partake of any greater authority than do "laws." Therefore, if a judicial decision is unconstitutional, "it is, in legal contemplation, as inoperative as though it had never been [handed down]." If a purported "law" is

---

[403] 28 U.S.C. § 1657.

[404] 18 U.S.C. § 401. See *United States* v. *Shipp*, 203 U.S. 563 (1906), 214 U.S. 386 (1909), and 215 U.S. 580 (1909).

[405] *Norton* v. *Shelby County*, 118 U.S. 425, 442 (1886). Accord, *Huntington* v. *Worthen*, 120 U.S. 97, 101-02 (1887); Ex parte *Siebold*, 100 U.S. 371, 376 (1880); *Fay* v. *Noia*, 372 U.S. 391, 408 (1963).

[406] *Swift* v. *Tyson*, 41 U.S. (16 Pet.) 1, 18 (1842).

unconstitutional, a judicial decision cannot make it constitutional. So, if a mere judicial decision is unconstitutional, a later judicial decision cannot make it constitutional. Even less can the original judicial decision render itself constitutional *per proprio vigore*.

To be sure, the Supreme Court takes the position that any of its decisions that "states a rule based upon the Constitution of the United States" is, "under the Supremacy Clause, . . . binding upon state courts."[407] On its face, this doctrine is constitutionally incoherent. If the Court's decisions that "state[ ] a rule based upon the Constitution" are, *"under the Supremacy Clause, . . . binding upon state courts,"* it can only be because each of those decisions, when handed down, itself became part and parcel of "the supreme Law of the Land," of dignity (or at least authority) equal to "[t]his Constitution, and the Laws of the United States which shall be made in Pursuance thereof."[408] Yet, if so, how could the Court ever *overrule* any of its previous decisions that "states a rule based upon the Constitution"— which it has often done[409]—without thereby overruling "[t]his Constitution" in the process? Or is it that the supposed supremacy of the Supreme Court's constitutional decisions applies only to "the Judges *in every State*" (which the Supremacy Clause explicitly mentions),[410] but not to the Supreme Court itself (which the Clause does not mention)?

---

[407] *Henry* v. *City of Rock Hill*, 376 U.S. 776, 777 n.1 (1964) (*per curiam*).

[408] U.S. Const. art. VI, cl. 2.

[409] See, e.g., *Payne* v. *Tennessee*, 501 U.S. 808, 827-30 & n.1 (1991).

[410] U.S. Const. art. VI, cl. 2 (emphasis supplied).

Yet, if so, how can the Supreme Court's constitutional decisions be binding upon either Congress or the President, neither of which the Supremacy Clause mentions, either?

The answer to these conundrums is that *no* constitutional decision of the Supreme Court is "supreme" over anyone (except perhaps the actual litigants in the "Case[ ]" or "Controvers[y]" *sub judice*), because "constitutional questions may not be considered as finally settled, until settled rightly."[411] Truth, not power (or worse, the hubris of office), is the touchstone of constitutional jurisprudence. And no one can rationally attribute to evanescent majorities of Justices on the Supreme Court a monopoly on the promulgation of truth, let alone an inerrant ability to discern it.

Moreover, the Constitution supports no such attribution. Instead, it provides only that "[t]his Constitution, and the Laws of the United States which shall be made in Pursuance thereof; and all Treaties made, or which shall be made, under the Authority of the United States, shall be the supreme Law of the Land; and the Judges in every State shall be bound thereby, any Thing in the Constitution or Laws of any State to the Contrary notwithstanding."[412] *Nowhere does the Constitution mention decisions of the Supreme Court or of any other court as any part whatsoever of this "supreme Law." Expressio unius exclusio alterius.* Self-evidently, then, the Constitution itself always remains supreme over any mere judicial decision purporting to

---

[411] *Pollock* v. *Farmers' Loan & Trust Co.*, 158 U.S. 601, 663 (1895) (Harlan, J., dissenting).

[412] U.S. Const. art. VI, cl. 2.

construe it. And even if a decision of the Supreme Court could arguably be assimilated to a "Law[ ] of the United States" in principle, it would not be such in practice unless it were "made in Pursuance [of the Constitution]." Therefore, "the Judges in every State" are not "bound" by mere decisions of the Supreme Court where those decisions conflict with the Constitution, because the conflict does not arise from "any Thing in the Constitution or Laws of any State to the Contrary," *but from the Constitution itself,* which "the Judges in every State" "shall be bound by Oath or Affirmation, to support," to the exclusion of everything else.[413] No "Judge[ ] in [any] State" takes an "Oath or Affirmation" to "be bound" by decisions of the Supreme Court, for two reasons: *First,* the Constitution plainly requires no such "Oath or Affirmation," but only an "Oath or Affirmation, to support this Constitution," which is not the same thing. *Second,* an "Oath or Affirmation, to support this Constitution [and the decisions of the Supreme Court construing it]" is basically *impossible*—because, although "the Judges in every State" can know when they take their "Oath[s] or Affirmation[s], to support this Constitution" what the Constitution provides as a matter of "original intent," that being written upon the face of the document, not one "Judge[ ] in [any] State" can possibly know (or, perhaps, even guess) what some majority of the Supreme Court may decide *in futuro* it imagines the Constitution means. No one can bind himself by an "Oath or Affirmation, to support" *unknown and unknowable* future judicial decisions that

---

[413] U.S. Const. art. VI, cl. 3.

plainly conflict with the Constitution he is "bound by Oath or Affirmation, to support."

Similarly, "the Senators and Representatives [in Congress], and the Members of the several State Legislatures, and all executive ... Officers, both of the United States and of the several States, shall be bound by Oath or Affirmation, to support this Constitution"[414]—not mere opinions of the Supreme Court about the Constitution, let alone plainly erroneous opinions.

Of course, for a State, as an actual party to the litigation, to refuse to acquiesce *at all* in a decision of the Supreme Court on the ground of that decision's *complete* unconstitutionality, it must first establish as much. For example, Texas could not assail the decision in *Lawrence* simply because the majority relied promiscuously on foreign law to define "liberty," if foreign law was not the exclusive and controlling basis for that aberrant result.[415] Texas (or any other State) could, however, attack or refuse to acquiesce in *Lawrence* because both Justice Kennedy's and Justice O'Connor's opinions broadly held that a State may no longer assert the promotion of morality as a justification for limiting the supposed "liberty" to engage in homosexual sodomy[416]—or, by logical extension, any other

---

[414] U.S. Const. art. VI, cl. 3.

[415] See ante, at 40-48.

[416] Justice Kennedy: "'[T]hat the governing majority in a State has traditionally viewed a particular practice as immoral is not a sufficient reason for upholding a law prohibiting the practice.'" 539 U.S. at 577 (opinion of the Court). Justice O'Connor: "Moral disapproval of a group

conduct that some gaggle of judges might some day categorize as part of "liberty."

2. Doubtlessly, the contemporary Judiciary would condemn any such attack on or refusal to acquiesce in *Lawrence* as an exhumation of the antebellum doctrine of "interposition," which the modern Supreme Court has held to be "without substance."[417] Robotic reliance on the Court's decisions begs the question, however, when a State specifically denies the correctness of those decisions, let alone the competence or good faith of the Justices who handed them down. Rather, recourse must be had to fundamental legal principles, history, and reason.

a. At the threshold, however, lies an objection: Whatever the doctrine of interposition may entail, by participating in *Lawrence* without somehow explicitly reserving her right to avail herself of interposition did Texas (or would any other State in similar circumstances) waive or forfeit her claim to assert that doctrine later on?

By dint of reason, the answer must be *No*. No litigant must explicitly reserve a right to complain of or seek redress against every possible judicial error or other wrongdoing that may occur in the future course of litigation, or be forever bound by

---

cannot be a legitimate governmental interest." Ibid. at 583 (concurring opinion).

[417] *United States* v. *Louisiana*, 364 U.S. 500, 501 (1960). In addition to judicial condemnation, interposition would be denigrated by the shapers of "public opinion" as a rehashing of issues settled forever by the Civil War and the controversies over racial segregation in the 1950s and 1960s.

it. Rather, any litigant may rely on the legal presumption that judges know and will honestly follow the Constitution, until the opposite appears.[418] Only in the latter eventuality does the right to invoke interposition become operative; and therefore only thereafter is a litigant required to assert the right in some timely and effective fashion, or lose it by his own inaction— which is usually evidenced when, in the face of the violation of his constitutional rights, the aggrieved party does nothing at all for what the law deems an unreasonable length of time,[419] or does something inconsistent with the assertion of his right, on which conduct an adverse party in fact or by benefit of law justifiably relies. Otherwise, the litigant can fall back on the principles that "'courts indulge every reasonable presumption against waiver' of fundamental constitutional rights, and . . . 'do not presume acquiescence in the loss of fundamental rights',"[420] and that "for a waiver [of constitutional rights] to be effective it must be clearly established that there was 'an intentional relinquishment or abandonment of a known right or privilege.'"[421]

---

[418] See, e.g., *Cannon* v. *University of Chicago*, 441 U.S. 677, 696-97 (1979) (governmental officials presumably know the law); *Albernaz* v. *United States*, 450 U.S. 333, 341-42 (1981) (government officials presumably carry out their functions with their constitutional powers and disabilities in mind). Key here is the qualifier "legal"—because the experiential presumption must be quite the opposite.

[419] E.g., does not file a lawsuit within the statute of limitations, or a pleading in a case *sub judice* within the time allowed by the court's rules.

[420] *Johnson* v. *Zerbst*, 304 U.S. 458, 464 (1938) (footnotes omitted).

[421] *Brookhart* v. *Janis*, 384 U.S. 1, 4 (1966).

By dint of historical precedent, too, the answer must be *No.* In *Worcester* v. *Georgia,*[422] the Court voided the convictions of missionaries who had resided among the Cherokee Indians without a State license. Although Georgia had participated in the litigation, in defiance of the Supreme Court's mandate the State's Governor—with the political support of President Andrew Jackson—refused to release the missionaries until they agreed to leave the State. The Court proved powerless, or at least reluctant, to do anything about this exercise of interposition.[423]

b. On the merits, the traditional understanding of interposition is that it involves an assertion of a State's *constitutional* privilege, right, and power to defend by direct action her and her citizens' constitutional rights against usurpation of power by any official or agent of the General Government. So, rightly understood, interposition is not an *extra*-constitutional or *anti*-constitutional doctrine, but a device for protecting and preserving the Constitution. Interposition embodies the States' privilege and power of legal, political, and even armed self-defense against oppression of their constituent people or their own destruction *qua* States.

1) Can States assert interposition on behalf of their citizens? According to the Supreme Court, *No.* A State's "duty or power" does not extend

---

[422] 31 U.S. (6 Pet.) 515 (1832).

[423] See 1 C. Warren, *The Supreme Court in United States History* (1926), at 729-79.

to enforc[ing her citizens'] rights in respect to their relations
with the Federal Government. In that field, it is the United
States and not the State which represents them as *parens
patriae* when such representation becomes appropriate; and
to the former, not to the latter, they must look for such
protective measures as flow from that status.[424]

Of course, when a State's citizens find themselves in a situation
of conflict, antagonism, or even oppression "in respect to their
relations with the Federal Government," to be told to seek
from that source "such protective measures as flow from that
status" rings hollow.

2) Whatever their power to assert interposition on behalf
of their citizens, States must have some authority, *under the
Constitution*, to do so on their own behalf. As even the
Supreme Court has conceded:

> The people of the United States constitute one nation,
> under one government, and this government, within the
> scope of the powers with which it is invested, is supreme.
> On the other hand, the people of each State compose a
> State, having its own government, and endowed with all
> the functions essential to separate and independent
> existence. The States disunited might continue to exist.
> Without the States in union there could be no such political
> body as the United States.

---

[424] *Massachusetts* v. *Mellon*, 262 U.S. 447, 486 (1923). Accord, *Florida* v.
Mellon, 273 U.S. 12, 18 (1927). But see *South Carolina* v. *Katzenbach*, 383 U.S.
301, 323-37 (1966) (State may challenge a *Congressional* statute as improper
under Section 2 of the Fifteenth Amendment); *Oregon* v. *Mitchell*, 400 U.S.
112 (1970).

... [I]n many articles of the Constitution the necessary existence of the States, and, within their proper spheres, the independent authority of the States, is distinctly recognized.[425]

So:

Not only ... can there be no loss of separate and independent autonomy to the States, through their union under the Constitution, but it may be not unreasonably said that the preservation of the States, and the maintenance of their governments, are as much within the design and care of the Constitution as the preservation of the Union and the maintenance of the National Government. The Constitution, in all its provisions, looks to an indestructible Union, composed of indestructible States.[426]

That being the case:

There are, indeed, certain virtual limitations, arising from the principles of the Constitution itself. It would, undoubtedly, be an abuse of the power [of Congress] if so exercised as to impair the separate existence and independent self-government ... of the States ....[427]

While the States "are, and they must ever be, co-existent with the National Government," then:

Neither may destroy the other. Hence the Federal Constitution must receive a practical construction. Its

---

[425] *Lane County* v. *Oregon*, 74 U.S. (7 Wall.) 71, 76 (1869).

[426] *Texas* v. *White*, 74 U.S. (7 Wall.) 700, 725 (1869). The appeal to an "indestructible Union, composed of indestructible States" was inaccurate, as WE THE PEOPLE can always dissolve the Union and the States by constitutional amendment. U.S. Const. art. V.

[427] *Veazie Bank* v. *Fenno*, 75 U.S. (8 Wall.) 533, 541 (1869).

limitations and its implied prohibitions must not be
extended so far as to destroy the necessary powers of the
states, or prevent their efficient exercise.[428]

Therefore:

[E]very State has a sphere of action where the authority of
the National Government may not intrude. Within that
domain the State is as if the Union were not. Such are the
checks and balances in our complicated but wise system of
State and national polity.[429]

For that reason:

In interpreting the Constitution it must never be
forgotten that the nation is made up of states, to which are
intrusted the powers of local government. And to them and
to the people the powers not expressly delegated to the
national government are reserved. . . . The power of the
states to regulate their purely internal affairs by such laws as
seem wise to the local authority is inherent, and has never
been surrendered to the general government.[430]

Indeed:

By the Constitution, a republican form of government
is guaranteed to every State in the Union, and the
distinguishing feature of that form is the right of the people
to choose their own officers for governmental
administration, and pass their own laws in virtue of the

[428] *Union Pacific Railroad Co.* v. *Peniston,* 85 U.S. (18 Wall.) 5, 31 (1873).
"While" is the correct term, because it must never be forgotten that WE THE
PEOPLE may change or even destroy both the General Government and the
States at any time. See U.S. Const. art. V; Declaration of Independence.

[429] *Farrington* v. *Tennessee,* 95 U.S. 679, 685 (1878).

[430] *Hammer* v. *Dagenhart,* 247 U.S. 251, 275 (1918).

legislative power reposed in representative bodies, whose legitimate acts may be said to be those of the people themselves . . . .[431]

In sum, inasmuch as "[t]he Constitution contemplates a national government free to use its delegated powers; also state governments capable of exercising their essential reserved powers; both operating within the same territorial limits; consequently, *the Constitution itself, by word or necessary inference, makes adequate provision for preventing conflict between them.*"[432] And if not always for "preventing," then surely for *resolving.*

Lawrence created conflict between the General Government and the States because a majority of Justices, under color of the Fourteenth Amendment (illegitimately construed at least in part according to foreign law), purported to strip Texas (and, by logical extension and *stare decisis*, all the States) of part of the reserved sovereign power that makes them *States*—in the sense of independent governments, rather than mere political subordinates of the General Government. In such a case, interposition becomes a matter of the States' self-defense and self-preservation *qua* States, and therefore a matter of preserving the Constitution against judicial usurpation.

Now, whatever may be the proper constitutional definition of an individual's "liberty" or a State's "reserved sovereignty," *life* as a human being or a human institution is

---

[431] *Duncan* v. *McCall*, 139 U.S. 449, 461 (1891).

[432] *Helvering* v. *Therrell*, 303 U.S. 218, 223 (1938) (emphasis supplied).

the precondition for it; and in a world steeped in physical and political aggression, *self-defense* is the precondition for life. Thus, self-defense is a primordial, unalienable right of every individual human being, of any people organized in a political or other community, and of the States as political communities, the independence of which was first asserted in the Declaration of Independence, then recognized in and protected by the Constitution.

The Declaration of Independence "solemnly publish[ed] and declare[d], That these United Colonies are, and of Right ought to be FREE AND INDEPENDENT STATES; . . . and that as Free and Independent States, they have full Power to levy War, conclude Peace, contract Alliances, establish Commerce, and to do all other Acts and Things which Independent States may of right do." Perforce of the Constitution, WE THE PEOPLE required the States to surrender some of these "full Power[s]" conditionally or unconditionally;[433] or to share authority concurrently with the General Government, subject to the latter's supremacy in appropriate situations.[434] But as the

---

[433] Compare the Declaration's reference to the States' "levy[ing] War, conclud[ing] Peace, [and] contract[ing] Alliances" with the Constitution's prohibitions on these matters: "No State shall enter into any Treaty, Alliance, or Confederation." U.S. Const. art. I, § 10, cl. 1. "No State shall, without the Consent of Congress, . . . enter into any Agreement or Compact . . . with a foreign Power, or engage in War, unless actually invaded, or in such imminent danger as will not admit of delay." U.S. Const. art. I, § 10, cl. 3.

[434] Compare the Declaration's reference to the States' "establish[ing] Commerce" with Congress's power under the Constitution to "regulate Commerce with foreign Nations, and among the several States." U.S. Const.

Tenth Amendment witnesses, WE THE PEOPLE did not strip the States of *all* "Power[s] . . . to do all . . . Acts and Things which Independent States may of right do." To the contrary, the Tenth Amendment explicitly recognizes and guarantees that "[t]he powers not delegated to the United States by the Constitution, nor prohibited by it to the States, are reserved to the States respectively, or to the people."

Now, when the Declaration of Independence asserted "[t]hat these United Colonies are, and *of Right* ought to be FREE AND INDEPENDENT STATES; . . . and that as Free and Independent States, they have full Power . . . to do all other Acts and Things which Independent States may *of right* do," of *what* "right," to be found in *what corpus juris*, did it speak? Of "the Laws of Nature and of Nature's God" that "entitle[d]" the United Colonies to a "separate and equal station" "among the powers of the earth." It is ultimately from, and certainly only consistent with, this body of "Laws"—once "[t]he powers . . . delegated to the United States by the Constitution, [ ]or prohibited by it to the States" are subtracted—that arise the powers "reserved to the States respectively, or to the people." No one doubts that the Founders of this country understood "the Laws of Nature and of Nature's God" to sanction individual and communal self-defense. Neither could such a doubt be seriously entertained, inasmuch as the Declaration was nothing if not an *apologia* for the Colonists' self-defense:

---

art. I, § 8, cl. 3. See, e.g., *Cooley* v. *Board of Wardens*, 53 U.S. (12 How.) 299, 315-21 (1851); *Simpson* v. *Shepard* (Minnesota Rate Cases), 230 U.S. 352, 398-412 (1913).

that "when a long train of abuses and usurpations, pursuing invariably the same Object evinces a design to reduce [a people] under absolute Despotism, it is their right, it is their duty, to throw off such Government, and to provide new Guards for their future security." Hardly surprising, therefore, is that the Constitution delegates to the General Government, or to any of its Branches or officers, no license whatsoever to aggress against the States or their people, or to strip the victims of such aggression of the legal power or the material ability to defend themselves. The Constitution prohibits neither the States nor the people from defending themselves. Indeed, the purpose of the Constitution—"to form a more perfect Union, establish Justice, insure domestic Tranquility, provide for the common defence, promote the general Welfare, and secure the Blessings of Liberty to ourselves and our Posterity"[435]—absolutely excludes and even renders ridiculous a contrary construction. And, perhaps even more to the point, the Constitution explicitly reserves to the States the power to "engage in War" when "actually invaded, or in such imminent Danger as will not admit of delay";[436] and recognizes the States' power, concurrent with that of Congress, to organize, arm, and in emergencies employ the "Militia."[437] Therefore, perforce of both the Declaration and the Constitution, the power of self-defense against political

---

[435] U.S. Const. preamble.

[436] See U.S. Const. art. I, § 10, cl. 3.

[437] Compare U.S. Const. art. I, § 8, cl. 16 with *Houston* v. *Moore*, 18 U.S. (5 Wheat.) 1, 16 (1820).

aggression is "reserved to the States respectively, or to the people."

Ultimately, this power is instrumentally guaranteed in the Second Amendment's recognition that, "[a] well regulated Militia, *being necessary to the security of a free State*, the right of the people to keep and bear Arms, shall not be infringed."[438] That the Militia, which is the collective reification of "the right of the people to keep and bear Arms," is *"necessary"* (not merely sufficient) implies that that "right" must be "unalienable," in the sense the Declaration of Independence uses that term. That the "necess[ity]" relates to *"security"* implies that the "right" involves self-defense. And that the "security" *"of a free State"* is involved implies that the goal is the survival of the States *qua* States within the understanding of the Declaration. True, the Constitution delegates to Congress the power (in pertinent part) "[t]o provide for calling forth the Militia to execute the Laws of the Union, [and] suppress Insurrections."[439] But a power "to execute the Laws" cannot be twisted into a license to violate "the supreme Law of the Land."[440] And a power to "suppress Insurrections"—that is, violent opposition to *lawful* authority—cannot be twisted into a warrant to outlaw resistance to usurpation and tyranny.

---

[438] Emphasis supplied.

[439] U.S. Const. art. I, § 8, cl. 15. Self-evidently, the President's authority as "Commander in Chief . . . of the Militia of the several States, when called into the actual service of the United States" is purely derivative of Congress's authority to "call[ ] forth the Militia." See U.S. Const. art. II, § 2, cl. 1.

[440] U.S. Const. art. VI, cl. 2.

c. The traditional argument against interposition is that, even if the States (rather than, as the Preamble asserts, WE THE PEOPLE) were the moving parties in formation of the Constitution, nevertheless they designated the Supreme Court as their common judge, to which they must refer their disputes over application of the Constitution and laws of the Union, and the decisions of which thereupon they must accept.[441]

1) Now, this argument is powerful when a constitutional dispute arises between certain States. For the Constitution authorizes "[t]he judicial Power [to] extend ... to Controversies between two or more States,"[442] and "[i]n all Cases ... in which a State shall be Party" grants "original Jurisdiction" to "the supreme Court."[443] And this jurisdiction various States have invoked, and the Court has exercised, without anyone's ever gainsaying its existence, efficacy, prudence, or justice.[444] Indeed, as the Supreme Court observed in *Ableman v. Booth*:[445]

> The importance which the framers of the Constitution attached to [the Supreme Court of the United States], for the purpose of preserving internal tranquility, is strikingly

---

[441] See generally, e.g., 1 J. Story, *Commentaries*, ante note 121, chs. III and IV.

[442] U.S. Const. art. III, § 2, cl. 1.

[443] U.S. Const. art. III, § 2, cl. 2.

[444] See, e.g., *New Jersey* v. *New York*, 30 U.S. (5 Pet.) 284 (1831); *Rhode Island* v. *Massachusetts*, 37 U.S. (12 Pet.) 657 (1838); *South Dakota* v. *North Carolina*, 192 U.S. 286 (1904); *Kansas* v. *Colorado*, 206 U.S. 46 (1907); *Virginia* v. *West Virginia*, 220 U.S. 1 (1911); *New Jersey* v. *New York*, 283 U.S. 336 (1931); *Texas* v. *New Jersey*, 379 U.S. 674 (1965).

[445] 62 U.S. (21 How.) 506 (1859).

manifested by the clause which gives this court jurisdiction over the sovereign states which compose this Union, when a controversy arises between them. Instead of reserving the right to seek redress for injustice from another state by their sovereign powers, they have bound themselves to submit to the decision of this court, and to abide by its judgment. And . . . experience has demonstrated that this power was not unwisely surrendered by the states; for in the time that has already elapsed since this government came into existence, several irritating and angry controversies have taken place between adjoining states, in relation to their respective boundaries, and which have sometimes threatened to end in force and violence, but for the power vested in this court to hear them and decide between them.[446]

2) Furthermore, the argument against interposition is not implausible even when the dispute is between the States and the political Branches of the General Government (Congress and the President), if one presumes that justices of the Supreme Court can be impartial in such a case. By the historical record, fair dealing on the Justices' part in this situation is not impossible, only unlikely.[447]

How unlikely, though—particularly in situations in which the Court's good offices are necessary—appears in a case that arose during Reconstruction. At issue in *Georgia* v. *Stanton*[448]

---

[446] Ibid. at 519.

[447] Contrast, *e.g., Printz v. United States*, 521 U.S. 898, 918-19, 923-24 (1997), with *Garcia v. San Antonio Metropolitan Transit Authority*, 469 U.S. 528, 545-47, 550-54, 556 (1985).

[448] 73 U.S. (6 Wall.) 50 (1868).

was the State's request for an injunction against the Secretary of War and two Army Generals, because certain Acts of Congress, alleged to be unconstitutional, had as their intent and design:

> [T]o overthrow and annul th[e] existing state government, and to erect another and different government in its place, unauthorized by the Constitution and in defiance of its guarantees; and that ... defendants ... , acting under orders of the President, [were] about setting in motion a portion of the army to take military possession of the state, and threaten[ed] to subvert her government and subject her people to military rule; that the state [was] holding inadequate means to resist the power and force of the Executive Department of the United States; and she therefore insist[ed] that such protection can, and ought to be afforded by [the Supreme Court].[449]

Denying the injunction, the Court held:

> [T]hese matters ... call for ... judgment ... upon political questions, and upon rights, not of persons or property, but of a political character .... *For the rights, for the protection of which our authority is invoked, are the rights of sovereignty, of political jurisdiction, of government, of corporate existence as a state, with all its constitutional powers and privileges.* No case of private rights or private property infringed, or in danger of actual or threatened infringement, is presented ....[450]

That is, *as to the preservation of their own existence,* the States have no legal recourse in the courts of the General

---

[449] Ibid. at 70.

[450] Ibid. at 77 (emphasis supplied).

Government—including the Supreme Court, to which the
Constitution assigns "original Jurisdiction" "[i]n all Cases . . . in
which a State shall be Party,"[451] and notwithstanding that "it is
entirely unimportant, what may be the subject of controversy.
Be it what it may, these parties have a constitutional right to
come into the Court of the Union."[452]

Self-evidently, *Georgia* v. *Stanton* is wrong. As the Court
itself early held in *Cohens* v. *Virginia*:[453]

> It is most true that this Court will not take jurisdiction if it
> should not: but it is equally true, that it must take
> jurisdiction if it should. The judiciary cannot, as the
> legislature may, avoid a measure because it approaches the
> confines of the constitution. We cannot pass it by because it
> is doubtful. With whatever doubts, with whatever
> difficulties, a case may be attended, we must decide it, if it
> be brought before us. We have no more right to decline the
> exercise of jurisdiction which is given, than to usurp that
> which is not given. The one or the other would be treason
> to the constitution.[454]

Yet, as an adverse precedent to interposition through
litigation, even as a matter of a State's self-defense, *Georgia* v.
Stanton remains.

---

[451] U.S. Const. art. III, § 2, cl. 2.

[452] *Cohens* v. *Virginia*, 19 U.S. (6 Wheat.) 264, 378 (1821).

[453] 19 U.S. (6 Wheat.) 264 (1821).

[454] Ibid. at 404.

d. Worse yet, if a State's complaint is against the common judge itself (as is Texas's complaint with regard to *Lawrence*), *who* can arbitrate the dispute?

1) The answer to this question depends on identifying the defendant. In the strictest constitutional sense, it cannot be the Supreme Court, because the Court, operating in its institutional capacity, *cannot* violate the Constitution, inasmuch as, if it were to violate the Constitution, it would not be exercising "[t]he judicial Power of the United States," and *pro tanto* would cease to be the "supreme Court."[455] In contrast, individual Justices operating under color of the Constitution, but in disregard of its "original intent," can and do violate it. When they do so, however, they are not exercising "[t]he judicial Power of the United States," but flouting it. As to their unconstitutional acts, they are not governmental officials, but mere lawbreakers.

In Ex parte *Young*,[456] The Supreme Court itself recognized this dichotomy in the case of State officials proceeding under color of unconstitutional State statutes:

> The act to be enforced is alleged to be unconstitutional; and if it be so, the use of the name of the state to enforce an unconstitutional act ... is a proceeding without the authority of, and one which does not affect, the state in its

---

[455] U.S. Const. art. III, cl. 1. This is true of every branch in a government of delegated (and thereby limited) powers, because, if any branch exceeds its delegated powers it necessarily acts without authority; and if it acts without authority, it necessarily forfeits its claim to be acting in the capacity of the government at all.

[456] 209 U.S. 123 (1908).

sovereign or governmental capacity. It is simply an illegal act upon the part of a state official in attempting, by the use of the name of the state, to enforce a legislative enactment which is void because unconstitutional. If the act ... be a violation of the Federal Constitution, the officer, in proceeding under such enactment, comes into conflict with the superior authority of the Constitution, and he is in that case stripped of his official or representative character and is subjected in his person to the consequences of his individual conduct. The state has no power to impart to him any immunity from responsibility to the supreme authority of the United States.[457]

The same principle applies to officers of the General Government.[458] So, for Justices of the Supreme Court:

The [judicial decision] to be enforced is alleged to be unconstitutional; and if it be so, the use of the name of the [United States] to enforce an unconstitutional [decision] ... is a proceeding without the authority of, and one which does not affect, the [United States] in its sovereign or governmental capacity. It is simply an illegal act upon the part of a [group of justices] in attempting, by the use of the name of the [United States], to enforce a [judicial decision] which is void because unconstitutional. If the [judicial decision] ... be a violation of the Federal Constitution, the [errant justices], in proceeding under such [decision], come[ ] into conflict with the superior authority of the Constitution, and [they are] in that case stripped of [their] official or representative character and [are] subjected in [their] person[s] to the consequences of [their] individual

---

[457] Ibid. at 159-60.

[458] See, e.g., *Minnesota* v. *Hitchcock*, 185 U.S. 373, 386 (1902).

conduct. The [United States] has no power to impart to [them] any immunity from responsibility to the supreme authority of the [Constitution].

2) Were the State of Texas somehow to complain to the common judge (the Supreme Court) against the lawbreakers Justices Kennedy, Breyer, Ginsberg, Souter, Stevens, and O'Connor, because of their unconstitutional decision in *Lawrence*, while any of those Justices still sat on the Court, they would have to recuse themselves. For no man may be a judge in his own case.[459] The probably insurmountable political-*cum*-practical problem in any such situation, though, would be whether *any* Justices of the Supreme Court—or any judges of any court—would deign to hear a case a State brought against their own brethren, past or present. (Those with experience in litigation are aware of the clannishness that exists among judges.)

Moreover, even if every Justice recused himself, and the case were assigned to and actually heard by "such inferior Courts as the Congress may from time to time ordain and establish,"[460] the judges in those courts, who almost universally accept the dogma of "judicial supremacy," would not likely rule in favor of a State aggrieved by an unconstitutional decision of some majority of the Supreme Court. The "inferior Courts" could rule in the State's favor if they held (as they should) that an *unconstitutional* opinion is neither a *valid* "opinion *of the Court*" nor a *valid* "precedent" to which the

---

[459] See *Tumey* v. *Ohio*, 273 U.S. 510, 523 (1927).

[460] U.S. Const. art. III, § 1.

doctrine of *stare decisis* can apply. But to do so would require rejecting the Supreme Court's directive that all lower courts must follow its precedents "no matter how misguided the judges of those courts may think [those precedents] to be"[461]— and therefore must reflexively absolve of all wrongdoing the authors of those "misguided" precedents.

3) In any event, except in a case where the remedy for a constitutional dispute between a State and a group of Justices is sought in an amendment of the supreme law,[462] the common judge cannot be a group of States acting in concert. For the Constitution strips every State of the power to "enter into any Treaty, Alliance, or Confederation,"[463] or "without the Consent of Congress ... [to] enter into any Agreement or Compact with another State."[464]

e. The possibility for successful interposition, then, depends upon cooperation among the States and Congress, the States and the President, or all of them together. For this there may be precedent[465]—but next to no contemporary likelihood. Indeed, the overwhelming likelihood today is that both Congress and the President would side with the Supreme Court in any dispute involving a State.

---

[461] *Hutto* v. *Davis*, 454 U.S. 370, 375 (1982).

[462] See U.S. Const. art. V. See post, 173-92.

[463] U.S. Const. art. I, § 10, cl. 1.

[464] U.S. Const. art. I, § 10, cl. 3. See, e.g., as to Southern secession, *Williams* v. *Bruffy*, 96 U.S. 176, 182 (1878).

[465] See ante, at 155.

CHAPTER 6

Amendment of the Constitution

The modern Supreme Court denigrates the doctrine of interposition as being "without substance"[466] primarily because it adheres to the dogma of "judicial supremacy" that "[a] decision [of the Court]" on a constitutional issue *cannot be reversed short of a constitutional amendment.*"[467] Americans are told (and too many of them believe) that the Court is the "ultimate interpreter of the Constitution,"[468] and that "the interpretation of the [Constitution] enunciated by th[e] Court . . . is the supreme law of the land."[469]

1. Fundamentally, this is nonsense. The abiding truth of the Constitution (its "original intent"), not any erroneous judicial interpretation of it, is the supreme law. After all, "no amount of repetition of . . . errors in judicial opinions can

---

[466] *United States* v. *Louisiana*, 364 U.S. 500, 501 (1960).

[467] *Gregg* v. *Georgia*, 428 U.S. 153, 176 (1976) (emphasis supplied).

[468] *Baker* v. *Carr*, 369 U.S. 186, 211 (1962); *Powell* v. *McCormack*, 395 U.S. 486, 548-49 (1969).

[469] *Cooper* v. *Aaron*, 358 U.S. 1, 18 (1958).

make the errors true."[470] If a law "repugnant to the constitution, is void" and "not law," and cannot be both "void, yet, in practice, completely obligatory,"[471] then how could the Constitution and some decision of the Supreme Court both be the supreme law of the land on the very same point at the very same time unless both said the very same thing? Moreover, by dint of what rational legal rule could any judicial decision be the exclusive, controlling, and final authority as to its own consistency with the Constitution? The Judiciary's answer to that question does not inspire confidence. For the only rationale the Court has ever offered is the circular mumbo jumbo of "judicial supremacy": The Justices can interpret the Constitution with finality because they are supreme; and they are supreme because, as finally interpreted by them, the Constitution makes them so.

In point of historical fact and law, as the Constitution's authors, the Founding Fathers were WE THE PEOPLE'S agents. WE THE PEOPLE "ordain[ed] and establish[ed]" the Constitution.[472] And only WE THE PEOPLE, through their representatives in State "Legislatures" or "Conventions," are authorized to amend it.[473] Inasmuch as "[t]he power to enact

---

[470] *Wallace* v. *Jaffree*, 472 U.S. 38, 107 (1985) (Rehnquist, C.J., dissenting). It needs to be added that "no amount of repetition of . . . [correct statements about the Constitution] in judicial opinions" can transform those opinions into the "supreme Law of the Land." Being correct makes the opinion constitutional; it does not make the opinion to any degree the Constitution.

[471] *Marbury* v. *Madison*, 5 U.S. (1 Cranch) 137, 177-78 (1803).

[472] U.S. Const. preamble.

[473] U.S. Const. art. V.

carries with it *final authority to declare the meaning of the legislation*,"[474] the "ultimate interpreter of the Constitution" cannot possibly be the Supreme Court,[475] and its "interpretation of the [Constitution]" cannot possibly be "the supreme law of the land."[476] As the Founding Fathers' legal mentor, Sir William Blackstone, pointed out, "whenever a question arises between the society at large and any magistrate vested with powers originally delegated by that society, it must be decided by the voice of the society itself: there is not upon earth any other tribunal to resort to."[477]

The theory that, irrespective of their intellectual merits, judicial opinions have some inherent and supreme constitutional stature would be laughable, did not the Judiciary and the legal *intelligentsia* tout it as part of America's jurisprudential "received wisdom." Of course, this notion suffers from the logical vice of begging the question: Judges and intellectuals apply and teach it because it is supposedly the received wisdom; but it is the received wisdom only because judges and intellectuals apply and teach it. The unsatisfying nature of arguments in favor of this revealed wisdom is exemplified even in Justice Joseph Story's otherwise justly famed *Commentaries*, in which he opined that "the judicial department has not only constantly exercised this right of

---

[474] *Proper* v. *Clark*, 337 U.S. 472, 484 (1949) (emphasis supplied).

[475] *Pace Baker* v. *Carr*, 369 U.S. 186, 211 (1962), and *Powell* v. *McCormack*, 395 U.S. 486, 548-49 (1969).

[476] *Pace Cooper* v. *Aaron*, 358 U.S. 1, 18 (1958).

[477] 1 *Commentaries*, ante note 158, at 212.

interpretation in the last resort, but its whole course of reasonings and operations has proceeded upon the ground that, once made, the interpretation was conclusive, as well upon the States as the people."[478] Yet the problem remains—if the "reasonings" are *false*, the Court's "operations" on that score are invalid, no matter for how long it has followed that "course." "[N]either the antiquity of a practice nor . . . steadfast . . . judicial adherence to it through the centuries insulates it from constitutional attack."[479] "[N]o one acquires a vested or protected right in violation of the Constitution by long use, even when that span of time covers our entire national existence."[480]

That the "reasonings" *are* false Story himself gave witness *sotto voce* when he asked, "what is to be the remedy, if there be any misconstruction of the Constitution on the part of the government of the United States or its functionaries, and any power exercised by them not warranted by its true meaning?"[481] "[A]ny power," presumably including the supposed power of "judicial supremacy" through "judicial review," and of "judicial review" itself in any particular "Case[ ]" or "Controvers[y]." Story dilated on what could be done "if th[e usurpation] should be by Congress," or "if the usurpation should be by the President," or "if the legislative, executive, and judicial departments should concur in a gross usurpation,"

---

[478] 1 *Commentaries*, ante note 121, § 392, at 294 (footnote omitted).

[479] *Williams v. Illinois*, 399 U.S. 235, 239 (1970).

[480] *Walz v. Tax Commission*, 397 U.S. 664, 678 (1970).

[481] 1 *Commentaries*, ante note 121, § 393, at 295-97.

or even if "there should be a corrupt co-operation of three-fourths of the States for permanent usurpation"[482]—but never once suggested that *the Judiciary on its own* might engage in usurpation and tyranny under the cloak of "judicial supremacy" or "judicial review," or what recourse WE THE PEOPLE might have if it did, other than to amend the Constitution, which of course presumes that judicial usurpation or tyranny is *not* "usurpation" or "tyranny" at all, but instead actually part of the Constitution which is "conclusive" on everyone! That is, according to Story (and those who share his views) the Supreme Court's opinions are "the supreme Law of the Land" because the Supreme Court by itself can never commit usurpation or tyranny, because the Supreme Court's opinions are "conclusive" on everyone else— so that, even if the Court *did* commit usurpation and tyranny, *no one could say so with any legal effect!*

Moreover, the notion that the Supreme Court's opinions on constitutional issues are, in and of themselves, "supreme law" also suffers from the political vice of self-promotion: Judges and the legal *intelligentsia* apply and teach it because it is peculiarly in their self-interest to do so, inasmuch as it maximizes their political power and prestige.

Besides the problems of *petitio principii* and *cui bono*, "judicial supremacy's" truly fantastic pretensions, absurd impracticality, and inconsistency with any rational understanding of "law" should astound any reasoning

---

[482] Ibid., §§ 393-95, at 297-98.

individual. First, if some majority of Justices of the Supreme Court declared that the Chief Justice, not the President, was the "Commander in Chief";[483] or that the President, not Congress, could "declare War";[484] or that States could impose "slavery [ ]or involuntary servitude" other than "as a punishment for crime";[485] or that one political party could employ a "religious Test" in the form of a "litmus test" in the Senate, to exclude individuals from judicial office unless they repudiated certain fundamental tenets of their faiths that condemned abortion;[486] or that the President could arrest and execute alleged suspects of crimes based on unilateral, untestable claims to secret knowledge that need not be communicated to any court[487]—would anyone in his right mind contend that these decisions *were* henceforward "the supreme Law of the Land"[488] subject only to superseding amendments of the Constitution?! That everyone in the United States was required to obey them? And that no one could interpose the unconstitutionality of these decisions as a perfect defense against punishment for refusing to acquiesce in them? Self-evidently not. To be sure, these are pellucid cases. But if the principle that any thinking American can reject a

---

[483] Notwithstanding U.S. Const. art. II, § 2, cl. 1.

[484] Notwithstanding U.S. Const. art. I, § 8, cl. 11.

[485] Notwithstanding U.S. Const. amend. XIII.

[486] Notwithstanding U.S. Const. art. VI, cl. 3.

[487] Notwithstanding U.S. Const. amends. V and VI. But cf. *Chicago & Southern Air Lines* v. *Waterman Steamship Corp.*, 333 U.S. 103, 110-12 (1948).

[488] U.S. Const. art. VI, cl. 2.

decision of the Supreme Court that fails to square with the Constitution applies to any case, it applies to every case. The greater the stupidity of the decision simply increases the speed with which the reader recognizes its unconstitutionality.

Second, in everyday practice, "judicial supremacy" is incoherent. With changing majorities of Justices of different minds, the Supreme Court has reversed itself on constitutional issues many times.[489] This must mean that in case *A* where a majority of the Court originally held *X* on a certain constitutional issue, the majority was wrong; and in case *B* where another majority now holds the opposite of *X* on that same issue, it is right (or at least the Justices in the present majority believe, or have reason to say, it is). It cannot mean that different majorities were *both* correct in *both* case *A and* case *B*, because the Constitution cannot mean both *X* and the opposite of *X—unless* its meaning changes with the needs of the times as perceived by ever-mutating gaggles of Justices. Inasmuch as the Supreme Court can be wrong, its decision of any constitutional issue cannot *be* the Constitution (for the Constitution cannot be wrong) but only someone's opinion— or perhaps someone's fallacy, someone's fantasy, even someone's falsity—*about* the Constitution.

Third, if perforce of "judicial supremacy" every blunder of constitutional law perpetrated by some majority of the Supreme Court must remain within the *United States Reports* as a valid precedent "conclusive" (in Story's estimation) "as well

---

[489] See, e.g., *Payne* v. *Tennessee*, 501 U.S. 808, 827-30 & n.1 (1991).

upon the States as the people" until fortuitously another case with the same issue arises and a new majority of Justices recognizes the error and reverses the earlier opinion, or until three-fourths of the States muster for a constitutional amendment—then, as a practical matter, WE THE PEOPLE *must suffer very large numbers of very bad constitutional opinions for a very long time*, during which period *error* will be treated as the "supreme Law of the Land." But, if, as a practical matter, error is as acceptable as truth—because, were it not, someone would be clamoring for its correction and providing an efficacious means to correct it—what possible meaning can attach to "Law"? Can "the supreme Law of the Land" that depends upon "the Law of Nature and of Nature's God," which forms the foundation of the whole edifice of America's existence, be rational *or irrational*, right *or wrong*, good *or evil* as *accident* dictates? Or does not the manifest illogic, incoherence, stupidity, deceitfulness, perversity, or wickedness of a judicial opinion constitute compelling evidence that what it says is not and could not be "the supreme Law" or even any "law"?

2. All this being true, advocating a constitutional amendment to prohibit the Justices from promiscuously using foreign law to interpret the Constitution, or to command them to allow the States to promote morality by punishing homosexual sodomy, or to correct any of their other misconstructions of the Constitution, would be out of place and counterproductive, for several reasons.

a. Advocacy of an amendment assumes as true what is patently false: namely, that a decision of a majority of the

Supreme Court *is* the Constitution, until some new majority decides otherwise. Even Justices themselves from time to time deplore

> the tendency to encrust unwarranted interpretations upon the Constitution and thereafter to consider merely what has been judicially said about the Constitution, rather than to be primarily controlled by a fair conception of the Constitution. . . . But the ultimate touchstone of constitutionality is the Constitution itself and not what [some majority of the Supreme Court] ha[s] said about it.[490]

Yet if some judicial "interpretations" are "*un*warranted," they are not correct constructions of the Constitution at all—and therefore an amendment cannot possibly be necessary to change what is not there in the first place.

b. Rather than attacking the pernicious dogma of "judicial supremacy," which is the crux of the problem, advocacy of a constitutional amendment to correct judicial errors of constitutional law accepts, perpetuates, and strengthens it:

➢ It implicitly affirms the Judiciary's arrant claim that its decisions on constitutional issues are always in some sense "warranted" in law (albeit sometimes undesirable in political policy, and therefore reasons for amendments).

➢ It fosters elitism, egotism, haughtiness, and hubris among judges and their clerks, the legal *intelligentsia*, and even lawyers in general. (Anyone who observes

---

[490] *Graves* v. *New York ex rel. O'Keefe*, 306 U.S. 466, 491-92 (1939) (Frankfurter, J., concurring) (footnote omitted).

judges closely—from the lowest to the highest courts in this country—knows that the last thing they need is more mulch to manure their individual superciliousness and collective cult of superiority.)

➢ It encourages judicial irresponsibility, entrenches judicial disdain for WE THE PEOPLE, and eliminates any incentive for individual judges of constitutional integrity to fight for reform, by solidifying in the public's mind the defeatist fantasy that nothing can be done to correct judicial usurpations and tyranny other than to set about the extraordinarily difficult task of amending the Constitution, and by confirming in the judicial mind that WE THE PEOPLE'S retribution for misconstructions of the Constitution is, at best, a paper tiger, because vanishingly few misconstructions can possibly be reversed by an amendment. Where deterrence fails— because the public's response to judges' usurpation and tyranny can be neither swift, nor sure, nor even likely— judicial misbehavior will increase and intensify. And, most insidious of all,

➢ It rewards and emboldens the culturally subversive forces that have attained intellectual dominance in the courts and law schools, by maintaining the present unsatisfactory composition of the bench and judicial clerkdom, and doing nothing to loosen those forces' stranglehold over the process of appointing new and no less undesirable judges.

c. Advocacy of a constitutional amendment to correct present judicial errors of constitutional law forgets that changing the Constitution in those particulars will not necessarily—if at all—force judicial proponents of "the living Constitution" properly to construe and apply any new amendment, let alone the remainder of the Constitution. For example, the Supreme Court has thoroughly misinterpreted the Bill of Rights, the Fourteenth Amendment, and especially the relationship between the two since the beginning, notwithstanding that the Fourteenth Amendment was a pellucid attempt to correct earlier judicial blunders relating to the Bill of Rights.[491]

d. Amendment of the Constitution is, designedly, an exceedingly expensive and time-consuming process—difficult in any particular instance, and all but impossible as a method for policing the Judiciary *seriatim* as to even its egregious errors. Were every significant judicial misconstruction of the Constitution to result in a corrective amendment, the Constitution could be as long as the *United States Reports* themselves. And were some significant and glaring misconstructions of the Constitution to go uncorrected, the whole process of reform would be discredited, leading to public frustration, apathy, and ultimately surrender to "judicial supremacy" in most cases.

---

[491] Particularly *Barron* v. *Baltimore*, 32 U.S. (7 Pet.) 243 (1833), and *Scott* v. *Sandford*, 60 U.S. (19 How.) 393 (1857). See 2 W. Crosskey, *Politics and the Constitution*, ante note 161, chs. XXX-XXXII.

3. Assuming *arguendo* the propriety of advocating a constitutional amendment to correct a judicial error or intentional misstatement of constitutional law, designing a proper amendment for that purpose may be challenging.

a. An amendment could be drafted on a relatively narrow case-by-case basis. For example, specifically to negate *Lawrence* as a precedent in future litigation, an amendment might provide in general terms, "This Constitution shall neither be construed nor applied so as to preclude or limit any State from prohibiting and punishing, civilly or criminally, sodomy between individuals of the same sex."[492]

b. An amendment could also be drafted on the basis of broad principles. For example—

1) To preclude judges from promiscuously employing foreign law in constitutional interpretation, an amendment might provide:

> SECTION 1. Except where it shall be necessary to resolve an issue arising under Congress's power "[t]o define and punish ... Offenses against the Law of Nations" in Article I, Section 8, Clause 10, arising under the disability of every "Person holding any Office of Profit or Trust under [the United States]" to "accept ... any ... Emolument, Office, or Title, of any kind whatever, from any King, Prince, or foreign State" in Article I, Section 9, Clause 8, or arising under the power of the President, "by and with the

---

[492] This language is merely indicative of a general verbal direction that might be taken. As the Texas statute at issue in *Lawrence* suggests, greater particularity would probably be desirable, especially in the definition of "sodomy." See 539 U.S. at 563.

Advice and Consent of the Senate, to make Treaties" in Article II, Section 2, Clause 2, no court or judge of the United States or of any State shall construe or apply any provision of this Constitution by or with reliance upon or reference to any law, statute, legislative enactment, executive order or decree, or judicial or administrative decision, of any sort whatsoever, of any foreign nation, country, or state, or of any international organization.

SECTION 2. Congress shall have power to enforce this article by appropriate legislation.

2) To preclude judges from employing foreign law in particular instances of constitutional interpretation under the Fourteenth Amendment (as in *Lawrence*), a new amendment might provide:

SECTION 1. No court or judge of the United States or of any State shall construe or apply the terms "privileges or immunities," "life," "liberty," "property," "due process of law," "equal protection of the laws," or "person" in this Constitution by reliance upon or reference to any law, statute, legislative enactment, executive order or decree, or judicial or administrative decision, of any sort whatsoever, of any foreign nation, country, or state, or of any international organization.

SECTION 2. Congress shall have power to enforce this article by appropriate legislation.

This approach could easily be applied to other Amendments that hierophants of "the living Constitution" have subverted, or are likely to subvert, through the importation of foreign legal notions, such as the Eighth ("cruel and unusual punishments") and the Second ("the right to keep and bear Arms").

3) To prohibit judges from excising morality as a legitimate basis for any legislation, an amendment might provide:

> SECTION 1. No court or judge of the United States or of any State shall adjudge, hold, declare, or otherwise rule any statute, resolution, or other enactment of Congress or of any State legislative body repugnant to this Constitution on the ground that such statute, resolution, or other enactment prohibits or punishes a particular practice, conduct, or behavior because of its inconsistency with public morals.
>
> SECTION 2. Congress shall have power to enforce this article by appropriate legislation.

4) More specifically addressed to the issue in *Lawrence*, an amendment protecting WE THE PEOPLE'S right to promote morality through legislation might provide:

> SECTION 1. No court or judge of the United States or of any State shall adjudge, hold, declare, or otherwise rule any statute, resolution, or other enactment of Congress or of any State legislative body repugnant to this Constitution on the ground that such statute, resolution, or other enactment prohibits or punishes a particular sexually deviant, prurient, lewd, or obscene practice, conduct, or behavior because of its inconsistency with public morals.
>
> SECTION 2. Congress shall have power to enforce this article by appropriate legislation.

The latter two instances, however, raise the further question of whether "public morals" would need to be carefully defined for either amendment not to be open to subversion. Prior to *Lawrence*, "public morals" and "morality" in legal parlance always referred at least implicitly to *Christian* morals and morality—which, one may surmise, is why the majority in *Lawrence* so thoroughly and enthusiastically excised "morality" in general from the set of "'sufficient reason[s]'" and "legitimate state interest[s]" for legislation.[493] The Supreme Court's self-serving claim that "[o]ur obligation is to define the liberty of all, not to mandate our own moral code," is doubly deceptive.[494] First, the Court's "obligation"—as it is the entire General Government's and the States' obligation—is to "mandate," or at least not to thwart or worse negate or destroy, the "moral code" given by "the Laws of Nature and of Nature's God." This can hardly be accomplished by denying that the promotion of morality is a "legitimate state interest." Second, when Justices "define the liberty of all" in a certain way so as to outlaw certain types of legislation, they necessarily "mandate" their own moral code—unless one believes that the freedom to behave in one fashion or another without legal restraint ("liberty") has and ought to have no relation to any set of ideals or principles of right human conduct ("morality"). In fact, the purpose and certainly the effect of "defin[ing] the liberty of all" in *Lawrence* was precisely and intentionally to "mandate [the Justices'] own moral code," because by "defin[ing] liberty," as they did in that case, they imposed on State legislators and WE THE PEOPLE a theretofore unheard-of constitutional principle that purports to control State legislators' conduct thereafter. *Lawrence* thus served the

---

[493] Ibid. at 577, 578.

[494] *Planned Parenthood* v. *Casey*, 505 U.S. 833, 851 (1992), followed in *Lawrence*, 539 U.S. at 571.

strategy of the forces of cultural dissolution, which aim initially at breaking down all barriers to socially deviant (i.e., culturally, and ultimately politically, revolutionary) behavior, against which Christianity (rightly understood) stands as a bulwark. As thoroughgoing totalitarians, though, the forces of cultural dissolution aim in the long run, not only at removing all Christian influences from the law, but also at imposing their own *counter*-morality on everyone through the most rigorous application of legalistic and other coercion. Therefore, if those forces gained control of legislatures and enacted statutes based on the notion that a renovated set of "public morals" embraces some "politically correct" agenda sounding in secular humanism, the illuminism of the Frankfurt School, or worse, the suggested amendments could be counterproductive as a means for successfully waging "the culture war" on behalf of traditional ideas of decency.

c. Perhaps the broadest principle a new amendment could add to (or, put more correctly, reassert in) the Constitution would be the requirement that courts construe "the supreme Law of the Land"[495] solely according to "original intent," and eschew all employment of "the living Constitution" (except in the few situations where it is possibly appropriate[496]). Could such an amendment be drawn so as succinctly to define "original intent," and sufficiently to preclude judicial evasion, it would obviate most of the problems of misconstruction that have plagued the courts since the Republic's earliest days. The

---

[495] U.S. Const. art. VI, cl. 2.

[496] See ante, at 138-40.

difficulty of drafting the requisite amendment, though, may be inferred from the preceding discussion of "original intent."[497]

4. The fundamental problem that a case such as *Lawrence* poses is probably incapable of solution by constitutional amendments in any event (even if proper ones could be written), because America is now sufficiently divided by the effects of the war of cultural aggression being waged by the forces of decadence, degeneration, and ultimately darkness that no consensus among three-fourths of the States can likely be had. The majority opinion in *Lawrence*, Justice Scalia observed,

> is the product of a Court, which is the product of a law-profession culture, that has largely signed on to the so-called homosexual agenda . . . directed at eliminating the moral opprobrium that has traditionally attached to homosexual conduct. . . .
>
> One of the most revealing statements in today's opinion is the Court's grim warning that the criminalization of homosexual conduct is "an invitation to subject homosexual persons to discrimination in both the public *and in the private spheres."* . . . *It is clear from this that the Court has taken sides in the culture war*, departing from its role of assuring, as neutral observer, that the democratic rules of engagement are observed. *Many Americans do not want persons who openly engage in homosexual conduct as partners in their business, as scoutmasters for their children, as teachers in their children's schools, or as boarders in their home. They view this as protecting themselves and their families from a lifestyle*

---

[497] See ante, at 55-80.

that they believe to be immoral and destructive. The Court views
this as "discrimination" which it is the function of our judgments
to deter.[498]

That "[m]any Americans do not want. . ." is precisely the point
of the *Lawrence* majority's participation in the war of cultural
aggression: Americans are being told that they will not be
permitted to protect themselves, not only from what "they
believe to be immoral and destructive," but also from what
according to two thousand years of Christian teaching and
tradition *is* immoral, and what *must* be destructive of the fabric
of American families that reject the homosexual "lifestyle" but
after *Lawrence* will increasingly be compelled to acquiesce in.
In the largest sense, then, *Lawrence* is a "test case": If Americans
will allow the "homosexual agenda" to be jammed down their
throats, at the expense of their own families, what other
immoral and destructive conduct will they not meekly
swallow? And *what other* is the long-term consideration. For
the reasoning of the *Lawrence* majority is not limited in
principle, or intended to be restricted in practice, to
homosexual conduct: "'[T]he fact that the governing majority
in a State has traditionally viewed a particular practice as
immoral is not a sufficient reason for upholding a law
prohibiting the practice'."[499] "[A] *particular* practice" can, of
course, embrace *any* practice "traditionally viewed . . . as
immoral." Which decrees the absolute separation of *all*
"traditional" morality and law.

---

[498] 539 U.S. at 602 (dissenting opinion) (emphasis supplied).

[499] Ibid. at 577.

If "the Court has taken sides in the culture war" for the benefit of the aggressors (as Justice Scalia correctly charged), it did not act alone. The Justices in the *Lawrence* majority are "the product of a law-profession culture" which decisively influences, if it does not dominate, the teaching of law, the practice of law, judges (and their clerks) who hand down opinions, legislators who enact statutes, and public officials generally. But even "the law-profession culture" is not independent, only a component part of another, overriding "culture" that it reflects and serves. The one thing that can be said with certainty of this "culture" is that is does not include, but militantly excludes, the "[m]any Americans [who] do not want" anything to do with the "homosexual agenda" or with the immorality for which it stands, yet intends to intrude its anti-values into those Americans' lives through legalistic coercion aimed at eliminating "discrimination"—that is, every vestige of freedom the "culture" deems "politically incorrect" or, in more descriptive terms, nonrevolutionary. Thus, instead of "one Nation, under God," *Lawrence* exposes *two* Americas— one, the America of "traditional" morality, with its roots in the Declaration of Independence and "the Laws of Nature and of Nature's God"; the other, the America of amoral "law," with its roots in cultural bolshevism imposed through intellectual, political, and judicial elitism. And *Lawrence* exposes the true problem this dichotomy creates as one, not of law (because *Lawrence* is not a constitutional decision), but of civil war being waged under legalistic camouflage, in which conflict the aggressors are deploying the basest of human appetites as their heavy artillery for blasting away at social cohesion.

The cultural Bolsheviks want their victims to imagine that the victims' sole recourse to a decision such as *Lawrence* is amendment of the Constitution, because the aggressors can muster sufficient political power and influence over public opinion to thwart that result every time. This means that Americans—once they wake up and face up to the dire peril the culture war poses, and point the finger of guilt at the cultural Bolsheviks waging it—ought to turn aside from constitutional amendments as blind alleys, and instead employ means for fighting the war that require no more than simple majorities.

CHAPTER 7

Ad Hoc Remedial Legislation by Congress or Pardons by the President

One approach to partial remediation of judges' misconstructions of the Constitution might be found in *ad hoc* legislation by Congress (or a State legislature), or pardons by the President (or a State governor) to remove or lighten the burdens imposed on the victims of these judicial travesties. This strategy derives from the plain fact that, even were the Supreme Court the "ultimate interpreter of the Constitution,"[500] it nevertheless could not as a practical matter always and necessarily make its "interpret[ations]" final even in the very "Case[ ]" or "Controvers[y]" in which it enunciated them.

1. a. For example, assume that, as a result of some erroneous constitutional pronouncement by a majority of the Justices, X is required to pay monetary damages to Y, and that through threats of or actual citations for contempt, the courts

---

[500] *Baker* v. *Carr*, 369 U.S. 186, 211 (1962); *Powell* v. *McCormack*, 395 U.S. 486, 548-49 (1969).

compel *X* to satisfy the judgment. Recognizing the injustice of this situation, Congress could pass a "private bill" reimbursing *X* for the amount paid to *Y*, on the ground that the original judgment was unconstitutional. Such an expenditure of public funds could be justified on the following reasoning: One of the purposes the Constitution sets out in the Preamble is "to . . . establish Justice"—and "[t]he Preamble . . . was totally inappropriate, under eighteenth-century rules [of legislative draftsmanship], unless a government was intended, having powers fully adequate to the 'objects' which the Preamble covers."[501] WE THE PEOPLE have authorized Congress "[t]o make all Laws which shall be necessary and proper for carrying into Execution . . . all . . . Powers vested by the Constitution in the Government of the United States, or in any Department or Officer thereof."[502] One of these "Powers" is "[t]he judicial Power of the United States."[503] If "[t]he judicial Power" is *mis*used (in this instance through an unconstitutional judgment), "Justice" is withheld, not "established." In order to "carry[ ] into Execution" "[t]he judicial Power" *so as* "to . . . establish Justice,*" Congress may "make a[ ] Law[ ]" which reverses the financial effect of the erroneous judicial decision. And a payment to *X* is permissible, inasmuch as "Money [may]

---

[501] 1 W. Crosskey, *Politics and the Constitution*, ante note 161, at 379.

[502] U.S. Const. art. I, § 8, cl. 18.

[503] U.S. Const. art. III, § 1.

be drawn from the Treasury ... in Consequence of Appropriations made by Law."[504]

This strategy, however, has rough edges in both practice and principle. In practice, such a remedy can be employed only in a decidedly limited number of cases in which misconstruction of the Constitution is the foundation for imposition of a monetary award that Congress could later remit by reimbursement.

In principle, such a remedy assumes that Congress may treat the Justices' *mis*construction of the Constitution as a fair exercise of "[t]he judicial Power," as opposed to a plain usurpation. No court, however, can have *constitutional* power to impose *unconstitutional* judgments on anyone. A *mis*construction of the Constitution with coercive effect is a *violation* of the Constitution, and as such is outside "[t]he judicial Power" by hypothesis—unless WE THE PEOPLE were sufficiently psychotic as to authorize the use of constitutional powers to violate the Constitution. Moreover, inasmuch as WE THE PEOPLE have not authorized the Justices to impose *mis*constructions of the Constitution on litigants in the guise of proper interpretations—that is, have not licensed them to equate legal errors with "Justice"—then why should WE THE PEOPLE pay to rectify the justices' misbehavior? The Justices themselves should he held liable.

---

[504] U.S. Const. art. I, § 9, cl. 7. See *Knote* v. *United States*, 95 U.S. 149, 153-54 (1877).

b. Very revealing of how far Congress can go in effectively reversing a decision of the Supreme Court through exercise of legislative power is *Pennsylvania* v. *Wheeling Bridge Company*.[505] There, the Supreme Court had rendered a decree "which declared [a] bridge ... to be an obstruction of ... free navigation ... , and directed that the obstruction be removed."[506] Congress then passed a statute declaring that certain bridges, including the one covered by the Court's decree, were "'lawful structures ... and shall be so held and taken to be, anything in the law or laws of the United States to the contrary notwithstanding.'"[507] To the contention that this statute was unconstitutional, the Court replied:

> The bridge had been constructed ... subject only to the power of Congress in the regulation of commerce. It was claimed, however, that ... [the bridge] was in conflict with [prior] Acts of Congress which were the paramount law.
>
> That being the view of the case taken by a majority of the court [in its earlier decision], they found no difficulty in arriving at the conclusion, that the obstruction of the navigation of the river, by the bridge, was a violation of the right secured to the public by the Constitution and laws of Congress . . . .
>
> Since, however, the rendition of this decree, the [subsequent] Act[ ] of Congress ... ha[s] been passed ...

---

[505] 59 U.S. (18 How.) 421 (1856).

[506] Ibid. at 429.

[507] Ibid.

requiring all persons navigating the river to regulate such navigation so as not to interfere with [the bridge].

So far, therefore, as this bridge created an obstruction to the free navigation of the river, . . . although it still may be an obstruction in fact, is not so in the contemplation of law.[508]

To the further contention that "the Act of Congress cannot have the effect and operation to annul the judgment of the court already rendered, or the rights determined thereby in favor of the [party complaining of the bridge]," the Court answered:

[T]h[e] part of the decree, directing the abatement of the obstruction, is . . . a continuing decree . . . . Now, whether it is a future existing or continuing obstruction depends upon whether or not it interferes with the right of navigation. If, . . . since the decree, this right has been modified by the competent authority, so that the bridge is no longer an unlawful obstruction, . . . the decree of the court cannot be enforced. There is no longer any interference with the enjoyment of the public right inconsistent with law . . . .[509]

2. The President (or a State governor), too, may intervene on an *ad hoc* basis in certain cases or categories of cases in which someone or a class of persons has been victimized through judges' misconstructions of the Constitution. Specifically, "[t]he President . . . shall have Power to grant Reprieves and Pardons for Offenses against the United States,

---

[508] Ibid. at 430.

[509] Ibid. at 431-32.

except in Cases of Impeachment."[510] With the exception stated:

> The power ... conferred is unlimited .... It extends to every offense known to the law, and may be exercised at any time after [the offense's] commission, either before legal proceedings are taken, or during their pendency, or after conviction and judgment. This power of the President is not subject to legislative control. Congress can neither limit the effect of his pardon, nor exclude from its exercise any class of offenders.[511]

Thus, using this authority, a President could overturn unconstitutional convictions that the Supreme Court upheld or refused to review.[512] Even though this authority would be limited to "Offenses against the United States," it would not be inconsequential.[513]

---

[510] U.S. Const. art. II, § 2, cl. 1.

[511] Ex parte *Garland*, 71 U.S. (4 Wall.) 333, 380 (1867). Accord, Ex parte *Grossman*, 267 U.S. 87, 120 (1925).

[512] One may complain that a President who would issue any such pardon would do better to prevent or abate the underlying prosecution in the first place, through control over the Attorney General and the Department of Justice. In a particular case, however, the key question of unconstitutionality may come to the fore only during the course of an otherwise plausible prosecution, or as the result of a faulty conviction (e.g., one lacking sufficient evidence), or as the product of some additional judicial blunder committed during appellate review. Or the prosecution itself, as well as judicial review thereof, may have occurred during a previous administration.

[513] A State governor could pardon offenses, not only against his own State directly and fully, but also against the United States indirectly, to the extent that the latter offenses triggered consequences in State law that a State

a. As to the particular victim of an unconstitutional conviction, a presidential pardon wipes out the offense, and thus completely reverses the Court's contrary decision: "A pardon reaches both the punishment prescribed for the offense and the guilt of the offender; and when the pardon is full, it releases the punishment and blots out the existence of guilt, so that in the eye of the law the offender is as innocent as if he had never committed the offense."[514] In addition, "the President . . . may remit fines, penalties and forfeitures of every description arising under the laws of Congress."[515] And the President can grant conditional pardons, too.[516]

Unfortunately, a pardon

> affords no relief for what has been suffered by the offender in his person by imprisonment, forced labor, or otherwise; it does not give compensation for what has been done or suffered, nor does it impose upon the government any obligation to give it. The offence being established by judicial proceedings, that which has been done or suffered while they were in force is presumed to have been rightfully done and justly suffered, and no satisfaction for it can be required.[517]

---

pardon could nullify. E.g., if conviction for a national felony resulted in imposition of a disability on the putative offender as a consequence of State law, the Governor might be authorized to remove the disability.

[514] Ex parte *Garland*, 71 U.S. (4 Wall.) 333, 380 (1867).

[515] *Pollack* v. *Bridgeport Steamship Co.* (The Laura), 114 U.S. 411, 413 (1885).

[516] Ex parte *Wells*, 59 U.S. (18 How.) 307, 314-15 (1856).

[517] *Knote* v. *United States*, 95 U.S. 149, 153-54 (1877).

Some "satisfaction . . . *can* be required," though, in that a victim could seek both financial recompense through a "private bill" in Congress,[518] and legal vindication through criminal prosecution of those who unconstitutionally persecuted him.[519]

b. The potential breadth of application of the President's power to pardon is extensive, both substantively and procedurally.

1) Substantively, for instance, numerous individuals are prosecuted and convicted annually for violations of the present national income tax, although serious grounds exist for concluding that the so-called Sixteenth Amendment was never properly ratified.[520] Typically, in conducting these prosecutions and sustaining these convictions, many courts simply refuse to entertain that defense, on the ground that the Amendment's validity *vel non* is a "political question" within the exclusive ken

---

[518] See ante, at 193-97.

[519] See post, at 261-68.

[520] See W. Benson & M. Beckman, *The Law That Never Was: The Fraud of the 16th Amendment and Personal Income Tax* (1985). The adjective "present" is a key qualifier, because the purpose of the Sixteenth Amendment is to empower Congress "to lay and collect taxes on incomes . . . *without apportionment among the several States, and without regard to any census or enumeration.*" U.S. Const. amend. XVI (emphasis supplied). Even without the Amendment, though, Congress would have power to tax some types of income "in Proportion to the Census or Enumeration." U.S. Const. art. I, § 9, cl. 4. Whether this authority could reach incomes derived directly from individuals' labor, however, is another question. See U.S. Const. amend. XIII.

of the Executive or Legislative branches of the General Government.[521]

To be sure, this is a misconstruction of the Constitution so stupendously specious as to evidence a markedly malicious motive. Judges never say that the unconstitutionality of a statute they are asked to enforce is a "political question" simply because it supposedly exceeds a particular power of Congress, even one that has received an extensive construction over the years, such as the Commerce Clause.[522] But, if one litigant may argue that some statute is unconstitutional because no such congressional power to enact it exists under (say) the rubric of "regulat[ing] Commerce," why cannot another litigant argue that the present unapportioned individual income tax is unconstitutional because no congressional power to enact it exists at all under any rubric, the purported Sixteenth Amendment never having been ratified? The foundational argument—the nonexistence of the requisite power—is the same. If, in a particular "Case[ ]" or "Controvers[y]," the Judiciary may say that Congress and the Executive are wrong about the *meaning* of a provision within the original body of the Constitution—*and therefore that*

---

[521] See, e.g., *United States* v. *Stahl*, 792 F.2d 1438 (9th Cir. 1986). Some cases, though, have decided the issue on the merits, wrongly in favor of the Amendment's validity. See, e.g., *United States* v. *House*, 617 F. Supp. 237 (W.D. Mich. 1985). Others have combined both rationales to rule against the complainant. See, e.g., *United States* v. *Foster*, 789 F.2d 457, 462-63 (7th Cir. 1986).

[522] U.S. Const. art. I, § 8, cl. 3. See, e.g., *Printz* v. *United States*, 521 U.S. 898, 918-19, 923-24 (1997).

such provision does not exist to the extent of the enhanced meaning claimed for it—why cannot the Judiciary also say that Congress and the Executive are wrong about the *existence* of an amendment, because of improprieties or deficiencies in the process by which it was supposedly ratified?

In any event, assuming *arguendo* that the question of the validity *vel non* of the Sixteenth Amendment *is* a "political question," then the power of the President to pardon alleged violators of the present income-tax code is not only an appropriate exercise of executive prerogative, but also a necessary consequence of the President's constitutional duties "to the best of [his] Ability, [to] preserve, protect and defend the Constitution,"[523] and to "take Care that the Laws be faithfully executed."[524] The latter point is particularly compelling, inasmuch as the Secretary of State—an officer of the executive branch, subordinate and answerable to the President, and for whose actions the President is ultimately responsible—originally certified (negligently or fraudulently, but in any event erroneously) the ratification of the Sixteenth Amendment in 1913, and by his silence in the face of notorious challenges to the ratification's sufficiency implicitly certifies that ratification on a continuous basis. To be sure, since 1913 a huge redistribution of wealth from society to the General Government and politicians' clients in special-interest groups has occurred under color of the Sixteenth Amendment, an orgy of political looting that almost in its entirety cannot now

---

[523] U.S. Const. art. II, § 1, cl. 7.

[524] U.S. Const. art. II, § 3.

be corrected by restitution to the victims. But the thoughtless manner in which officials have applied the Constitution with respect to that supposed Amendment is inconsequential in comparison to how they should have applied it.[525] For if "a bold and daring usurpation might be resisted, after [long and complete] acquiescence,"[526] surely a mindless "[g]eneral acquiescence cannot justify departure from the [supreme] law."[527] When the non-ratification—and therefore legal nonexistence—of a constitutional amendment is broached, the matter cannot simply be disregarded because theretofore the General Government has always acted as if the amendment existed, and only recently has the amendment's legitimacy ever been challenged.[528] "[N]either the antiquity of a practice nor . . . steadfast legislative and judicial adherence to it through the centuries insulates it from constitutional attack."[529] "[N]o one acquires a vested or protected right in violation of the Constitution by long use, even when that span of time covers our entire national existence and indeed predates it."[530] Constitutional questions "must be resolved not by past uncertainties, assumptions or arguments, but by the application of the controlling principles of constitutional

---

[525] See *The Propeller Genesee Chief* v. *Fitzhugh*, 53 U.S. (12 How.) 443, 458 (1851).

[526] *McCulloch* v. *Maryland*, 17 U.S. (4 Wheat.) 316, 401 (1819).

[527] *Smiley* v. *Holm*, 285 U.S. 355, 369 (1932).

[528] See *Fairbank* v. *United States*, 181 U.S. 283, 311 (1901).

[529] *Williams* v. *Illinois*, 399 U.S. 235, 239 (1970).

[530] *Walz* v. *Tax Commission*, 397 U.S. 664, 678 (1970).

interpretation."[531] Even less of a consideration is that, without the Sixteenth Amendment, most of the present income-tax code would lack any legal foundation, stripping the General Government of a major source of its revenue. "[T]hat ... constitutional protections against arbitrary government are inoperative when they become inconvenient or when expediency dictates otherwise is a very dangerous doctrine and if allowed to flourish would destroy the benefit of a written Constitution."[532]

Indeed, one salient purpose for the President to employ his power to pardon to resolve the question of the unconstitutionality of the Sixteenth Amendment would be thereby to assert his authority, *independent of the Supreme Court*, to construe and apply the Constitution within the ambit of "[t]he executive Power,"[533] so as to obviate the species of "arbitrary government" that has arisen under color of "judicial supremacy" through "judicial review," and manifested itself precisely in the courts' refusal to inquire into the unconstitutionality of that Amendment (among other defaults in their duties).[534]

2) Procedurally, too, the presidential power to pardon could have far-reaching consequences. For instance, the

---

[531] *Wright* v. *United States*, 302 U.S. 583, 597-98 (1938).

[532] *Reid* v. *Covert*, 354 U.S. 1, 14 (1957) (opinion of Black, J.).

[533] U.S. Const. art. II, § 1, cl. 1.

[534] Obviously, under these circumstances, the President would also terminate all criminal prosecutions, as well as civil and administrative actions, for alleged violations of the present individual income tax.

President could effectively nullify each and every judgment he deemed unconstitutional by pardoning all criminal contempts the courts of the General Government employed to enforce those judgments.[535] The power to pardon could thus operate as a method of "presidential review" of judicial action as to the latter's conformity *vel non* with law.

It is no argument against this power that:

> [I]t will tend to destroy the independence of the judiciary and violate the primary constitutional principle of a separation of the legislative, executive, and judicial powers. . . .
>
> The Federal Constitution nowhere expressly declares that the three branches of the government shall be kept separate and independent. . . . Complete independence and separation between the three branches . . . are not attained, or intended, as [various] provisions of the Constitution and the normal operation of government under it easily demonstrate. . . . The Executive can reprieve or pardon all offenses after their commission . . . .
>
> These are some instances of . . . restraints possibly available under the Constitution to each branch of the government in defeat of the action of the other. They show that the independence of each . . . is qualified and is so subject to exception as not to constitute a broadly positive injunction or a necessarily controlling rule of construction. The fact is that the Judiciary, quite as much as Congress and the Executive, are dependent on the co-operation of the other two, that government may go on. Indeed, while the Constitution has made the Judiciary as independent of the

---

[535] See Ex parte *Grossman*, 267 U.S. 87 (1925).

other branches as is practicable, it is . . . the weakest of the three. It must look for a continuity of necessary co-operation, in the possible reluctance of either of the other branches, to the force of public opinion.

Executive clemency exists to afford relief from undue harshness *or evident mistake* in the operation or enforcement of the criminal law.[536]

3. Furthermore, under the Necessary and Proper Clause,[537] and without encroaching upon the President's power to pardon, Congress can pass statutes that authorize other officers to remit forfeitures or penalties imposed under the laws of the United States.[538] As some of these statutes could—indeed, would be intended to—take into account judicial errors of constitutional or other law as the basis for amnesty, they would be methods for ongoing congressional review of judicial action as to the latter's conformity *vel non* with law.

---

[536] Ibid. at 119-20 (emphasis supplied).

[537] U.S. Const. art. I, § 8, cl. 18.

[538] *Pollock* v. *Bridgeport Steamship Co.* (*The Laura*), 114 U.S. 411, 414-16 (1885) (Secretary of the Treasury).

CHAPTER 8

"Constitutional Review" of Judicial Actions by Congress and the President

Reprieves and pardons, remissions of forfeitures and penalties, and amnesties can be based upon political, economic, social, or for that matter any reasons—not necessarily always, or perhaps even usually, the legal merits of the particular situation under scrutiny. Such relief will be effective whether or not a legal reason is cited, and even if that reason is wrong or pretextual. Therefore, these forms of relief by themselves cannot in the nature of things constitute or evidence *authoritative* presidential or congressional "constitutional review" of judicial action, because the Judiciary (or anyone else) can always dismiss the legal reasons the President or Congress proffers as mere surplusage, unnecessary to the efficacy of the relief.[539] There is, however, a constitutionally solid foundation for *presidential or congressional "constitutional review" of judicial action.*

---

[539] The same is true of a presidential veto, which may be motivated for any number of reasons other than constitutional considerations. See U.S. Const. art. I, § 7, cl. 2.

1. In the contemporary legal hothouse of "judicial supremacy" through "judicial review," presidential or congressional "constitutional review" of judicial action is imperatively necessary for the survival of constitutionalism and a free society. The notions that any adventitious majority of Justices of the Supreme Court is the "ultimate interpreter of the Constitution,"[540] that "the interpretation of the [Constitution] enunciated by [such a majority] . . . is the supreme law of the land,"[541] and that "[a] decision [of such a majority]" on a constitutional issue "cannot be reversed short of a constitutional amendment"[542] subvert sound government and destabilize society. For undeniable it is that "no amount of repetition of . . . errors in judicial opinions can make the errors true";[543] that if judicial decisions are not true they cannot "establish Justice";[544] and that, if WE THE PEOPLE have no alternative to accepting as *ersatz* "Justice" what is *untrue*, except to amend the Constitution in each and every instance of judicial error, then those decisions (and the "judicial supremacy" from which they derive) will undermine "domestic Tranquility"[545]—and eventually will discredit, not

---

[540] *Baker* v. *Carr*, 369 U.S. 186, 211 (1962); *Powell* v. *McCormack*, 395 U.S. 486, 548-49 (1969)

[541] *Cooper* v. *Aaron*, 358 U.S. 1, 18 (1958).

[542] *Gregg* v. *Georgia*, 428 U.S. 153, 176 (1976) (emphasis supplied).

[543] *Wallace* v. *Jaffree*, 472 U.S. 38, 107 (1985) (Rehnquist, C.J., dissenting).

[544] U.S. Const. preamble.

[545] U.S. Const. preamble. The best contemporary example is the "culture war" over abortion. See, e.g., *Planned Parenthood* v. *Casey*, 505 U.S. 833 (1992).

only the United States Constitution, but also constitutionalism itself, as nothing more than legalistic cover-stories for the arbitrary *Diktats* of "a law-profession culture," the values, goals, and morals of which are alien and antagonistic to those common Americans share.[546] Indeed, once "the rule of law" in America is exposed, deconstructed, and vilified as nothing but "the rule of men," how many of its victims will ask whether this situation has come about *through* "the rule of law" *or in opposition to it*? Will not people's natural tendency be to jettison "the rule of law" entirely, as a proven snare and delusion, and to turn instead to the politics of personalities, in which "law" becomes nothing more than the label some leader attaches to his agenda? That is, will not "judicial supremacy" as exercised by the creatures of the contemporary "law-profession culture" lead inexorably to Caesarism—and, as a consequence of Caesarism, to the demise of "the Blessings of Liberty [for] ourselves and our Posterity"?[547]

2. The question then becomes, *what* branches of the General Government can interpret the Constitution *as part of their institutional competence, right, and duty*? The answer is: *each* branch. The reason is that the basis for "constitutional review" of judicial action by the President or Congress is precisely the same as the basis for "judicial review" of presidential or congressional action. If "judicial review" is in any sense valid, then presidential or congressional "constitutional review" must be equally valid.

---

[546] 539 U.S. at 602 (Scalia, J., dissenting).

[547] U.S. Const. preamble.

a. The source of "judicial review," out of which supposedly arises "judicial supremacy," is Chief Justice John Marshall's opinion in *Marbury* v. *Madison.*[548] Marshall's basic argument was not original, as it had previously appeared in *The Federalist.*[549] And his reasoning constituted too thin a prop to support the top-heavy superstructure of "judicial *supremacy*" later generations of judges have piled on it. For, prior to *Marbury,* "judicial review" of the modern variety was rare and controversial, and "judicial supremacy" quite unknown even as a theory.[550] And *Marbury's* reasoning, even if it justified a certain type of "judicial review," proved the exact opposite of "judicial supremacy."

Marshall defined the question before the Court in *Marbury* as "whether an act [of legislation], repugnant to the constitution, can become the law of the land."[551] Yet even he found this inquiry "not of an intricacy proportioned to its interest."[552] The more challenging questions are: *What branches of the government may identify a repugnancy, by dint of what constitutional authority, under what circumstances, and as against whom?* As to the first of these, Marshall asked: "If an act of the legislature, repugnant to the constitution, is void, does it,

---

[548] 5 U.S. (1 Cranch) 137 (1803).

[549] No. 78 (A. Hamilton).

[550] See 2 W. Crosskey, *Politics and the Constitution,* ante note 161, chs. XXVII-XXIX.

[551] 5 U.S. (1 Cranch) at 176.

[552] Ibid.

notwithstanding its invalidity, bind *the courts*, and oblige *them* to give it effect?" He answered:

> It is emphatically the province and duty of the judicial department to say what the law is. . . . So, if a law be in opposition to the constitution; if both the law and the constitution apply to *a particular case*, so that *the court must decide that case* conformably to the law, disregarding the constitution; or conformably to the constitution, disregarding the law; *the court must determine which of these conflicting rules governs the case.* This is the very essence of judicial duty.

> If then the courts are to regard the constitution; and the constitution is superior to any ordinary act of the legislature; the constitution, and not such ordinary act, *must govern the case* to which they would both apply.[553]

Now, Marshall doubtlessly recognized (even though he did not say) that, in the first instance, it is emphatically the province and duty of WE THE PEOPLE'S representatives "to say what the [*statutory*] law is,"[554] and, more importantly, emphatically the province and duty of WE THE PEOPLE themselves "to say what the [*constitutional*] law is."[555] In any event, Marshall's own description of the situation plainly evidenced his understanding that "the province and duty of the judicial department to say what the law is" arises only in the course of

---

[553] Ibid. at 177-78 (emphasis supplied).

[554] "All legislative Powers herein granted shall be vested in a Congress." U.S. Const. art. I, § 1. See U.S. Const. art. I, § 7, cl. 2, which defines when "Bill[s]" become "Law[s]."

[555] See U.S. Const. preamble and art. V.

deciding "a particular case" in which the validity of a contested constitutional provision, statute, or other governmental action is at issue. If, however, "[t]he judicial Power shall extend" only *to* certain "Cases" and "Controversies,"[556] it can extend only to the litigants (and their privies) *in* those "Cases" and "Controversies," they being the only parties actually before the Court against whom its "judicial Power" can operate. Thus, nothing in Marshall's reasoning in *Marbury* supported the extrapolation that, the Court having spoken in "a particular case," its decision binds one or both coordinate branches of the government (or anyone else) in all things thereafter, as well as the litigants in that "case."

Marshall observed that "[t]he judicial Power" extends to "all cases arising under the constitution,"[557] and concluded that it was "too extravagant to be maintained" that the Framers had intended that "a case arising under the constitution should be decided without examining the instrument under which it arises."[558] True enough. But, once again, Marshall limited his own reasoning to the specific context of "a case." Moreover, the selfsame reasoning applies with equal force to Congress and the President: In deciding whether a statute it intends to pass, or has passed, is valid, must not Congress "examin[e] the instrument under which [the statute] arises"? In "tak[ing] care that the Laws be faithfully executed,"[559] must not the President

---

[556] U.S. Const. art. III, § 2, cl. 1.

[557] Compare 5 U.S. (1 Cranch) at 178 with U.S. Const. art. III, § 2, cl. 1.

[558] 5 U.S. (1 Cranch) at 178-79.

[559] U.S. Const. art. II, § 3.

examine those "Laws" and compare them to "the instrument
under which [they] arise[ ]"? And should not Congress and the
President, in exercising their own constitutional authorities
when confronted with a decision of the Supreme Court,
themselves "examin[e] the instrument under which [that
decision] arises" to determine whether the Constitution and
the Court's construction of it are mutually consistent? Surely
so—unless Congress and the President are to function as
robotic subordinates of the Court. For the Court "to say what
the law is" in the context of deciding "a particular case"—that
is, to state its opinion on what the Constitution means in that
situation—differs not one whit from the enactment of a statute
by Congress, or the execution of one by the President, in terms
of each branch's satisfying itself that its action comports with
what it believes the Constitution requires or allows.

Marshall then explained what he held to be the ultimate
source of the authority for "judicial review":

> [T]he framers of the constitution contemplated that
> instrument, as a rule for the government of *courts*, as well as
> of the legislature.
>
> Why otherwise does it direct the judges to take an oath
> to support it? This oath certainly applies, in an especial
> manner, to their conduct in their official character.
>
> . . .
>
> Why does a judge swear to discharge his duties
> agreeably to the constitution of the United States, if that
> constitution forms no rule for his government? . . .

If such be the real state of things, this is worse than solemn mockery. To prescribe, or to take this oath, becomes equally a crime.

It is also not entirely unworthy of observation, that in declaring what shall be the *supreme* law of the land, the *constitution* itself is first mentioned; and not the laws of the United States generally, but those only which shall be made in *pursuance* of the constitution, have that rank.

Thus, the particular phraseology of the constitution . . . confirms and strengthens the principle . . . that a law repugnant to the constitution is void; and that *courts*, as well as other departments, are bound by that instrument.[560]

What, though, does all this mean operationally for other branches of the General Government?

Marbury actually held no more than that the Supreme Court may constitutionally refuse to enforce a statute that interferes with the performance of those powers the Constitution specifically invests in the Judiciary—because the Court has received "[t]he judicial Power" directly from WE THE PEOPLE, and must exercise that power according to the Justices' own honestly conscientious understanding thereof, not according to the will of Congress or the President. That is, rather than having created the precursor of today's "judicial supremacy" through "judicial review," *Marbury* really applied only the rules of "checks and balances" and "separation of powers," whereby the Court refused to exercise an authority Congress had attempted unconstitutionally to thrust upon it.

---

[560] Ibid. at 179-80 (emphasis in the original).

Such a construction of "judicial review" leaves only narrow scope for nullification of laws or executive actions.[561] Most of the time, it would allow the Court only to refuse to enforce, against the litigants in a particular "Case[ ]" or "Controvers[y]," a statute or executive action a majority of the Justices deemed unconstitutional under the facts of that "Case[ ]" or "Controvers[y]."

b. Such a construction of "judicial review" would also have to concede to Congress and the President analogous rights, powers, and duties of "constitutional review" within their own constitutionally defined domains. As Marshall himself did in his elliptical admission in *Marbury* that "courts, *as well as other departments*, are bound" by the Constitution—and in exactly the same way, and for the same reason.

That judges "shall be bound by Oath or Affirmation, to support the Constitution"[562] does not prove that thereby they exercise an *exclusive* power of "review" over the Constitution's meaning—that is, an unchallengeable authority to define, modify, expand, contract, or nullify the powers of Congress and the President, with no constitutional recourse on the latter's behalf. For members of Congress themselves, too, "shall be bound by [the selfsame] Oath or Affirmation, to

---

[561] See, e.g., *Hayburn's Case*, 2 U.S. (2 Dall.) 409, 410-14 n.† (1792) (Court refuses to administer a congressional pension Act because the duties imposed are not judicial, and Court's opinions are subject to revision by non-judicial officer).

[562] U.S. Const. art. VI, cl. 3.

support this Constitution";[563] and the President as well "shall take the following Oath or Affirmation:—'I do solemnly swear (or affirm) that I will faithfully execute the Office of President of the United States, and will to the best of my Ability, preserve, protect and defend the Constitution of the United States."[564] Undeniably, on *Marbury's* reasoning, both of these "Oath[s] or Affirmation[s]" must invest Congress and the President with rights and duties to "review" the Judiciary's decisions and disregard in the future exercise of their authority those they consider to be erroneous interpretations of the Constitution—such rights and duties necessarily of stature equal to the right and duty of "judicial review" that arises out of the judges' "Oath[s] or Affirmation[s]."

This is proven by substituting in *Marbury's* reasoning appropriate terms relating to "judicial decisions" for terms relating to "legislative acts":

> The powers of the [Judiciary] are defined and limited; and that those limits may not be mistaken or forgotten, the constitution is written. To what purpose are powers limited, and to what purpose is that limitation committed to writing, if those limits may, at any time, be passed by those intended to be restrained? The distinction between a government with limited and unlimited powers is abolished, if those limits do not confine the persons on whom they are imposed, and if acts prohibited and acts allowed, are of equal obligation. It is a proposition too plain to be contested, that the constitution controls any [judicial

[563] U.S. Const. art. VI, cl. 3.

[564] U.S. Const. art. II, § 1, cl. 7.

decision] repugnant to it; or that the [Judiciary] may alter the constitution by an ordinary [decision].

Between these alternatives, there is no middle ground. The constitution is either a superior paramount law, unchallengeable by ordinary means, or it is on a level with ordinary [judicial decisions], and, like other [decisions], is alterable when the [Judiciary] shall please to alter it. If the former part of the alternative be true, then a [judicial decision], contrary to the constitution, is not law: if the latter part be true, then written constitutions are absurd attempts, on the part of the people, to limit a power, in its own nature, illimitable.

Certainly, all those who have framed written constitutions contemplate them as forming the fundamental and paramount law of the nation, and consequently, the theory of every such government must be, that a[judicial decision], repugnant to the constitution, is void. This theory is essentially attached to a written constitution, and is, consequently, to be considered by th[e Supreme C]ourt, as one of the fundamental principles of our society. It is not, therefore, to be lost sight of . . . .

If a[judicial decision], repugnant to the constitution, is void, does it, notwithstanding its invalidity, bind [Congress, the President, or the States], and oblige them to give it effect? Or, in other words, though it be not law, does it constitute a rule as operative as if it was law? This would seem to overthrow, in fact, what was established in theory; and would seem . . . an absurdity too gross to be insisted on. . . .

It is, emphatically, the province and duty of [Congress to enact laws and of the President to execute the laws]. Those who apply the rule to particular cases, must of necessity expound and interpret that rule. If two laws conflict with each other, [Congress or the President] must decide on the operation of each. So, if a [judicial decision] be in opposition to the constitution; if both the [decision] and the constitution apply to a particular case, so that [Congress or the President] must either decide that case, conformable to the [judicial decision], disregarding the constitution; or conformable to the constitution, disregarding the [judicial decision]; [Congress or the President] must determine which of these conflicting rules governs the case: this is the very essence of [their] duty. If then, [Congress or the President] are to regard the constitution, and the constitution is superior to any ordinary [judicial decision], the constitution, and not such ordinary [decision], must govern the case to which they both apply.

Those, then, who controvert the principle, that the constitution is to be considered, [by Congress and the President], as a paramount law, are reduced to the necessity of maintaining that [Congress and the President] must close their eyes on the constitution, and see only the [judicial decision]. This doctrine would subvert the very foundation of all written constitutions. It would declare that an act which, according to the principles and theory of our government, is entirely void, is yet, in practice, completely obligatory. It would declare, that if the [Judiciary] should do what is expressly forbidden, such act, notwithstanding the express prohibition, is in reality effectual. It would be giving to the [Judiciary] a practical and real omnipotence, with the same breath which professes to restrict their powers within narrow limits. It is prescribing limits, and declaring that those limits may be passed at pleasure. That it thus reduces to nothing, what we have deemed the greatest improvement on political institutions, a written constitution, would, of itself, be sufficient, in America, where written constitutions have been viewed with such reverence, for rejecting the construction. . . .

. . .

[I]t is apparent, that the framers of the constitution contemplated that instrument for the government of [Congress and the President], as well as of the [Judiciary]. Why otherwise does it direct [Congressmen and the President] to take an oath to support it? This oath certainly applies in an especial manner, to their conduct in their official character. How immoral to impose it on them, if they were to be used as the instruments, and the knowing instruments, for violating what they swear to support!

. . . Why does a [Congressman or the President] swear to discharge his duties agreeably to the constitution . . . , if that constitution forms no rule for his government? If it is closed upon him, and cannot be inspected by him? If such be the real state of things, this is worse than solemn mockery. To prescribe, or take this oath, becomes equally a crime.

It is not entirely unworthy of observation, that in declaring what shall be the supreme law of the land, the constitution itself is first mentioned; and not the laws of the United States, generally, but those only which shall be made in pursuance of the constitution, have that rank[; and not judicial decisions at all].

Thus, the particular phraseology of the constitution . . . confirms and strengthens the principle, supposed to be essential to all written constitutions, that a [judicial decision] repugnant to the constitution is void; and that courts, as well as other departments, are bound by that instrument.[565]

The only qualification to this reasoning is that "a [judicial decision] repugnant to the constitution is *void*" (in the sense of inoperative or legally non-controlling) for everyone *except the actual parties litigant (and their privies) whose "Case*[ ]*" or "Controvers*[y]*" it purports to decide.* They, unfortunately, can be bound by the judicial error, unless as a practical matter Congress or the President can take some form of remedial action, or the Court itself rehears the case and overrules the prior judgment.

3. The doctrine of congressional and presidential "constitutional review" that flows so readily from *Marbury* itself is not peculiar to John Marshall's reasoning, but has been explicitly advanced by other leading statesmen in the most public manner.

a. In his veto of the recharter of the second Bank of the United States, President Andrew Jackson explained:

Mere [judicial] precedent is a dangerous source of authority, and should not be regarded as deciding questions of constitutional power except where the acquiescence of the people and the States can be considered as well settled. . . .

. . . [T]he opinion of the Supreme Court . . . ought not to control the coordinate authorities of this Government. The Congress, the Executive, and the Court must each for itself be guided by its own opinion of the Constitution. Each

---

public officer who takes an oath to support the Constitution swears that he will support it as he understands it, and not as it is understood by others. It is as much the duty of the House of Representatives, of the Senate, and of the President to decide upon the constitutionality of any bill or resolution which may be presented to them for passage or approval as it is of the supreme judges when it may be brought before them for judicial decision. The opinion of the judges has no more authority over Congress than the opinion of Congress has over the judges, and on that point the President is independent of both. The authority of the Supreme Court must not, therefore, be permitted to control the Congress or the Executive . . . , but to have only such influence as the force of their reasoning may deserve.[566]

b. In his First Inaugural Address, President Abraham Lincoln recalled:

[T]he position [is] assumed by some, that constitutional questions are to be decided by the Supreme Court; nor do I deny that such decisions must be binding, in any case, upon the parties to a suit, as to the object of that suit, while they are also entitled to a very high respect and consideration in all parallel cases by all other departments of the government. And, while it is obviously possible that such decision may be erroneous in any given case, still the evil effect following it, being limited to that particular case, with the chance that it may be overruled and never become a precedent for other cases, can better be borne than could the evils of a different practice. At the same time, the candid citizen must confess that if the policy of the government,

---

[566] 3 *A Compilation of the Messages and Papers of the Presidents* (J. Richardson ed. 1897), at 1139, 1144-45.

upon vital questions affecting the whole people, is to be irrevocably fixed by decisions of the Supreme court, the instant they are made, in ordinary litigation between parties in personal actions, the people will have ceased to be their own rulers, having to that extent practically resigned the government into the hands of that eminent tribunal.[567]

c. Earlier, in his debates with Stephen Douglas, Lincoln excoriated Douglas:

[Stephen Douglas is a] man [who] sticks to a decision which forbids the people of a Territory from excluding slavery,[[568]] and he does so not because he says is it right in itself—he does not give any opinion on that—but because it has been *decided by the court*, and being decided by the court, he is, and you are bound to take it in your political action as *law*—not that he judges at all of its merits, but because a decision of the court is to him a *"Thus saith the Lord."* He places it on that ground alone, and ... thus committing himself unreservedly to this decision, *commits him to the next one* just as firmly as to this.[569]

Lincoln also observed:

[I] asked [Douglas] again to point out ... the reasons for his ... adherence to the Dred Scott decision as it is. I have turned his attention to the fact that General Jackson differed with him in regard to the political obligation of a Supreme Court decision. I have asked his attention to the fact that

---

[567] *Living American Documents* (I. Starr, L. Todd & M. Curti eds., 1961), at 177.

[568] *Scott* v. *Sandford*, 60 U.S. (19 How.) 393 (1857).

[569] Ottawa, Illinois (21 August 1858), in *The Lincoln-Douglas Debates of 1858* (R. Johannsen ed. 1965), at 65 (emphasis in the original).

[Thomas] Jefferson differed with him in regard to the political obligation of a Supreme Court decision. Jefferson said, that "Judges are as honest as other men, and not more so." And he said, substantially, that "whenever a free people should give up in absolute submission to any department of government, retaining for themselves no appeal from it, their liberties were gone." . . .

So far in this controversy I can get no answer at all from Judge Douglas upon these subjects. Not one can I get from him, except that he swells himself up and says, "All of us who stand by the decision of the Supreme Court are the friends of the Constitution; all you fellows that dare question it in any way, are the enemies of the Constitution." Now, in this very devoted adherence to this decision, in opposition to all the great political leaders whom he has recognized as leaders . . . , there is something very marked. And the manner in which he adheres to it— not as being right upon the merits . . . but as being absolutely obligatory upon every one simply because of the source from whence it comes—as that which no man can gainsay, whatever it may be—this is another marked feature of his adherence to that decision. It marks it in this respect, that it commits him to the next decision, whenever it comes, as being as obligatory as this one, since he does not investigate it, and won't inquire whether this opinion is right or wrong. So he takes the next one without inquiring whether *it* is right or wrong. He teaches men this doctrine, and in so doing prepares the public mind to take the next decision when it comes, without any inquiry.[570]

---

[570] Galesburg, Illinois (7 October 1858), in ibid. at 232-33 (emphasis in the original).

That Lincoln's description was no caricature of Douglas's view, Douglas himself admitted:

> I ask him [i.e., Lincoln], whether he is not bound to respect and obey the decisions of the Supreme Court as well as me? The Constitution has created the court to decide all Constitutional questions in the last resort, and when such decisions have been made, they become the law of the land, and you, and he, and myself, and every other good citizen are bound by them.[571]

Lincoln explained what he meant by the phrase "in regard to the political obligation of a Supreme Court decision," saying:

> We oppose the Dred Scott decision in a certain way .... We do not propose that when Dred Scott has been decided to be a slave by the court, we, as a mob, will decide him to be free. We do not propose that, when any other one, or one thousand, shall be decided by that court to be slaves, we will in any violent way disturb the rights of property thus settled, but we nevertheless do oppose that decision as a political rule, which shall be binding on the voter to vote for nobody who thinks it wrong, which shall be binding on the members of Congress or the President to favor no measure that does not actually concur with the principles of that decision. We do not propose to be bound by it as a political rule in that way, because we think it lays the foundation not merely of enlarging and spreading out what we consider an evil, but it lays the foundation for spreading that evil into the States themselves. We propose

---

[571] Galesburg, Illinois (7 October 1858), in ibid. at 243.

so resisting it as to have it reversed if we can, and a new judicial rule established upon this subject.[572]

Of great significance to the falsity of the theory of "judicial supremacy" that Douglas openly espoused, Lincoln savaged the Dred Scott case, not just as an erroneous decision, but rather as conscious, purposeful judicial participation in a subversive political *"tendency*, if not a conspiracy"! "We cannot absolutely know," he charged,

> that all these exact adaptations are the result of preconcert. But when we see a lot of framed timbers, different portions of which we know have been gotten out at different times and places and by different workmen—[Senator] Stephen [Douglas], [President] Franklin [Pierce], [Chief Justice of the Supreme Court] Roger [Taney] and [President] James [Buchanan], for instance—and when we see these timbers joined together, and see they exactly make the frame of a house or a mill, all the tenons and mortises exactly fitting, and all the lengths and proportions of the different pieces exactly adapted to their respective places, and not a piece too many or too few—not omitting even the scaffolding— or, if a single piece be lacking, we see the place in the frame exactly fitted and prepared yet to bring such a piece in—in such a case, we find it impossible not to believe that Stephen and Franklin and Roger and James all understood one another from the beginning, and all worked upon a common plan or draft drawn up before the first blow was struck.

It should not be overlooked that, by the Nebraska bill, the people of a *State* as well as Territory were to be left

---

[572] Quincy, Illinois (13 October 1858), in ibid. at 255.

"perfectly free," "subject only to the Constitution." Why mention a State? They were legislating for Territories, and not for or about States.... While the opinion of the [Supreme C]ourt, by Chief Justice Taney, in the Dred Scott case, and the separate opinions of all the concurring Justices, expressly declare that the Constitution of the United States neither permits Congress nor a Territorial Legislature to exclude slavery from any United States Territory, they all omit to declare whether or not the same Constitution permits a State, or the people of a State, to exclude it.... Put this and that together, and we have another nice little niche, which we may, ere long, see filled with another Supreme Court decision, declaring that the Constitution of the United States does not permit a *State* to exclude slavery from its limits. And this may especially be expected if the doctrine of "care not whether slavery be voted down or voted up," shall gain upon the public mind sufficiently to give promise that such a decision can be maintained when made.

Such a decision is all that slavery now lacks of being alike lawful in all the States. Welcome, or unwelcome, such decision is probably coming, and will soon be upon us, unless the power of the present political dynasty shall be met and overthrown.[573]

Later, Lincoln amplified his indictment, saying that his "main object [in his earlier speech] was to show ... that there was a *tendency*, if not a conspiracy among those who have engineered

---

[573] Springfield, Illinois (16 June 1858), *in* ibid. at 18-19 (emphasis in the original).

this slavery question for the last four or five years, to make slavery perpetual and universal in this nation."[574]

In all this, Lincoln supplied both his hearers and future generations with a veritable compass of criminal politics useful not only to chart with gyroscopic accuracy the course of contemporary events, but also to change that direction for the better. Just as the Dred Scott case was in Lincoln's time, so today the majority's opinion in *Lawrence* is one of those "timbers [to be] joined together . . . that exactly make the frame of . . . a mill," of which one grindstone is the exclusion of morality as a legitimate interest for enacting legislation, the other the infusion of foreign law into constitutional interpretation. Just as Stephen Douglas once defended the Dred Scott case on the ground that "the Constitution has created the court to decide all Constitutional questions in the last resort," so today *Lawrence* stands upon the foundation of "judicial supremacy." And just as Lincoln long ago recognized that America would suffer a succession of legal calamities "unless the power of the present political dynasty shall be met and overthrown," so today no one should believe that the danger stems solely from those Justices who apply the new hermeneutics of amorality and alienation, or from the "law-profession culture" of which they are the scions, or even from the cultural bolshevism the "law profession culture" advances—rather than from those individuals for whom cultural bolshevism, the "law profession culture," and judges

---

[574] Ottawa, Illinois (21 August 1858), *in* ibid. at 56 (emphasis in the original).

are simply political tools proficuous for amassing power. Just as Lincoln with the Dred Scott case, WE THE PEOPLE should

> not propose to be bound by [*Lawrence*] as a political rule . . .
> , because [they] think it lays the foundation not merely of enlarging and spreading out what [they] consider an evil, but it lays the foundation for spreading that evil . . . . [WE THE PEOPLE should] propose so resisting it as to have it reversed if [they] can, and a new judicial rule established upon this subject.

With their ultimate goal being that "the power of the present political dynasty shall be met and overthrown." That is, in every particular—from reversal of *Lawrence* on the issues of morality as the source of law and of the use of foreign law in constitutional interpretation; to the return of such interpretation to "original intent"; to the overthrow of "judicial supremacy"—*the "new judicial rule" must strike unerringly and unceasingly at the power of the present political dynasty.*

4. On the merits of the matter, concurrent "constitutional review" by Congress, the Executive, and the Supreme Court, each operating independently within the ambit of its own authority, and none claiming "supremacy" over the others in its power of review, is far more plausible in a representative government, and especially a representative government based upon separation of powers and checks and balances, than is an exclusive "judicial review" that rationalizes the Court's "judicial supremacy."

a. In the first place, "judicial supremacy"—the claim that "the federal judiciary is supreme in the exposition of the law of the Constitution" and that "the interpretation of the [Constitution] enunciated by th[e Supreme] Court . . . is the supreme law of the land"[575]—affronts both the Constitution's declaration that "WE THE PEOPLE . . . do ordain and establish this Constitution"[576] and the Constitution's mandate that only WE THE PEOPLE, through their representatives in Congress, State "Legislatures," and State "Conventions," are authorized to amend it.[577] Moreover, the panegyrists of "judicial supremacy" forget that, because "[t]he power to enact carries with it *final authority to declare the meaning of the legislation*,"[578] the "ultimate interpreter of the Constitution" cannot possibly be the Supreme Court,[579] and its "interpretation of the [Constitution]" cannot possibly be "the supreme law of the land."[580] Rather, the ultimate interpreter, whose decision *ex necessitate* becomes the supreme law, must always be WE THE PEOPLE.

To be sure, WE THE PEOPLE could conceivably delegate their plenary and final power of constitutional interpretation to some agent. But nowhere does the Constitution delegate to judges any power that amounts to "judicial supremacy." Rather, WE THE PEOPLE delegated merely "[t]he judicial

---

[575] *Cooper* v. *Aaron*, 358 U.S. 1, 18 (1958).

[576] U.S. Const. preamble.

[577] U.S. Const. art. V.

[578] *Proper* v. *Clark*, 337 U.S. 472, 484 (1949) (emphasis supplied).

[579] *Pace Baker* v. *Carr*, 369 U.S. 186, 211 (1962), and *Powell* v. *McCormack*, 395 U.S. 486, 548-49 (1969).

[580] *Pace Cooper* v. *Aaron*, 358 U.S. 1, 18 (1958).

Power,"[581] and that only in "Cases" and "Controversies."[582]
Nothing in "[t]he judicial Power" so limited leads inexorably
(or even at all) to the conclusion that an opinion of the
Supreme Court on some constitutional issue necessary to
decide a "Case[ ]" or "Controvers[y]," involving particular
litigants, under a set of facts peculiar to that litigation, binds
everyone else in the world on that question, notwithstanding that
no one else has had a hearing in that "Case[ ]" or
"Controvers[y]." To the contrary, such an universalistic
misconstruction of "[t]he judicial Power" offends the first
principle of due process of law, that "[p]arties whose rights are
to be affected are entitled to be heard."[583] So, "judicial
supremacy" is plainly not a delegation of power to, but a
seizure of power by, the Judiciary—or, more descriptively, the
individuals acting as judges, their law clerks, and the "law-
profession culture" of which they all are products.

Because "judicial supremacy" is usurpation, its exercise
will often come into conflict with WE THE PEOPLE'S will.[584] In

---

[581] U.S. Const. art. III, § 1.

[582] U.S. Const. art. III, § 2, cls. 1-2.

[583] *Baldwin* v. *Hale*, 68 U.S. (1 Wall.) 223, 233 (1863). See, e.g., *Fuentes* v.
Shevin, 407 U.S. 67, 80-82 (1972); *Armstrong* v. *Manzo*, 380 U.S. 542, 552
(1965); *Mullane* v. *Central Hanover Bank & Trust Co.*, 339 U.S. 306, 314 (1950).

[584] Obviously, in some "Cases" and "Controversies" "judicial review" will
be consistent with the Constitution, because the judges' opinions will
correctly construe and apply the supreme law. Parties other than the
litigants in those "Cases" and "Controversies" will be bound by what the
judges opine about the Constitution, not as a consequence of "judicial
supremacy" (i.e., because whatever judges may say must be taken to be the

those situations, WE THE PEOPLE cannot count on the Judiciary to correct itself. Quite the contrary: Simply by adhering to the dogma of "judicial supremacy" that "[a] decision [of the Court]" on a constitutional issue "cannot be reversed short of a constitutional amendment,"[585] the Judiciary denies any need for self-correction, but instead brazenly instructs WE THE PEOPLE to change their own Constitution from day to day if they cannot stomach the judges' serial misconstructions of it. Now, as Blackstone pointed out, "whenever a question arises between the society at large and any magistrate vested with powers originally delegated by that society, it must be decided by the voice of the society itself: there is not upon earth any other tribunal to resort to."[586] To settle questions between the Judiciary and themselves, however, WE THE PEOPLE need not act directly through amendments of the Constitution. For WE THE PEOPLE have two other agents in the General Government: Congress and the President. And these are branches of government *co-equal with and coordinate to* the Judiciary. As such, they are not subordinate to the Judiciary in any way. For a "coordinate" branch of government is "one [that] has no power to enforce its decision upon the other [coordinate branch]."[587] If anything, the Judiciary is something less than co-equal with and

---

Constitution), but as a consequence of the Constitution's "original intent," which the judges' opinions happen faithfully to reflect.

[585] *Gregg* v. *Georgia*, 428 U.S. 153, 176 (1976) (emphasis supplied).

[586] 1 *Commentaries*, ante note 158, at 212.

[587] *Town of South Ottawa* v. *Perkins*, 94 U.S. 260, 268 (1877).

coordinate to Congress and the President, because those branches have the ability to control or discipline the Supreme Court, the "inferior Courts" of the General Government,[588] and individual "Judges, both of the supreme and inferior Courts"[589] by restricting the Supreme Court's appellate jurisdiction (or in the case of the "inferior Courts" both their original and appellate jurisdiction),[590] "packing" the courts by adding new judges (or even creating new courts altogether),[591] removing old and then appointing new judges through impeachment or some other process,[592] or criminally prosecuting judges who violate citizens' constitutional rights.[593]

Moreover, Congress and the President are closer to, and more likely to be in political tune and sympathy with, WE THE PEOPLE than is the Judiciary. After all, WE THE PEOPLE elect the members of Congress and the President. Bills passed by Congress and signed by the President have the approval of two of the three coordinate branches of the General Government; and bills passed by Congress over a President's veto have the approval of two thirds of WE THE PEOPLE'S representatives— whereas, although the justices are appointed by the President and confirmed by the Senate, a decision of the Supreme Court

---

[588] U.S. Const. art. III, § 1.

[589] U.S. Const. art. III, § 1.

[590] See post, at 269-80.

[591] See post, at 281-83.

[592] See post, at 285-321.

[593] See post, at 261-68.

can be the product of the eccentric opinion of a single Justice (on his own or under his law clerks' baneful influence) who confects a majority one way or the other. And if WE THE PEOPLE consider members of Congress or the President to be wrong on some constitutional issue, they can remove them in two, four, or six years through elections.

b. That, as outlined above, the Constitution empowers Congress, the President, or both together to control or discipline the Supreme Court, the "inferior Courts" of the General Government, and individual "Judges, both of the supreme and inferior Courts," proves that the Constitution provides for congressional and presidential "constitutional review" of judicial action. For example, no one can deny that judges who knowingly and willfully violate litigants' constitutional rights do not demonstrate the "good Behaviour" constitutionally necessary to "hold their Offices,"[594] should be "removed from Office on Impeachment for, and Conviction of, . . . high Crimes and Misdemeanors,"[595] and (in any event) should be criminally prosecuted.[596] Yet the predicate for any of these actions is a finding that the judges did, in fact and law, violate their victims' constitutional rights—which, self-evidently, requires an interpretation and application of the Constitution, by either Congress (impeachment) or the

---

[594] U.S. Const. art. III, § 1.

[595] U.S. Const. art. II, § 4.

[596] See 18 U.S.C. §§ 241-42, discussed post, at 261-62.

President (prosecution).[597] So, unless Congress and the President have a power of "constitutional review" of judicial actions, neither could fulfill these constitutional duties.

Where does the power of "constitutional review" of judicial actions reside?

1) As to Congress, the power can be found in numerous constitutional provisions.

a) In the first instance, "[t]he Senators and Representatives [of Congress] ... shall be bound by Oath or Affirmation, to support this Constitution."[598] That is, "to support this Constitution" *according to the meaning that each of them in good conscience believes it to have,* not some meaning someone else tells them it has. As the Supreme Court itself pointed out, "it is the province of this Court ... not to bow to [other opinions] implicitly; and the Judges must exercise ... that understanding [of the Constitution] which Providence has bestowed upon them, with that independence which the people of the United States expect from this department of the government."[599] Providence, however, smiles upon and graces Senators and Representatives (and the President, too), no less than judges. And WE THE PEOPLE expect from all the branches of the

---

[597] Of course, although the Executive may prosecute, the case must proceed before some judge. Nothing, however, precludes Congress and the President from establishing special courts entrusted with exclusive and final jurisdiction to hear such cases, and staffed with individuals distinguished for their strict adherence to "original intent."

[598] U.S. Const. art. VI, cl. 3.

[599] *Gibbons* v. *Ogden*, 22 U.S. (9 Wheat.) 1, 186-87 (1824).

General Government such "independence" as the Constitution allows. Thus, every time Senators and Representatives are confronted by a decision of the Judiciary on constitutional law that in any way affects the performance of their duties, they must weigh the judges' reasoning against their own "Oath[s] or Affirmation[s], to support this Constitution," accepting the former only if it squares with the latter.

b) The Constitution provides that:

> The judicial Power of the United States, shall be vested in one supreme Court, and in such inferior Courts as the Congress shall from time to time ordain and establish. The Judges, both of the supreme and inferior Courts, shall hold their Offices during good Behaviour . . . .[600]

Thus, execution of "[t]he judicial Power" involves judges' "hold[ing] their Offices during good Behaviour" *and not* "hold[ing] . . . Offices during" or as a consequence of "[bad] Behaviour." The Constitution also provides that "all civil Officers of the United States[ ] shall be removed from Office on Impeachment for, and Conviction of, . . . high Crimes and Misdemeanors."[601] The Appointments Clause refers to "Judges of the supreme Court, and all *other* Officers of the United States."[602] This indicates that "Judges of the supreme Court" are constitutional "Officers" who can come within the Impeachment Clause. The Constitution further provides that Congress shall have power "[t]o make all Laws which shall be

---

[600] U.S. Const. art. III, § 1.

[601] U.S. Const. art. II, § 4.

[602] U.S. Const. art. II, § 2, cl. 2 (emphasis supplied).

necessary and proper for carrying into Execution . . . *all* . . . Powers vested by this Constitution in the Government of the United States, or in *any* Department or Officer thereof."[603] Taken together, these powers invest Congress with plenary authority to define what constitutes judicial "good Behaviour" (or lack thereof) and judicial "high Crimes and Misdemeanors," for the purposes of judges' "carrying into Execution" "[t]he judicial Power" and of Congress's "carrying into Execution" its powers of "Impeachment . . . and Conviction." Inasmuch as any judge's chronically negligent, egregious, reckless, or intentional violations of the Constitution cannot amount to "good Behaviour," and in some instances plainly constitute "high Crimes and Misdemeanors," Congress must be constitutionally empowered to define such violations and specify them as disqualifications for judicial office. In addition, Congress must be constitutionally empowered to engage in "constitutional review" of judicial actions in order to determine when such violations have occurred and what to do about them.

2) As to the President as well, the power of "constitutional review" can be found in several constitutional provisions.

a) In the first instance, the President "shall take the . . . Oath or Affirmation . . . that [he] will faithfully execute the Office of President of the United States, and will to the best of [his] Ability, preserve, protect and defend the Constitution."[604]

---

[603] U.S. Const. art. I, § 8, cl. 18 (emphasis supplied).

[604] U.S. Const. art. II, § 1, cl. 7.

"[F]aithfully [to] execute [his] Office," the President must be
"faithful[ ]" to *what*? Plainly, to the Constitution, which alone
defines that "Office." Yet not to someone else's ideas about the
Constitution. For someone else may be wrong—even
intentionally so. Instead, the President, having personally
"take[n an] . . . Oath or Affirmation," must be responsible to
his own conscience. The President may "faithfully execute
[his] Office" in good conscience, albeit unknowingly in error, if
he himself honestly endeavors to understand and apply his
constitutional powers and duties. He cannot "faithfully," or
even intelligently, "execute [his] office" if, in the fashion of a
robot, he merely adopts and carries out someone else's
interpretation of those powers and duties. To like effect, the
President cannot "preserve, protect and defend the
Constitution" "to the best of [*his own*] Ability" if he
mechanically relies on the "Ability" of someone else to
construe "[t]he executive Power"[605] for him. Indeed, how can
the President rely on someone else's "Ability" at all, unless he
uses his own "Ability" to judge that other's "Ability"?
Furthermore, the President "take[s] . . . [an] Oath or
Affirmation" to "preserve, protect and defend *the
Constitution*"—not judges' opinions about the Constitution.
And to "preserve, protect and defend" it against
misconstruction, usurpation, and tyranny of any sort by
anyone, including himself. What, then, other than his own
conscience, can reliably inform him when someone, especially

---

[605] U.S. Const. art. II, § 1, cl. 1.

himself, has crossed the forbidden line?[606] Self-evidently, then, the President's "Oath or Affirmation" imposes upon him an extensive and intensive duty of "constitutional review," the performance of which excludes his acquiescence, to any degree, in "judicial supremacy."

b) The Constitution further requires that the President "shall take Care that the Laws be faithfully executed."[607] "[T]he Laws" include the Constitution, which is "the supreme Law of the Land."[608] They do not include judicial decisions, which are merely some judges' opinions—some perhaps fair; others perhaps faulty, false, or fraudulent—as to what "the Laws" are, or what they mean, or how they should be applied: "only evidence of . . . the laws . . . and . . . not of themselves laws."[609] That being so, there will necessarily arise numerous occasions

---

[606] Reliance on the President's conscience to inform his constitutional inquiries is not an invitation for him to displace the Constitution's "original intent" with his own unfettered judgment. For a good conscience must be properly formed, paying close attention to "the Laws of Nature and of Nature's God" (among which is the injunction against bearing false witness), and not arrogating to itself an antinomian "right to define [its] own concept of existence, of meaning, of the universe, and of the mystery of human life." *Planned Parenthood* v. *Casey*, 505 U.S. 833, 851 (1992), followed in *Lawrence*, 539 U.S. at 574. Inasmuch as this theory of "autonomy" has led the Judiciary to license when it could have prevented, and thereby to be complicit in, the wanton and arbitrary killing of tens of millions of innocent and defenseless human beings—a holocaust besides which any other pales into only secondary significance—it self-evidently cannot be the basis for a conscience *properly* formed.

[607] U.S. Const. art. II, § 3.

[608] U.S. Const. art. VI, cl. 2. See In re *Neagle*, 135 U.S. 1, 64 (1890).

[609] *Swift* v. *Tyson*, 41 U.S. (16 Pet.) 1, 18 (1842).

when the President must "take Care that [judicial decisions contrary to] the Laws [are not] faithfully executed," or even executed at all. And, to do so, he must avail himself of a power of "constitutional review" independent of "judicial review" and in no way subject to "judicial supremacy."

c. That Congress and the President have powers and duties of "constitutional review" of judicial action negates "judicial supremacy"; but it does not by itself imply congressional or presidential supremacy over the Judiciary. In cases of disagreement on constitutional issues among the three branches, each branch's interpretation controls within its own ambit of constitutional authority, because therein each branch is independent of the others. WE THE PEOPLE'S delegations of authority—"[a]ll legislative Powers herein granted *shall be vested* in a Congress,"[610] "[t]he executive Power *shall be vested* in a President,"[611] and "[t]he judicial Power of the United States, *shall be vested* in one Supreme Court, and in such inferior Courts as the Congress may . . . ordain and establish"[612]—set up three coordinate branches with separate competencies peculiar to each. Congress may not exercise "executive" or "judicial" power; the President may not exercise "legislative" or "judicial" power; and the Judiciary may not exercise "legislative" or "executive power." So, when one branch engages in "constitutional review," it can do so only within its own sphere of competence, and therefore necessarily without

---

[610] U.S. Const. art. I, § 1 (emphasis supplied).

[611] U.S. Const. art. II, § 1, cl. 1 (emphasis supplied).

[612] U.S. Const. art. III, § 1 (emphasis supplied).

any effect (other than moral suasion) on the co-equal exercise of such "review" by another branch within its own sphere of competence.

Within its sphere of competence, however, each branch has power to *affect* the others. For example, Congress can remove the President and judges by "Impeachment . . . and Conviction." Congress can pass "Laws" which the President must "faithfully execute[ ]" and the courts must enforce. The President can prosecute any public official who violates the General Government's criminal laws. And the courts can refuse to enforce supposed "laws" that the judges believe violate the Constitution. This does not amount, though, to one branch's having the ability to *control* the exercise of another Branch's "vested" powers, in the sense of dictating how those powers are to be employed. Thus, Congress can remove the President from office—but it cannot direct his course of conduct as President in office. The President can prosecute judges for intentional violations of litigants' constitutional rights—but he cannot prescribe how judges are honestly to decide constitutional "Cases" or "Controversies." The Supreme Court can declare a supposed "law" unconstitutional, and refuse to enforce it against the litigants before it in a particular "Case[ ]" or "Controvers[y]"—but it cannot tell Congress what "Laws" to enact, or the President when and how "faithfully" to "execute[ ]" the "Laws."

Notwithstanding the hoopla and bluster about "judicial supremacy" emanating from the "law-profession culture," of the three branches within the General Government the

Judiciary is obviously the institutionally weakest, in the sense of its actual constitutional disability to influence what the other branches do. In its lucid moments, the Supreme Court has recognized as much, admitting that "the action of the political branches of the government [i.e., Congress and the President], in a matter that belongs to them, is conclusive."[613]

Perhaps the clearest example of the Judiciary's actual fecklessness appears in *Mississippi v. Johnson.*[614] At issue was whether the President could be enjoined "from carrying into effect [certain] [A]ct[s] of Congress alleged to be unconstitutional."[615] Referring to "the duty of the President in the exercise of the power to see that the laws are faithfully executed, and among those laws the [challenged a]cts," and characterizing the duties the acts imposed on the President as being "in no just sense ministerial," but purely "executive and political," the Court wryly observed that an attempt by the Judiciary to dictate to the President

> might be justly characterized ... as "an absurd and excessive extravagance."
>
> It is true that ... the interposition of the court is not sought to enforce action by the Executive under constitutional legislation, but to restrain such action under legislation alleged to be unconstitutional. But we are unable to perceive that this circumstance takes the case out of the

[613] *Williams v. The Suffolk Insurance Co.*, 38 U.S. (13 Pet.) 415, 420 (1839).

[614] 71 U.S. (4 Wall.) 475 (1867).

[615] Ibid. at 497.

general principles which forbid judicial interference with
the exercise of executive discretion.

It was admitted . . . that the application now made to
us is without a precedent; and this is of much weight
against it.

. . .

The impropriety of such interference will be clearly
seen upon consideration of its possible consequences.

Suppose . . . the injunction prayed for [were] allowed.
If the President refuse obedience, it is needless to observe
that the court is without power to enforce its process. If, on
the other hand, the President complies with the order of the
court and refuses to execute the [A]cts of Congress, is it not
clear that a collision may occur between the Executive and
Legislative Departments . . . ? May not the House of
Representatives impeach the President for such refusal?
And in that case could this court interfere in behalf of the
President, thus endangered by compliance with its
mandate, and restrain by injunction the Senate . . . from
sitting as a court of impeachment? Would the strange
spectacle be offered to the public wonder of an attempt by
this court to arrest proceedings in that court?

These questions answer themselves.[616]

---

[616] Ibid. at 499-501. Actually, they do not entirely "answer themselves."
First, the President might have "complie[d] with the order of the court and
refuse[d] to execute the [A]cts of Congress," not because he deemed himself
legally bound by the Court's judgment, but because, in the exercise of his
own independent "constitutional review"—surely occasioned by the lawsuit
and perhaps influenced by the Justices' reasoning—he determined that "the
[A]cts of Congress" *were* unconstitutional, and that therefore he could not
"faithfully execute[ ]" them. In that event, the House and the Senate might
seek to impeach and convict the President—but not because of something

The Court might also have considered the possibility that a suit naming the President in his official capacity could be rendered nugatory *ab initio* if the President simply refused to appear (except specially, as a courtesy to point out the Court's lack of jurisdiction), on the ground that his general appearance would concede *pro tanto* the unconstitutional dogma of "judicial supremacy" over the Executive Department, which concession itself would violate the President's duty to "take Care that the Laws be faithfully executed."[617] In the face of such a refusal, what coercive sanction could the Justices employ against the office of President itself to require that it submit its conduct to their scrutiny? On the other hand, if the suit named the President solely in his individual capacity (that is, putatively as a common lawbreaker), the President refused to appear (again, except specially), and the Court held him in

---

the Supreme Court compelled him to do. Second, even if the President were impeached in the House and tried in the Senate precisely because he deemed himself legally bound by the Court's judgment, that the Court would be powerless to prevent his conviction would not detract from its authority to enter the original judgment that resulted in his refusal to "execute[ ]" the challenged "[A]cts of Congress." Judicial power is "the power of a court to decide and pronounce a judgment *and carry it into effect* between parties who bring a case before it for decision." *Muskrat* v. *United States*, 219 U.S. 346, 356 (1911) (emphasis supplied). In the hypothetical example, the Court *would have* "pronounce[d] a judgment" (that "the [A]cts of Congress" were unconstitutional), and *would have* "carr[ied] it into effect" (by successfully enjoining the President from "execut[ing]" those "[A]cts"). That the President's compliance with the Court's decree would have had further consequences beyond the Court's authority to affect simply emphasizes that the General Government is based upon *separation* of powers.

[617] U.S. Const. art. II, § 3.

contempt or entered a default judgment against him enforceable by contempt, what could the Justices do if thereafter the President, in his official capacity, pardoned himself, in his individual capacity, for any contempt they imposed, thereby reducing their judgment to a practical cipher?[618]

Similarly, assume *arguendo* that "homosexual activists" concluded that the decision in *Lawrence* was not proving sufficiently effective in promoting "the so-called homosexual agenda,"[619] and therefore sued the members of Congress, seeking a declaration and mandatory injunction that Congress enact a statute under color of Section 2 of the Fourteenth Amendment to "enforce" with appropriately coercive sanctions against all the States the definitions of "liberty" and "equal protection of the laws" set out in Justice Kennedy's and Justice O'Connor's opinions. Further, assume *arguendo* that the Justices who joined in those opinions issued a declaratory judgment and injunction in the complainants' favor. What could the Court then do to force members of Congress to draft such a bill? Or to vote for it? Or to force the President to sign, rather than to veto, it? Or to force Congress to override a veto? Or to force the President to "execute" such a "Law[ ]," if enacted? To issue a mandatory injunction is one thing, to impose it another.

---

[618] See U.S. Const. art. II, § 2, cl. 1, discussed ante, at 197-206.

[619] See 539 U.S. at 602 (Scalia, J., dissenting).

In short, the Justices can do nothing to force Congress to enact (or not to enact), or the President to execute (or to refuse to execute), "Laws." But Congress and the President can do everything necessary to prevent individual judges from having anything to do with the "Laws," even in the proper exercise of "[t]he judicial Power"—by removing them from the Bench through either "Impeachment . . . and Conviction" or criminal prosecution. Thus, the personnel composing the Judiciary may be rendered utterly subordinate to Congress, the Executive, or both. To be sure, impeachment and prosecution of judges are subject to political abuse. For deterrence or correction of political abuses, however, judges must look to WE THE PEOPLE to control Congress and the President.

Present-day "judicial supremacy" is constitutionally intolerable because it elevates judges, their clerks, and the elitist "law-profession culture" over WE THE PEOPLE, inasmuch as (according to the "law-profession culture") a judicial opinion on a constitutional question is subject to reversal only by a constitutional amendment. (That the Supreme Court can reverse itself on constitutional issues is no sufficient corrective, because that procedure leaves the justices as judges in their own case, rather than invoking a true check and balance separate from and independent of the Judiciary.) That is, "judicial supremacy" is not simply *subject to* abuse, but *itself is* an abuse, because its serial errors can almost never be corrected, and its basic institutional fault—oligarchical rule by the "law-profession culture"—can never be mitigated. Conversely, congressional and presidential "constitutional review" of judicial action is controlled, not by the cumbersome process of constitutional amendment, but in the regular course of elections, the ultimate check and balance in any republican government. Thus, such "constitutional review" guarantees the supremacy of WE THE PEOPLE over *all three* branches of the General Government, because any conflict among them will ultimately be referred back to WE THE PEOPLE in the fastest, most direct, and most definitive manner.

In sum, that powers and duties of congressional and presidential "constitutional review" of judicial action exist cannot be doubted. Nonetheless, the question remains how best to exercise and fulfill them.

CHAPTER 9

Congressional Definition of a Republican Form of Government

The Constitution provides that "[t]he United States shall guarantee to every State in this Union a Republican Form of Government."[620] However political theory may define that phrase, American political practice surely accepted as examples thereof the State governments that existed in the late 1700s. All of the States must have had "a Republican Form of Government" in the constitutional sense, because they were admitted into the "more perfect Union" under the Constitution[621] with their forms of government as they were, and (with the exception perhaps of Rhode Island[622]) subsequently never significantly changed those forms, or suffered them to be changed by Congress. "Thus we have

---

[620] U.S. Const. art. IV, § 4.

[621] U.S. Const. preamble.

[622] See *Luther* v. *Borden*, 48 U.S. (7 How.) 1 (1849).

HOW TO DETHRONE THE IMPERIAL JUDICIARY

unmistakable evidence of what was republican in form, within the meaning of that term as employed in the Constitution."[623]

"[A] Republican Form" cannot refer solely to the structure or mechanical operations of the government, but must take into account as well—indeed, primarily—the substance of the government's legal powers and disabilities. As the Declaration of Independence made clear:

> [Americans] hold these truths to be self-evident, that all men are created equal, that they are endowed their Creator with certain unalienable Rights, that among these are Life, Liberty, and the pursuit of Happiness.—That to secure these rights, Governments are instituted among Men, deriving their just powers from the consent of the governed,—That whenever any Form of Government becomes destructive of these ends, it is the Right of the People to alter or abolish it . . . .

To be *acceptable*, then, *"any* Form of Government" must "secure" all men's "unalienable Rights," must exercise only "just powers," and must never "become[ ] destructive of these ends." That is, an acceptable "Form of Government"— whether it is "Republican" or something else—must satisfy these substantive requirements. Presumably, Americans would have maintained their allegiance even to the British Crown, had not that "Form of Government become[ ] destructive of these ends": "The history of the present King of Great Britain is a history of repeated injuries and usurpations, all having in direct object the establishment of an absolute Tyranny over

---

[623] *Minor* v. *Happersett*, 88 U.S. (21 Wall.) 162, 176 (1875) (dictum).

these States." The British government's "Form" changed, not in outward appearance, but in inward intent.

Because the Constitution "guarantee[s] to every State . . . a Republican Form of Government" *in perpetuo* and without limitation or qualification, the conclusion is inescapable that WE THE PEOPLE believe such a constitutional "Form" cannot be "destructive of these ends." Such a belief would be rational, however, only if it incorporated the understanding that "a Republican Form" *means* a government that satisfies the substantive standards the Declaration sets out.

In any event, Congress—and Congress alone—could so declare in applying the Guarantee Clause. For "[i]t was long ago settled that the enforcement of this guaranty belong[s] to the political department."[624] Just as "it is . . . the province of Congress to determine when a state has ceased to be republican in form, and to enforce the guaranty of the Constitution on that subject,"[625] so too is it Congress's prerogative to define what constitutes "a Republican Form of Government." Indeed, the latter is necessary to the former. For that reason, the Judiciary lacks power to rule that it violates the Guarantee Clause for Congress "to recognize [some power] as a part of the legislative authority of a state."[626] "Even if [a State legislative power] were [a denial of a republican form of government], the enforcement of that

---

[624] *Taylor* v. *Beckham*, 178 U.S. 548, 578 (1900).

[625] *Pacific States Telephone & Telegraph Co.* v. *Oregon*, 223 U.S. 118, 133 (1912).

[626] *Ohio ex rel. Davis* v. *Hildebrant*, 241 U.S. 565, 569-70 (1916).

guaranty ... is for Congress, not the courts."[627] And any attempt to involve the Judiciary in such a dispute would be "obviously futile."[628]

In the late 1700s, the legislatures of every State enforced Christian morality—"the Laws of Nature and of Nature's God"—by prohibiting various forms of aberrant conduct, homosexual sodomy among them. For that reason, "a Republican Form of Government" under the Constitution can be said to be one in which the legislature enjoys such a power. (Or at least a government in which the legislature enjoys such a power is not thereby disqualified from being of "a Republican Form.") Similarly, in the late 1700s the laws of every State were in no wise controlled or influenced by foreign laws, save for those parts of English common law that the Colonies had earlier adopted. For that reason, "a Republican Form of Government" under the Constitution in the States can be said to be one in which foreign laws have no influence over the construction and application of domestic law, either directly, or indirectly through construction and application of the Constitution and laws of the United States to such domestic law, except as the Constitution explicitly allows.[629] (If foreign laws are influential, let alone controlling, the government is *colonial* in form.) Ratification of the Fourteenth Amendment, with its mandate that no State "shall . . . deprive any person of . . . liberty . . . without due process of law,"

---

[627] *Highland Farms Dairy* v. *Agnew*, 300 U.S. 608, 612 (1937).

[628] *O'Neill* v. *Leamer*, 239 U.S. 244, 248 (1915).

[629] See ante, at 80-89.

effected no change in this situation. After the Amendment's adoption, as before, State legislatures promoted morality by proscribing various types of indecent behavior. And no one ever suggested that WE THE PEOPLE intended the Amendment to incorporate *foreign* law into the term "due process of law."

In Justice Kennedy's opinion in *Lawrence*, for the first time in American history the States were told that: (i) "'the fact that the governing majority in a State has traditionally viewed a particular practice as immoral is not a sufficient reason for upholding a law prohibiting the practice'"; and (ii) to punish homosexual sodomy the States must "show[ ] that in this country the governmental interest in circumscribing personal choice is somehow more legitimate or urgent" than it is in "[o]ther nations" or "in many other countries" according to their laws.[630] On the one hand, if the majority in *Lawrence* intended to overturn an understanding of two hundred years' duration concerning what governmental powers have always been or are now implicit in or consistent with "a Republican Form of Government," it acted without authority. For Congress enjoys exclusive authority to apply—and therefore to construe—the Guarantee Clause. Moreover, even Congress cannot change the "original intent" of "a Republican Form."[631] On the other hand, if the majority in *Lawrence* intended to say that, even if the States' power to punish homosexual sodomy and their immunity from intrusion of foreign laws into the construction and application of their domestic laws have been

---

[630] 539 U.S. at 577, 576-77.

[631] See *Eisner* v. *Macomber*, 252 U.S. 189, 206 (1920).

and now remain consistent with "a Republican Form," nonetheless they can be set aside by the Judiciary—by application of the Judicial Power, through Section 1 of the Fourteenth Amendment, to nullify the Guarantee Clause *pro tanto*—it acted without authority. For the Constitution mandates that "[t]*he United States* shall guarantee to every State . . . a Republican Form of Government."[632] And, self-evidently, no court *of the United States* can use "[t]he judicial Power *of the United States*"[633] to defeat a requirement "WE THE PEOPLE *of the United States*"[634] explicitly imposed upon the United States.

To deal with the future effects of *Lawrence*, Congress could enact a statute defining "a Republican Form of Government," and protecting the States in their operations as such, in the following terms:

A "Republican Form of Government" under Article IV, Section 4, of the Constitution of the United States derives its legitimacy from the laws of nature and of nature's God, recognizes that all men are created equal, that they are endowed by their Creator with certain unalienable rights, and that among these rights are life, liberty, and the pursuit of happiness.

A Republican Form of Government is instituted among men, deriving its just powers from the consent of the governed, to secure these unalienable rights.

---

[632] U.S. Const. art. IV, § 4 (emphasis supplied).

[633] U.S. Const. art. III, § 1 (emphasis supplied).

[634] U.S. Const. preamble (emphasis supplied).

To achieve that end, a Republican Form of Government has the privilege, right, power, and duty to legislate for the protection and promotion of the public safety, health, welfare, and morals; and its legislature's determination that particular conduct, behavior, or practices endanger the public safety, health, welfare, or morals constitutes sufficient reason for a law regulating, restraining, or prohibiting such conduct, behavior, or practices.

Because a Republican Form of Government derives its just powers from the consent of the governed, it is immune from having its constitution and laws—and in particular its laws enacted to protect and promote the public safety, health, welfare, and morals—or the provisions of the Constitution and laws of the United States that may affect them, construed and applied according to, in conformity with, or by reference to any foreign law whatsoever, except insofar as the Constitution of the United States explicitly allows for such construction and application under Article I, Section 8, Clause 10; Article I, Section 9, Clause 8; Article I, Section 10, Clause 1; and Article II, Section 2, Clause 2.

In no civil action, criminal prosecution, or administrative proceeding in any court or agency of the United States or of any State or subdivision thereof, of the District of Columbia, or of any Territory or possession of the United States, shall the constitutionality *vel non* of any law of any State or subdivision thereof be determined according to, in conformity with, or by reference to any foreign law whatsoever, except as provided herein; nor shall any law of any State or subdivision thereof, or of the District of Columbia, or of any Territory or possession of the United States be declared unconstitutional or otherwise invalid, or refused enforcement or application, solely because its only rationale is its conformity to the principles of a Republican Form of Government set out herein.

CHAPTER 10

Presidential Refusal
to Enforce an Unconstitutional
Judicial Decision

The President's constitutional duty as chief law-enforcement officer is to "take Care that the Laws be faithfully executed."[635] Judicial decisions are not "Laws" of any kind. "In the ordinary use of language"—to which constitutional terms must usually be referred[636]—"it will hardly be contended that the decisions of Courts constitute laws. They are, at most, only evidence of what the laws are; and are not of themselves laws. They are often re-examined, reversed, and qualified by the Courts themselves, whenever they are found to be either defective, or ill-founded, or otherwise incorrect."[637] So, by the Constitution's plain text, the President need not "faithfully execute[ ]" "the decisions of Courts" at all (only the "Laws" the courts properly enforce), and certainly not when he believes those decisions "either defective, or ill-

---

[635] U.S. Const. art. II, § 3.

[636] See ante, at 68-77.

[637] *Swift* v. *Tyson*, 41 U.S. (16 Pet.) 1, 18 (1842).

founded, or otherwise incorrect" *in comparison to the Constitution*, which he has taken an "Oath or Affirmation . . . to the best of [his] Ability, [to] preserve, protect and defend" *against anyone and everyone*.[638]

The President's refusal to enforce an unconstitutional judicial decision would not amount to its *reversal*. As against the litigants (and their privies) in that "Case[ ]" or "Controvers[y]," the ruling would nonetheless stand as *res judicata*, to be effectuated by whatever other officer of government the courts might importune to honor it, or to be applied in future judicial proceedings. Thus, the President's refusal would even be consistent with "judicial supremacy" in its one constitutional definition: namely, that "a decision by a court of competent jurisdiction in respect to any essential fact or question in the . . . action is conclusive between the parties in all subsequent actions."[639] And the Judiciary could continue to cite that ruling as a precedent supposedly binding on judges in other cases. But no judge could count on *the President's* assistance in *imposing* that decision on the litigants, or anyone else.

This would seriously impede judicial arrogance, to the extent of quashing the expansive definition of "judicial supremacy" altogether. The United States Marshals Service is "a bureau within the Department of Justice under the authority and direction of the Attorney General."[640] "The

---

[638] U.S. Const. art. II, § 1, cl. 7.

[639] *Forsyth v. Hammond*, 166 U.S. 506, 518 (1897).

[640] 28 U.S.C. § 561(a).

President shall appoint, by and with the advice and consent of the Senate, a United States marshal for each judicial district of the United States and for the Superior Court of the District of Columbia . . . ."[641] Therefore, the President can remove (and with the Senate's concurrence replace) the marshals as he sees fit, it they fail to conform to his policies.[642] "It is the primary role and mission of the United States Marshals Service to provide for the security and to obey, execute, and enforce all orders of the United States District Courts [and] the United States Courts of Appeals . . . ."[643] "Except as otherwise provided *by law* or Rule of Procedure,the United States Marshals Service shall execute all *lawful* writs, process, and orders issued *under the authority of the United States*, and shall command all necessary assistance to execute its duties."[644] Thus, if the President determines that some judicial "writ[ ], process, [or] order[is *not*] issued *under the authority of the United States*," because it violates the Constitution; and if, in fulfillment of his duty to "take Care that the Laws be faithfully executed" he commands the Marshals Service not to execute such "writ[ ], process, [or] order[ ]"; then the Service is thereby excused "by law"—the Constitution, as construed and applied by the President—from doing so. And the "writ[ ], process, [or] order[ ]" must remain ineffective. So, if judicial power is "'the power of a court to decide and pronounce a judgment *and*

---

[641] 28 U.S.C. § 561(c).

[642] See *Myers v. United States*, 272 U.S. 52, 181-82 (1926).

[643] 28 U.S.C. § 566(a).

[644] 28 U.S.C. § 566(c) (emphasis supplied).

carry it into effect,'"[645] "judicial supremacy" is largely a pipe dream without Executive cooperation.

On the other side, "[t]he Supreme Court may appoint [its own] marshal, who shall be subject to removal by the Court,"[646] not by the President.[647] And the Court's "marshal shall . . . [s]erve and execute all process and orders issued by the Court or member thereof."[648] But whether this slender force could adequately perform the Supreme Court's business in the face of the President's adamant refusal to assist is doubtful—inasmuch as merely "[s]erv[ing] and execut[ing] all process and orders issued by the Court" is not the same as seeing them *obeyed*. And confronted by such a refusal, what could the Supreme Court do? Enjoin the President,[649] or his subordinates?[650] Hold him or them in contempt, only to see its citations effectively overturned by Executive pardons?[651] As the Court itself has conceded, "[t]he executive power is vested in a President, and as far as his powers are derived from the Constitution, he is beyond the reach of any other department,

---

[645] *Muskrat* v. *United States*, 219 U.S. 246, 256 (1911) (emphasis supplied).

[646] 28 U.S.C. § 672(a).

[647] Compare U.S. Const. art. II, § 2, cl. 2 with *Myers* v. *United States*, 272 U.S. 52, 162-63 (1926).

[648] 28 U.S.C. § 672(c)(2).

[649] See *Mississippi* v. *Johnson*, 71 U.S. (4 Wall.) 475 (1867), discussed ante, at 241-44.

[650] See *Georgia* v. *Stanton*, 73 U.S. (6 Wall.) 50 (1868), discussed ante, at 166-68.

[651] U.S. Const. art. II, § 2, cl. 1, discussed ante, at 197-206.

except in the mode prescribed by the Constitution through the impeaching power."[652]

---

[652] *Kendall* v. *United States* ex rel. *Stokes*, 37 U.S. (12 Pet.) 524, 610 (1838).

CHAPTER 11

Criminal Prosecution of Judges for Violations of Litigants' Constitutional Rights

The President may refuse to enforce a judicial decision that is repugnant to the Constitution for any reason. If the Justices have rendered an opinion that negligently misconstrues the Constitution, perhaps the President's refusal to enforce it will mark the end of the matter. If, however, the Justices have violated litigants' constitutional rights knowingly, willfully, and intentionally, or with willful blindness to or reckless disregard of those rights, the President is bound, under his constitutional duty to "take Care that the Laws be faithfully executed," to do more: specifically, to prosecute the justices criminally.

1. The *United States Code* provides:

> If two or more persons conspire to injure, oppress, threaten, or intimidate any person in any State . . . in the free exercise or enjoyment of any right or privilege secured to him by the Constitution or laws of the United States, or because of his having so exercised the same[,]

. . .

> [t]hey shall be fined under this title or imprisoned not more than ten years, or both . . . [; and]

> [w]hoever, under color of any law, statute, ordinance, regulation, or custom, willfully subjects any person in any State . . . to the deprivation of any rights, privileges, or immunities secured or protected by the Constitution or laws of the United States . . . shall be fined under this title or imprisoned not more than ten years, or both . . . .[653]

These laws apply to officials of the General Government,[654] and specifically to judges.[655]

Indeed, one would be hard pressed to imagine a situation in which these laws could be applied more aptly than to judges who issue trumped-up rulings for the very purpose of depriving people of their constitutional rights. For what could more affront the "Oath[s] or Affirmation[s], to support this Constitution" that all "judicial Officers, both of the United States and of the several States," take—and more subvert, corrupt, and at length overturn this country's entire legal system—than a criminal Judiciary? What, then, could need to be exposed and rooted out sooner, more thoroughly, or more mercilessly?[656]

---

[653] 18 U.S.C. §§ 241, 242.

[654] *Screws* v. *United States*, 325 U.S. 91, 97 n.2, 108 (1945).

[655] *Dennis* v. *Sparks*, 449 U.S. 24, 29 n.5 (1980) (State judge).

[656] Yet, as everyone who studies judicial opinions carefully—parsing the records, briefs, and arguments—can attest, although criminal misconstructions and misapplications of the Constitution occur in *many* cases, next to none of the offenders ever faces prosecution. This is because

Now, in criminal cases the prosecution would have to
establish the defendant judges' *scienter*: their knowledge,
willful blindness, or reckless disregard of their wrongdoing at
the time they perpetrated it. This, however, would not be as
difficult as it might appear at first blush. Any attorney who has
studied cases in which judges have intentionally violated
litigants' constitutional rights knows what has happened, how
to marshal the evidence, and how to present it convincingly to

---

vanishingly few lawyers would ever file such charges with prosecutors;
fewer prosecutors would ever press them if filed; and even fewer judges
would try them with the single-mindedness of purpose and hunters' gusto
they employ when ordinary civilians are in the dock. Lawyers, prosecutors,
and judges, after all, are members of the same "law-profession culture," or
club, in which a collective professional courtesy and especially a sweep-our-
own-dirt-under-the-rug mentality take precedence over any eccentric
individuals' demands that the profession itself clean its own house. (In the
language of another racket, the "law-profession culture" is a master
practitioner of *omertà*.) Some lawyers believe that prosecuting judges for
criminal violations of the Constitution is largely futile, and recoil from
turning themselves into laughing stocks or pariahs by tilting at windmills.
Most lawyers who ambition positions as prosecutors or judges themselves
are careful to avoid making political enemies by broaching charges against
the politically powerful, even where deserved. (Besides, why make
precedents that may come back to haunt the accusers?) Many lawyers desire
to maintain the law profession as a self-policing entity, and with that status
to preserve the aura of infallibility that comes from being a judge in its own
case. And all too many lawyers view the public as both the source of their
livelihoods and a potentially implacable adversary, should it ever realize the
depth of the "law-profession culture's" cynical insouciance for common
people's rights. The us-*versus*-them mentality, unfortunately, generally
proves stronger than any self-imposed ethical responsibilities. Clients come
and go. The profession remains. One's true loyalty, or at least one's
adherence, must be to the permanent thing (in the terminology of that other
racket, *la cosa nostra*).

a jury. In practice, America's version of kangaroo justice is as easy to spot as the Australian animal: reliance on supposedly "controlling" precedents which actually have no bearing on the issues in the case;[657] quotations of law or recitations of fact ripped out of context, suppressed altogether, or falsified; refusals to address statutes or judicial precedents key to a litigant's case; dismissals of a litigant's legal arguments as "without merit" or "frivolous," with no analysis of their substance; attributions of "overwhelming evidence" to one side's case, where the evidence is disputable or even inadmissible; novel reinterpretations of the law on appeal, to rationalize the results reached at trial; and on and on it goes.

In *Lawrence*, for example, the Justices in the majority knew (or should have known) that foreign law could not control the constitutional merits—but through legalistic legerdemain arranged to make it decisive anyway. And those Justices together with Justice O'Connor were aware (or should have been aware) of no basis for denying State legislatures the right and power to promote (Christian) morality that lawmakers have exercised from the beginning of the Republic—but through naked judicial *fiat* struck that right and power from "due process of law" notwithstanding. These actions subordinated to foreign law and abridged, if not annihilated,

---

[657] See, e.g., Vieira, "Poltroons on the Bench: The Fraud of the 'Labor-Peace' Argument for Compulsory Public-Sector Collective Bargaining," *Government Union Review*, Vol. 18, No. 3 (1998); idem, "Travesty, Tragedy and Treason: *Abood* v. *Detroit Board of Education* and the Supreme Court's Betrayal of the Constitution in Public-Sector Labor Relations," *Government Union Review*, Vol. 19, No. 2 (2000).

the constitutional powers, privileges, and rights of the people of Texas to uphold, protect, and promote morality through legislation. More than that, perforce of "judicial supremacy" (which every justice in *Lawrence* doubtlessly foresaw), these actions will subordinate to foreign law and abridge the constitutional powers, privileges, and rights of the people in every State, to the legislation of which *Lawrence* will be applied as a controlling precedent—thereby depriving WE THE PEOPLE as a whole of "the separate and equal station" "among the powers of the earth" "to which the Laws of Nature and of Nature's God entitle them," and to which the Declaration of Independence attests. If, as Justice Scalia charged, the majority in *Lawrence* "has taken sides in the culture war," aggressively aligning itself against the "[m]any Americans" who desire to "protect[ ] themselves and their families from a lifestyle that they believe to be immoral and destructive,"[658] then its recruitment of foreign law to overturn the right WE THE PEOPLE claimed in the Declaration "to be FREE AND INDEPENDENT STATES" with "full Power . . . to do all . . . Acts and Things which Independent States may of right do" is the legalistic equivalent of setting on America's shores the Hessian mercenaries.[659] So, for the President in good faith to consider these acts worthy of prosecution is hardly beyond the realm of the plausible or the possible.

---

[658] 539 U.S. at 602 (dissenting opinion).

[659] As denounced in the Declaration: "He [i.e., King George III] is at this time transporting large Armies of foreign Mercenaries to compleat the works of death, desolation and tyranny . . . ."

Moreover, as an aggravating factor, if the majority in *Lawrence* "has taken sides in the culture war," it is not simply because its "opinion is the product of a Court, which is the product of a law-profession culture, that has largely signed on to the so-called homosexual agenda."[660] Far worse: The majority's opinion in *Lawrence* is the product of Justices, and of the "law-profession culture" they represent, who believe that "judicial supremacy" licenses them to behave in even the most recklessly anti-social fashion—because such behavior, no matter how egregious, results in no adverse consequences to themselves. They are steeped in the hubris of power without responsibility, expecting that the "[m]any Americans" who are their intended victims will always be unable to protect themselves. They are intoxicated with the adulation they receive as "enlightened jurists" in the journals of the "law-profession culture," and from the mouthpieces of cultural bolshevism throughout the country—secure in the knowledge that dissent will be voiced (and, more importantly, heard) only among the disaffected, whose political influence is in inverse proportion to their numbers. And they are protected by the "law-profession culture's" self-serving code of professional responsibility, which enjoins those few lawyers who discern the judicial emperor's nakedness to remain respectfully reticent, and instead slog through the judicial muck according to the "law-profession culture's" rules of march: attempting to discover cracks in the Justices' reasoning, through which in future "Cases" and "Controversies" to slip intellectually honest

---

[660] 539 U.S. at 602 (Scalia, J., dissenting).

arguments that may salvage some bits and snippets of traditional American law and culture. As if whatever arguments were proffered the Judiciary would accept, and whatever artifacts of traditional American law and culture the Judiciary would allow to survive, if those arguments and artifacts did not advance or at least conform to the "law-profession culture's" agenda of the moment. For, as Justice Scalia observed, "[i]t is just a game, after all. '[I]n the end,' it is the *feelings* and *intuition* of a majority of the Justices that count . . . ."[661]

Yet, would any judges dare to impose their unconstitutional "feelings and intuition" on WE THE PEOPLE if they believed that they would face *indictments* for their misdeeds?[662]

2. This is not to say that, even though in principle sound, prosecution of errant justices of the Supreme Court (or any judges, for that matter) for violations of litigants' constitutional rights would not be problematic under contemporary political circumstances. In the absence of a special Court of Constitutional Review "ordain[ed] and establish[ed]" by Congress,[663] staffed with scrupulously honest jurists committed to "original intent," and the judgments of which were not subject to appeal,[664] these prosecutions would *ex necessitate* be

---

[661] *Atkins* v. *Virginia*, 304, 348 (2002) (dissenting opinion).

[662] Or impeachments. See post, at 285-321.

[663] U.S. Const. art. III, § 1.

[664] See U.S. Const. art. III, § 2, cl. 2.

heard by members of the present Judiciary. These "products of [the] law-profession culture" might well be expected to hold themselves bound to treat the Supreme Court's decisions as correct, and to follow them.[665]

One may also wonder where, without a thorough housecleaning, the Department of Justice would find prosecutors of personal integrity capable of the task— prosecutors and judges being all too often these days co-conspirators in denials of citizens' constitutional rights.[666]

---

[665] Compare *Hutto* v. *Davis*, 454 U.S. 370, 375 (1982) (lower courts must follow Supreme Court's precedent "no matter how misguided the judges of those courts may think it to be"), with *Planned Parenthood* v. *Casey*, 505 U.S. 833, 854-69 (opinion of O'Connor, J.), 912-14 (opinion of Stevens, J.), 923-24 (opinion of Blackmun, J.) (1992) (dilation on the importance to the Court of *stare decisis*).

[666] See, e.g., Roberts, "Federal courts are jailing the innocent," *Conservative Chronicle* (14 January 2004), at 27.

CHAPTER 12

Congressional Limitations
on the Jurisdiction of
the Supreme Court
and Other Courts

One way to prevent judges from negligently, recklessness, or criminally misconstruing the Constitution is simply to prevent them from hearing certain constitutional issues at all.

1. a. For judges of the General Government "in such inferior Courts as the Congress may from time to time ordain and establish,"[667] grants and restrictions of original and appellate jurisdiction are entirely with Congress's discretion.

> [I]f the Constitution had ordained and established the inferior courts, and distributed to them their respective powers, they could not be restricted or devested by Congress. But as it has made no such distribution . . . , having a right to prescribe, Congress may also withhold from any court of its creation jurisdiction of any of the [constitutionally] enumerated controversies. Courts created

_____

[667] U.S. Const. art. III, § 1.

by statute can have no jurisdiction but such as the statute confers. No one of them can assert a just claim to jurisdiction exclusively conferred on another, or withheld from all.

The Constitution has defined the limits of the judicial power of the United States, but has not prescribed how much of its shall be exercised by the [inferior courts]; consequently, the statute which does prescribe the limits of their jurisdiction, cannot be in conflict with the Constitution, unless it confers powers not enumerated therein.[668]

Thus, Congress can declare that the "inferior Courts" may hear only certain questions.[669] Or that they may not grant certain remedies.[670] Or that whatever questions they may hear may not be appealed.[671]

b. In addition, by statutory control of "Exceptions" to the Supreme Court's "appellate Jurisdiction, both as to Law and Fact,"[672] Congress can preclude that Court from hearing certain issues. For, with the exception of its "original Jurisdiction" which the Constitution mandates directly,[673] the Supreme

---

[668] *Sheldon* v. *Sill*, 49 U.S. (8 How.) 441, 448-49 (1850).

[669] *Lockerty* v. *Phillips*, 319 U.S. 182, 187 (1943) (denial of equity jurisdiction).

[670] *Lauf* v. *E.G. Shinner & Co.*, 303 U.S. 323, 329-30 (1938); *Drivers' Union* v. *Lake Valley Co.*, 311 U.S. 91, 100-03 (1940) (injunctions).

[671] *United States* v. *Klein*, 80 U.S. (13 Wall.) 128, 145 (1872).

[672] U.S. Const. art. III, § 2, cl. 2.

[673] U.S. Const. art. III, § 2, cl. 2.

Court has only such jurisdiction as the Constitution allows Congress to confer.[674] As the Court itself early recognized:

> [T]he political truth is, that the disposal of the judicial power, (except in a few specified instances) belongs to congress. If congress has given the power to this Court, we possess it, not otherwise: and if congress has not given the power to us, or to any other Court, it still remains at the legislative disposal. Besides, congress is not bound, and it would, perhaps, be inexpedient, to enlarge the jurisdiction of the federal Courts, to every subject, in every form, which the constitution might warrant.[675]

Ex parte *McCardle*[676] provides a striking example of the Supreme Court's subordination to Congress in this regard. In that case, the Court first had held that it had jurisdiction over an appeal involving a writ of habeas corpus, had heard oral argument, and had taken the case under advisement for decision. Then Congress passed a statute repealing the Court's appellate jurisdiction in such cases—whereupon the Court obediently dismissed the case for want of jurisdiction:

> We are not at liberty to inquire into the motives of the Legislature. We can only examine into its power under the Constitution; and its power to make exceptions to the appellate jurisdiction of this court is given by express words.

---

[674] See, e.g., *United States* v. *Hudson and Goodwin*, 11 U.S. (7 Cranch) 32, 33 (1812); *Cary* v. *Curtis*, 44 U.S. (3 How.) 236, 245 (1845); *The Mayor* v. *Cooper*, 73 U.S. (6 Wall.) 247, 252 (1868).

[675] *Turner* v. *Bank of North America*, 4 U.S. (4 Dall.) 8, 10 (1799) (Chase, J.).

[676] 73 U.S. (6 Wall.) 318 (1868), and 74 U.S. (7 Wall.) 506 (1869).

What, then, is the effect of the repealing Act upon the case before us? We cannot doubt as to this. Without jurisdiction the court cannot proceed at all in any cause. Jurisdiction is the power to declare the law, and when it ceases to exist, the only function remaining to the court is that of announcing the fact and dismissing the cause.[677]

2. A troublesome problem remains, however: namely, whether Congress may *not* make *some* specific "Exceptions," "as to Law [or] Fact," from the Supreme Court's appellate jurisdiction,[678] *where to do so would plainly license a violation of the Constitution.*

For Congress to withhold appellate jurisdiction from the Supreme Court over certain constitutional issues, it must first determine for itself the meaning and application of the Constitution in the premises, and then conclude either that: (i) based on prior judicial decisions and the then-present composition of the bench, the Court will *wrongly* decide the issues; or (ii) the Court should not be permitted to hear the issues at all, *howsoever* it might decide them. In the first instance, Congress might believe that the Court's judicial decisions on the subject have been wrong, that the present group of Justices will not correct these errors, and that therefore removal of appellate jurisdiction will protect the constitutional rights of parties against whom otherwise the Court would enter new and no less erroneous rulings. This approach, however, will not necessarily have the practical

---

[677] 74 U.S. (7 Wall.) at 514.

[678] U.S. Const. art. III, § 2, cl. 2.

result Congress desires, because the parties Congress intends to protect may be denied their constitutional rights in the State courts, which have jurisdiction to hear federal issues[679] and cannot be controlled in the exercise thereof by Congress as are the courts of the General Government. In the second instance, conversely, if Congress did not reasonably believe that the Court's previous decisions were wrong, or its personnel wrongheaded, for Congress to withhold jurisdiction would be perverse, because that would deny constitutional protection to litigants otherwise entitled to it. Indeed, limitation of the Court's appellate jurisdiction in such a situation might evidence Congress's malign intent to immunize from "judicial review" a purported statute it *knows* is unconstitutional—that is, *for the very purpose of perpetrating and perpetuating usurpation or tyranny.* True, an otherwise constitutional statute will not be declared invalid on the assumption of an illicit legislative motive.[680] Presumably, "our elected representatives . . . know the law"[681] and enact legislation with their constitutional powers and disabilities in mind.[682] Nonetheless, "[w]hile good faith . . . is to be presumed, yet to carry that presumption to the extent of always holding that there must be some undisclosed and unknown reason for subjecting certain

---

[679] See *Testa* v. *Katt*, 330 U.S. 386 (1947); *Charles Dowd Box Co.* v. *Courtney*, 368 U.S. 502 (1962); *Free* v. *Bland*, 369 U.S. 663 (1962); *Sullivan* v. *Little Hunting Park*, 396 U.S. 229 (1969).

[680] See *United States* v. *O'Brien*, 391 U.S. 367, 382-85 (1968).

[681] *Cannon* v. *University of Chicago*, 441 U.S. 677, 696-97 (1979).

[682] See *Albernaz* v. *United States*, 450 U.S. 333, 341-42 (1981).

individuals ... to hostile ... legislation is to make the protecting clauses of the [Constitution] a mere rope of sand."[683] Of course, here, too, the State courts could frustrate Congress's improper plan.

To be sure, the Supreme Court might acquiesce in such a situation. Then again, it might not. Directly in point is *United States* v. *Klein.*[684] There, Congress had enacted a statute providing that the acceptance of a certain presidential pardon "shall be conclusive evidence of the acts pardoned, but shall be null and void as evidence of the rights conferred by it, both in the court of claims [the court of original jurisdiction] and in th[e Supreme C]ourt on appeal."[685] The Court refused to bow to this limitation of its jurisdiction:

> [T]he language of the [statute] shows plainly that it does not intend to withhold appellate jurisdiction except as a means to an end. Its great and controlling purpose is to deny to pardons granted by the President the effect which this court has adjudged them to have. The [statute] declares that pardons shall not be considered by this court on appeal. . . . It provides that, whenever it shall appear that any judgment of the court of claims shall have been founded on such pardons . . . the Supreme Court shall have no further jurisdiction of the case and shall dismiss the same for want of jurisdiction. . . .
>
> . . . [T]he denial of jurisdiction to this court, as well as to the court of claims, is founded solely on the application

---

[683] *Gulf, Colorado & Santa Fe Ry.* v. *Ellis,* 165 U.S. 150, 154 (1897).

[684] 80 U.S. (13 Wall.) 128 (1872).

[685] Ibid. at 144.

of a rule of decision, in causes pending prescribed by Congress. The court has jurisdiction of the cause to a given point; but when it ascertains that a certain state of things exists, its jurisdiction is to cease and it is required to dismiss the cause for want of jurisdiction.

. . . [T]his is not an exercise of the acknowledged power of Congress to make exceptions and prescribe regulations to the appellate power.

. . . In the case before us, the court of claims has rendered judgment for the claimant and an appeal has been taken to this court. We are directed to dismiss the appeal, if we find that the judgment must be affirmed, because of a pardon granted . . . . Can we do so without allowing that the legislature may prescribe rules of decision to the judicial department of the government in cases pending before it?

. . .

Congress has already provided that the Supreme Court shall have jurisdiction of the judgments of the court of claims on appeal. Can it prescribe a rule in conformity with which the court must deny to itself the jurisdiction thus conferred, because and only because its decision, in accordance with settled law, must be adverse to the government and favorable to the suitor? The question seems to us to answer itself.

The rule . . . is also liable to just exception as impairing the effect of a pardon, and thus infringing the constitutional power of the Executive.

. . .

. . . [T]he legislature cannot change the effect of . . . a pardon any more than the Executive can change a law. Yet this is attempted by the provision under consideration. The court is required to receive special pardons as evidence of guilt, and to treat them as null and void. . . . This certainly impairs the executive authority, and directs the court to be instrumental to that end.[686]

So, a congressional attempt to exercise "legislative supremacy" by limiting the Court's appellate jurisdiction over certain constitutional issues could turn out to be nothing more than an occasion for the Court to claim "judicial supremacy" over those and other constitutional issues.

To obviate this result in contentious areas would demand that Congress measure the jurisdiction to be removed with a legal micrometer equipped with a ultrafine constitutional scale. This would require not only that each issue be addressed in legally unassailable language, but also that the matter be revisited repeatedly if the Court attempted to evade or even strike down the congressional restrictions in areas in which the Justices considered "judicial supremacy" at stake.

For example, if Congress were to strip the Supreme Court of appellate jurisdiction in "Cases" and "Controversies" raising the issue of whether a State legislature may constitutionally enact a statute for the purpose of promoting traditional morality, the gaggle of offending Justices in *Lawrence* (Kennedy, Breyer, Ginsberg, Souter, Stevens, and O'Connor) might—perhaps should to expected to—rule that Congress's attempt to shield "traditional morality" from "judicial review" violates the First Amendment, because "traditional morality" is merely verbal camouflage for *Christian* morality, and

---

[686] Ibid. at 145-48. See also *Cary* v. *Curtis*, 44 U.S. (3 How.) 236, 252-60 (1845) (Story, J., dissenting).

because Congress cannot use the Exceptions Clause[687] to immunize a "law respecting an establishment of religion,"[688] or (in the words of *Klein*) "impair[ing] the [First Amendment] and direct[ing] the [Supreme C]ourt to be instrumental to that end." Moreover, that the First Amendment postdates the Exceptions Clause would be a strong argument that the former imposes limitations on the latter. Certainly, the contrary construction would have less force, inasmuch as "no court of justice can be authorized so as to construe any clause of the Constitution as to defeat its obvious ends, when another construction, equally accordant with the words and sense thereof, will enforce and protect them."[689]

In any event, limiting the Supreme Court's appellate jurisdiction in contentious areas vital to the "law-profession culture's" present-day agenda will be conducive, less to repose, than to endless legislative tinkering and litigation.

3. Nonetheless, "[w]hatever functions Congress are, by the Constitution, authorized to perform, they are, when the public good requires it, bound to perform."[690] Constitutional power carries with it a corresponding duty. In *Lawrence*, the Justices in the majority abused their jurisdiction by promiscuously insinuating foreign law into American constitutional jurisprudence and by banishing traditional morality from it. No

---

[687] U.S. Const. art. III, § 2, cl. 2.

[688] U.S. Const. amend. I.

[689] *Prigg* v. *Pennsylvania*, 41 U.S. (16 Pet.) 539, 612 (1842).

[690] *United States* v. *Marigold*, 50 U.S. (9 How.) 560, 567 (1850).

amendments of the Constitution are required to reverse these rulings, their unconstitutionality being undeniable. And the propriety of Congress's employment of the Exceptions Clause in this situation is beyond cavil, too. So, as a stop-gap measure—until the members of Congress can marshal their courage and oust the malefactors themselves, and not merely limit the amount of harm they can do—a limitation on the courts' jurisdiction may be in order. The following language could provide a model:

> Other than the Supreme Court of the United States in the exercise of its original jurisdiction as provided in Article III, Section 2, Clause 2 of the Constitution of the United States, no court or judge of the United States shall have or exercise to any degree original or appellate jurisdiction, in any case, controversy, or other proceeding of any kind, to hear or decide any claim, question, issue, assignment of error, or other like matter to the extent that it shall or may turn upon or be decided by consideration of whether—

> (a) any provision of the Constitution of the United States can, may, or should be construed, interpreted, or applied according or by reference to the laws, legislation, statutes, regulations, executive orders, decrees, or judicial or administrative decisions or rulings of (i) any country, state, or nation other than the United States or a State thereof, or (ii) any international organization or entity: *Provided, however, that* this paragraph shall not apply to any question, issue, assignment of error, or other like matter arising under or relating to the power of Congress "[t]o define and punish . . . Offenses against the Law of Nations" in Article I, Section 8, Clause 10; the disability of every "Person holding any Office of Profit or Trust under [the

United States]" to "accept . . . any . . . Emolument, Office, or Title, of any kind whatever, from any King, Prince, or foreign State" in Article I, Section 9, Clause 8; or the power of the President, "by and with the Advice and Consent of the Senate, to make Treaties" in Article II, Section 2, Clause 2; or

(b) any law, legislation, statute, executive or administrative order or regulation, or judicial or administrative decision or ruling of any State or Territory of the United States or subdivision thereof, or of the District of Columbia, has a constitutionally rational basis, because a particular practice, behavior, or conduct is prohibited or punished therein or thereby for being inconsistent with public morality as defined in the public policy of such State, Territory, or District.

4. The possibility of adequate legislative draftsmanship aside, fundamentally the problem with Congress's trying to assert its constitutional control over the Supreme Court's appellate jurisdiction in a case such as *Lawrence* is that, as *Lawrence* itself demonstrates, the true complaint is not that the Court has jurisdiction over such questions as whether States may legislate according to the precepts of morality and whether foreign law has a place in constitutional interpretation, but instead that certain Justices now composing a distinct majority on the Court intend to decide these (and other) questions *un*constitutionally, in order to promote an alien agenda, and the Devil take the hindmost. That is, the problem is not the existence of the jurisdiction, nor even its abstract potential for abuse, but rather the proven certainty that it will be abused because of the personalities and purposes

of the men and women now permitted to exercise it—*not the abuse of jurisdiction, but the abuse of office.* For which the proper remedy is not to limit the amount of harm these people can do *in* office, but to remove them *from* office, so that they can do no more harm at all. Indeed, that they have done *any* harm so far suffices to counsel their removal.[691]

---

[691] That constitutional rights do not turn on the mere amount of harm done, see *Gulf, Colorado & Santa Fe Ry.* v. *Ellis*, 165 U.S. 150, 153-54 (1897); *Fairbank* v. *United States*, 181 U.S. 283, 291-92 (1901); *Looney* v. *Crane*, 245 U.S. 178, 189-90 (1917); *Patton* v. *United States*, 281 U.S. 276, 292 (1930); *Abington School District* v. *Schempp*, 374 U.S. 203, 225 (1963).

CHAPTER 13

"Packing" the Courts

The first method for removal of errant Justices is indirect: namely, diminishing their influence by decreasing their relative numbers on the bench. "Packing" of the Supreme Court (or of any courts Congress controls) would be nothing new. Pursuant to the power granted in the Necessary and Proper Clause,[692] Congress originally provided for a Supreme Court of six judges.[693] It increased the number to ten by 1863.[694] Then it reduced the bench to seven.[695] Finally, Congress settled on nine Justices.[696]

By changing the tribunal's size and appointing new Justices of one or another ideological persuasion, Congress and the President (through his appointment power and the Senate's consent[697]) can control the outcome of "judicial review" of

---

[692] U.S. Const. art. I, § 8, cl. 18.

[693] Act of 24 September 1789, ch. 20, § 1, 1 Stat. 73, 73.

[694] Act of 3 March 1863, ch. 100, § 1, 12 Stat. 794, 794.

[695] Act of 23 July 1866, ch. 210, § 1, 14 Stat, 209, 209.

[696] Act of 10 April 1869, ch. 22, § 1, 16 Stat. 44, 44.

[697] U.S. Const. art. II, § 2, cl. 2.

politically controversial constitutional issues. Indeed, even the supposed "finality" of judicial rulings can be rendered precarious, as in the case of the alleged packing of the Court to reverse its decision on the constitutionality of the Civil War Greenbacks.[698]

Similarly, through its power "[t]o constitute Tribunals inferior to the Supreme Court,"[699] Congress could create a special court with jurisdiction over all or certain types of constitutional questions. Coupled with removal of all appellate jurisdiction over such issues from the Supreme Court, this would remedy the present problem embodied in the majority in *Lawrence*—at least until the judges appointed to the special court began to align their decisions with the "law-profession culture's" *anti*-American agenda.

The latter concern points up why court "packing" is never a final solution, especially where the matter is solely one of adding new, presumably good judges to an existing bench composed primarily of bad ones. Even in the new dough, the leaven of the Pharisees will be insidiously at work. Moreover, court "packing" teaches no sure *moral* lesson. True, new men of distinction and integrity are honored and empowered by their appointments. But old men who have proven themselves unworthy are not dishonored, deprived of office, and dumped into History's dustbin where they belong. Rather, they are

---

[698] See Sachs, "Stare Decisis and the Legal Tender Cases," 20 *Virginia L. Rev.* 856 (1934); Burton, "The Legal Tender Cases: A Celebrated Supreme Court Reversal," 42 *Amer. Bar Ass'n J.* 231 (1956).

[699] U.S. Const. art. I, § 8, cl. 9.

suffered to subsist in their evil ways, perhaps intent on and capable of inflicting even more damage on the Constitution and the country.

CHAPTER 14

Removal of Judges for Lack of "good Behaviour" or by "Impeachment . . . and Conviction"

1. a. Removal from the bench *sine die* of every judge who demonstrates such incapacities as inability properly to construe the Constitution, or instability in construction over time, or infatuation with "the living Constitution" is the only sound means to deal with the problem so grossly evidenced in *Lawrence*. Whatever the explanation for their transgressions, judicial malefactors must be compelled to desist. But, invoking "judicial supremacy," they will resist any attempts to control, direct, correct, or even influence their behavior. Therefore, the weapon of "judicial supremacy" must be stricken from their hands *tout court*, and their ability to perpetrate further harm totally curtailed, by removing them from office. *No man, no problem.*

As discussed below, Congress enjoys plenary power to remove judges of the General Government from office for their demonstrated lack of "good Behaviour,"[700] or for their commission of "Treason, Bribery, or other high Crimes and Misdemeanors,"[701] or both. "Senators and Representatives . . . shall be bound by Oath or Affirmation, to support th[e] Constitution"[702] in this particular as in all others—especially so to correct judges' misconstructions of the Constitution, Congress's toleration of which amounts, not to "support" of the Constitution, but to complicity in its subversion, perversion, deconstruction, or destruction. And "[w]hatever functions Congress are, by the Constitution, authorized to perform they are, when the public good requires it, bound to perform."[703] The same, of course, is true for the President where the Constitution presumes that he will cooperate with Congress in these matters.[704]

b. For at least two reasons, removal is substantively the remedy most pertinent to the harm needing correction. First, removal addresses the wayward judges' *personal responsibility* for the situation. The problem is not a matter of impersonal trends or institutional incapacities, but of certain identified individuals whose specific behavior objectively contradicts their "Oath[s] or Affirmation[s]" of office[705] and infuses into constitutional jurisprudence false and pernicious doctrines.

---

[700] U.S. Const. art. III, § 1.

[701] U.S. Const. art. II, § 4.

[702] U.S. Const. art. VI, cl. 3.

[703] *United States* v. *Marigold*, 50 U.S. (9 How.) 560, 567 (1850).

[704] See U.S. Const. art. II, § 1, cl. 7 and § 3.

[705] U.S. Const. art. VI, cl. 3.

Because of their incompetence, recklessness, hubris, malice, or other culpable states of mind, these individuals confuse and conflate their own aberrant legal, political, economic, and cultural notions with the Constitution, wrongly denying constitutional rights, powers, privileges, and immunities not only to particular litigants but also, through those litigants' "Cases" and "Controversies" (either directly or as precedents), to Congress, the President, the States, and ultimately WE THE PEOPLE as well. *These individuals' judicial opinions are chronically wrong, because they are the wrong individuals to be issuing judicial opinions.*

Second, removal fully affirms and applies the constitutional scheme of *checks and balances*, by asserting Congress's right, power, and duty to pass on the "good Behaviour" of judges in terms of their competence and good faith in construing the Constitution—thereby establishing that judges are not the "ultimate interpreters" of the Constitution, but instead are themselves bound by WE THE PEOPLE'S interpretation of the Constitution, and therefore are responsible to and punishable by WE THE PEOPLE'S representatives for infractions of the supreme law. *WE THE PEOPLE can conclude that the wrong individuals are issuing judicial opinions by determining that these individuals' opinions on constitutional questions are chronically wrong—and can remove them from office on that basis.*

c. *Lawrence* provides a paradigmatic, compelling, and urgent case for removal. As explained above, Justices Breyer, Ginsberg, Kennedy, O'Connor, Souter, and Stevens have attacked not only the Constitution, but also the Declaration of Independence; and not only the Declaration, but also the "higher law" on which the Declaration explicitly rests: "the Laws of Nature and of Nature's God." Indeed, this judicial majority has read out of constitutional jurisprudence "the history of Western civilization and . . . Judeo-Christian moral and ethical standards," in reliance on "other authorities [found in foreign law] pointing in an opposite direction."[706]

The heretofore unheard-of proposition advanced by the *Lawrence* majority—"'that . . . a State has traditionally viewed a particular practice as immoral is not a sufficient reason for upholding a law prohibiting that practice'"[707]—is (as Justice Scalia observed) plainly "out of accord with our jurisprudence,"[708] although not necessarily alien (as he thought) to "the jurisprudence of *any* society we know," because Justice Kennedy identified the British Parliament and the European Court of Human Rights as "other authorities" for the doctrine.[709] The vital (or fatal) question which no one in *Lawrence* bothered to address, though, remains: *What is the logical terminus of that "opposite direction" from "the history of Western civilization and . . . Judeo-Christian moral and ethical standards" towards which these "other [foreign] authorities" now direct the Court?* For Justice Kennedy wrote not of a merely

---

[706] 539 U.S. at 572 (opinion of Kennedy, J., for the Court).

[707] Ibid. at 577.

[708] Ibid. at 599 (dissenting opinion).

[709] Ibid. at 572-73, 576-77.

"different direction," with perhaps a generally similar compass heading; but of "an *opposite* direction."

Justice Scalia complained that the *Lawrence* majority was serving only one "side[ ] in the culture war, departing from its role of assuring, as neutral observer, that the democratic rules of engagement are observed."[710] To say, however, that the Court should defer to democracy is to concede the *Lawrence* majority's revolutionary thesis that "the history of Western civilization and . . . Judeo-Christian moral and ethical standards" *can be*, and according to someone's cultural calculus *ought to be*, voted out of American constitutional law. Yet, where under the Constitution is anyone empowered to prohibit by vote the measurement of human conduct according to "the Laws of Nature and of Nature's God" that "entitle[d]" Americans in the first instance to their independence? Nowhere. Democracy has no right to take this country in "an opposite direction" from "the history of Western civilization and . . . Judeo-Christian moral and ethical standards." Neither does "judicial supremacy." The precepts of morality supply the necessary foundation for the answer to every constitutional question, because they provide the sanction of "higher law" absent which the Constitution itself would be of no legitimacy. Therefore, the *Lawrence* majority's repudiation of "the history of Western civilization and . . . Judeo-Christian moral and ethical standards" amounted to repudiation of the Declaration of Independence, and consequentially the Constitution, and consequentially again

---

[710] Ibid. at 602 (dissenting opinion).

the Justices' own authority—further proof that whom the gods would destroy they first make mad.

2. The legal question, then, becomes: On what specific constitutional basis does chronic error in construction, or intentional misconstruction, of the Constitution constitute grounds for removal of a Justice (or any judge of the General Government) from office?

a. "The Judges, both of the supreme and inferior Courts, shall hold their Offices *during good Behaviour*"[711] Therefore, they can be removed for conduct that constitutes less than "good Behaviour." Two classes of misconduct could justify removal under this provision:

> ➤ the "Treason, Bribery, or other high Crimes and Misdemeanors"[712] that are grounds for "Impeachment" by the House of Representatives,[713] trial and conviction by the Senate,[714] and "remov[al] from Office on Impeachment . . . and Conviction,"[715] and as to which "Judgment . . . shall not extend further than to removal from Office, and disqualification to hold and enjoy any Office of honor, Trust or Profit under the United States";[716] or

---

[711] U.S. Const. art. III, § 1 (emphasis supplied).

[712] See U.S. Const. art. II, § 4.

[713] U.S. Const. art. I, § 2, cl. 5.

[714] U.S. Const. art. I, § 3, cl. 6.

[715] U.S. Const. art. II, § 4.

[716] U.S. Const. art. I, § 3, cl. 7.

> ➤ other wrongdoing that, although it does not descend to
> the depths of "High Crimes and Misdemeanors,"
> nonetheless falls below the constitutionally required
> minimum level of "good Behaviour."

Self-evidently, such physical disabilities as insanity, senility, or
drug addiction, or such personal deficiencies as incompetence,
insouciance, or indolence cannot be considered "Treason,
Bribery, or other high Crimes and Misdemeanors," and
therefore cannot be addressed by "Impeachment . . . and
Conviction"—unless, for example, the *knowingly* incompetent,
insouciant, or indolent "Judge[ ]" were considered to have
violated his oath of office by such conduct, thereby becoming
guilty of the serious crimes of false swearing or perjury.[717] Yet,
judges suffering from or exhibiting these problems cannot be
allowed to persist in office, either. Therefore, lack of "good
Behaviour" must sweep in conduct less serious as well as far
more extensive than "high Crimes and Misdemeanors."

The Constitution's linguistic structure compels the same
conclusion.

> [Each] provision[ ] of the Constitution . . . must be
> considered in the light of the other[s].[718]

> The Constitution is an organic scheme of government to be
> dealt with as an entirety. A particular provision cannot be
> dissevered from the rest of the Constitution.[719]

---

[717] *See* 18 U.S.C. §§ 1001(a)(2), 1621(1).

[718] *Hostetter* v. *Idlewild Bon Voyage Liquor Corp.*, 377 U.S. 324, 332 (1964).

[719] *Reid* v. *Covert*, 354 U.S. 1, 44 (1957) (opinion of Frankfurter, J.). See
United States v. *Wong Kim Ark*, 169 U.S. 649, 653-54 (1898).

It cannot be presumed, that any clause in the constitution is intended to be without effect; and therefore, such a construction is inadmissible, unless the words require it.[720]

In expounding the Constitution of the United States, every word must have its due force, and appropriate meaning; for it is evident from the whole instrument, that no word was unnecessarily used, or needlessly added.... Every word appears to have been weighed with the utmost deliberation, and its force and effect to have been fully understood. No word in the instrument, therefore, can be rejected as superfluous or unmeaning....[721]

[All] fundamental [constitutional] principles are of equal dignity, and n[one] must be enforced as to nullify or substantially impair the other.[722]

If "good Behaviour" meant nothing more than an absence of the commission of "high Crimes and Misdemeanors," the Founding Fathers would have had no need to employ two distinct phrases. They could easily have written that "[t]he Judges ... shall hold their Offices *unless impeached and convicted for Treason, Bribery, or other high Crimes and Misdemeanors*"—or perhaps simply "*unless impeached and convicted*," because "Impeachment," by constitutional definition, always involves

---

[720] *Marbury* v. *Madison*, 5 U.S. (1 Cranch) 137, 174 (1803). See also *Myers* v. *United States*, 272 U.S. 51, 151-52 (1926); *Knowlton* v. *Moore*, 178 U.S. 41, 87 (1900); *Blake* v. *McClung*, 172 U.S. 239, 260-61 (1898).

[721] *Holmes* v. *Jennison*, 39 U.S. (14 Pet.) 540, 570-71 (1840) (opinion of Taney, C.J.) (equally divided Court), followed in *Williams* v. *United States*, 289 U.S. 553, 572-73 (1933).

[722] *Dick* v. *United States*, 208 U.S. 340, 353 (1908).

that litany of "high Crimes and Misdemeanors." Indeed, the Founders could have dispensed entirely with the language "[t]he Judges . . . shall hold their Offices. . .," because, simply as "civil Officers of the United States," "Judges" are always subject to "Impeachment . . . and Conviction" without any special mention of their exposure.[723] Had the Framers written the Constitution in any of those ways, however, no insane, ignorant, or ignominious judge who did not stumble blindly into some "high Crime or Misdemeanor" could ever be removed, which no one could consider an appropriate situation. Thus, the dual phraseology plainly must have been intended to allow for removal under two different sets of circumstances.

This imports, however, that the special requirements of "Impeachment . . . and Conviction" do not necessarily apply to removal of judges for lack of "good Behaviour." Conduct that consists of "high Crimes and Misdemeanors" necessarily also constitutes a lack of "good Behaviour," and must be prosecuted to removal by "Impeachment . . . and Conviction," because of its dominant character. But conduct that consists of some other (and necessarily lesser) lack of "good Behaviour" ought to be prosecuted to removal by a procedure other and simpler than "Impeachment . . . and Conviction," because that process applies only to "high Crimes and Misdemeanors." Again, the Founders could not have believed it necessary to involve the House and especially the Senate in the cumbersome process of "Impeachment . . . and Conviction" in

---

[723] U.S. Const. art. II, § 4.

order to remove an insane judge. Plainly, "the power of impeachment is . . . intended for occasional and extraordinary cases, where a superior power, acting for the whole people, is put into operation to protect their rights, and to rescue their liberties from violation."[724]

b. Although the "good Behaviour" language indicates that judges of the General Government may be removed from office by some process short of "Impeachment . . . and Conviction," the Constitution specifies no particular procedure for such removal.

1) Congress, however, has authority "[t]o make all Laws which shall be necessary and proper for carrying into Execution . . . all . . . Powers vested . . . in the Government of the United States"[725] Plainly, a power of removal incident to and dependent upon the condition of disqualification (lack of "good Behaviour") must exist; or the condition would be nugatory. And "[t]he government which has a right to do an act . . . must . . . be allowed to select the means; and those who contend that it may not select any appropriate means, that one particular mode of effecting the object is excepted, take upon themselves the burden of establishing that exception."[726] For example, although the Constitution is silent on the matter, no one doubts that Congress is empowered to determine the

---

[724] 1 J. Story, *Commentaries*, ante note 121, § 751, at 550.

[725] U.S. Const. art. I, § 8, cl. 18.

[726] *McCulloch* v. *Maryland*, 17 U.S. (4 Wheat.) 316, 409-10 (1819).

"Compensation" which "[t]he Judges . . . shall . . . receive for their Services."[727]

Perhaps the procedure most plausible from the perspective of *pre*-constitutional Anglo-American legal history would involve a majority vote in both the House of Representatives and the Senate (an "address"), recommending removal and stating the basis therefore in specific conduct that violated the standard of "good Behaviour," followed by an order of the President if he concurs in Congress's recommendation. This would combine the procedure of the English Act of Settlement[728] (which was well known to the Founding Fathers) with the controlling constitutional standard of "good Behaviour," together with the basic principle stated in *Myers* v. *United States*[729] that "[t]he power of removal is incident to the power of appointment,[[730]] . . . and when the grant of executive power is enforced by the express mandate to take care that the laws be faithfully executed,[[731]] it emphasizes the necessity for including within the executive power . . . the exclusive power of removal."[732] Congress's participation in the process would be justified on the following bases:

---

[727] U.S. Const. art. III, § 1. Compare U.S. Const. art. I, § 6, cl. 1; art. II, § 1, cl. 6.

[728] 12 & 13 Will. III, ch. 2, § 3 (1700).

[729] 272 U.S. 52 (1926).

[730] U.S. Const. art. II, § 2, cl. 2.

[731] U.S. Const. art. II, § 3.

[732] 272 U.S. at 122.

> ➤ judges are not executive "Officers," thereby limiting application of the *Myers* rationale, and authorizing Congress's involvement;

> ➤ the Act of Settlement is the outstanding (albeit not quite parallel) precedent for the procedure of legislative address followed by executive removal; and

> ➤ the combination of the two sets up a sound system of checks and balances, in that Congress defines "good Behaviour" and initiates the process of removal, the President must independently concur in Congress's determination, and if the President refuses to act for improper reasons, he himself may be impeached, convicted, and removed from office.

As noted above, the Act of Settlement is not an exact parallel for removal of judges by address under the Constitution. The Act provided that "Judges Commissions be made *Quamdiu se bene gesserint* [i.e., during good behavior] . . . but upon the Address of both Houses of Parliament, it may be lawful to remove them."[733] And the Act was interpreted to allow removal *without any prior violation of the condition of good behavior.*[734] The procedure used in the Act of Settlement would be constitutionally allowable, though, where address and removal *were* conditioned upon a lack of "good Behaviour" in the judge subject to them.

---

[733] 12 & 13 Will. III, ch. 2, § 3.

[734] See R. Berger, *Impeachment: The Constitutional Problems* (1973), at 151 n.131. Nonetheless, prior to ratification of the Constitution many of the States employed that procedure (or some variant). See ibid. at 145.

Instructive in this regard is the debate in the Federal Convention concerning a proposed amendment of the "good Behaviour" language in a draft of the Constitution.

Mr DICKINSON moved as an amendment . . . after the words "good behavior" the words "provided that they may be removed by the Executive on the application by the Senate and House of Representatives."

Mr GERRY 2^{ded} the motion.

Mr Govr MORRIS thought it a contradiction in terms to say that the Judges should hold their offices during good behavior, and yet be removable without a trial. Besides it was fundamentally wrong to subject Judges to so arbitrary an authority.

Mr SHERMAN saw no contradiction or impropriety if this were made part of the constitutional regulation of the Judiciary establishment. He observed that a like provision was contained in the British statutes.

Mr RUTLIDGE. If the Supreme Court is to judge between the U.S. and particular States, this alone is an insuperable objection to the motion.

Mr WILSON considered such a provision in the British Government as less dangerous than here, the House of Lords & House of Commons being less likely to concur on the same occasions. . . . The judges [here] would be in a bad situation if made to depend on every gust of faction which might prevail in the two branches of our Gov^t

Mr RANDOLPH opposed the motion as weakening too much the independence of the Judges.

Mr DICKINSON was not apprehensive that the Legislature composed of different branches constituted on such different principles, would improperly unite for the purpose of displacing a Judge.

On the question for agreeing to M[r] Dickinson's Motion

N.H. no. Mas. abs[t] C[t] ay. N.J. abs[t] P[a] no. Del. no. M[d] no. V[a] no. N.C. abs[t] S.C. no. Geo. no.[735]

The comments of all the delegates who spoke—and especially of Sherman and Wilson who referred explicitly to British law—made clear that Dickinson's amendment was seen as providing for a power of removal similar to that in the Act of Settlement: namely, *not* conditioned upon an absence of "good Behaviour" in the offending judge, but without standards at all, other than agreement among the House, the Senate, and the President that the judge should be removed. This, of course, is what the amendment's language required. For a proviso generally creates an exception from the rule to which it applies. So, here, Dickinson's language "provided that they may be removed" would have operated to allow removal even where no lack of "good Behaviour" had occurred, that is, at the unbridled discretion of Congress and the President. This is why Morris condemned the amendment as creating "a contradiction in terms" and "subject[ing] Judges to so arbitrary an authority." Obviously, however, no such objection would apply were the removal of judges by congressional address and executive order conditioned upon the absence of "good Behaviour." So the fate of Dickinson's amendment provides no

---

[735] *Debates in the Federal Convention of 1787 as Reported by James Madison, in Documents Illustrative of the Formation of the Union of American States* (1927), at 622-23 (footnotes omitted).

reason for denying Congress the authority to create such a procedure by statute as a means "necessary and proper for carrying into Execution" the requirement that "Judges . . . shall hold their Offices during good Behaviour," but no longer.[736]

2) Moreover, Congress can—indeed, must—define and declare standards of "good Behaviour" (or its absence), according to the *pre*-constitutional understanding of the common law. Some of these would be obvious and non-controversial, such as insanity, senility, or other physical, mental, or emotional inabilities to perform judicial tasks to some satisfactory level. Others might be subject to political debate, and should be settled in that manner, inasmuch as

---

[736] Berger argued that "good Behaviour" tenure should be enforced in a special court created by Congress. *Impeachment*, ante note 734, at 133-34. The weaknesses in his position, however, are two-fold. First, creating a new *court* with jurisdiction to remove *judges* from office for lack of "good Behaviour" violates the rule, inherent in the principles of separation of powers and checks and balances, that no one (or branch of government) should be a judge in his (or its) own case. Second, Berger conceded that "the common law provided no [judicial] *remedy* for forfeiture of *judicial* office." Ibid. at 133. "[T]here is no [*pre*-constitutional] English case wherein a judge comparable to a federal judge was removed in a judicial proceeding." Ibid. at 127 (footnote omitted). Nonetheless, he argued that this omission was "fortuitous" and that "[r]emedies were not frozen by the Constitution to those extant in 1788" Ibid. (footnote omitted). Whether "fortuitous" or not, though, the omission *was* part of the *pre*-constitutional common law. And if Congress may create new remedies for ills that the common law did not address through judicial causes of action, certainly it may do so on the analogy of a British statutory precedent that *was* part of the law applicable to the Colonies, that *did* address the subject matter, and that with suitable incorporation of the limiting constitutional standard of "good Behaviour" can perform the required function.

"good Behaviour" is ultimately a matter of what questionable "Behaviour" WE THE PEOPLE will tolerate. This is an area in which "the living Constitution" may legitimately have some relevance. For example, what would have been recognized in *pre*-constitutional common law as insanity would surely both in 1789 and today constitute a lack of "good Behaviour." Conversely, what might be recognized today as a serious personality disorder destructive of a proper judicial temperament might not have been considered a debilitating form of insanity at common law.

In any event, whatever the minimum standards for "good Behaviour" may prove to be as a result of Congress's assessment of *pre*-constitutional common law and its consideration of contemporary social and political standards, an absence of "good Behaviour" must surely include judges' malign, reckless, willfully blind, negligent, or incompetent misinterpretations of the Constitution in the course of adjudicating "Cases" and "Controversies" before them.

So, Congress could undoubtedly find an absence of "good Behaviour" where (as in *Lawrence*) judges promiscuously employed foreign law to construe the Constitution, thus repudiating America's "separate and equal station" "among the powers of the earth" to which the Declaration of Independence laid claim;[737] or where they denied that traditional morality is "'a sufficient reason for upholding a law prohibiting [an aberrant] practice,'" thus repudiating "the Laws

---

[737] 539 U.S. at 572-73, 576-77.

of Nature and of Nature's God" the Declaration invoked;[738] or (worse yet) where they relied on foreign law specifically "pointing in an *opposite* direction" from "the history of Western Civilization and . . . Judeo-Christian moral and ethical standards."[739]

c. Perhaps, however, discussion of new procedures for removal of errant judges other than by "Impeachment . . . and Conviction" is premature and unnecessary, inasmuch as the Justices' deviation from "good Behaviour" evidenced in *Lawrence* meets the requirement of "high Crimes and Misdemeanors."

1) "Impeachment . . . and Conviction" is the best method for removal of such justices at the present time because it is the only method available. It can be utilized without having to enact any new, and doubtlessly controversial, statute. Its use will preemptively defeat the argument that the Constitution allows no other process for removal. It exudes the high dignity and solemnity appropriate to the problem:

> These prosecutions are . . . conducted by the representatives of the nation, in their public capacity, in the face of the nation and upon a responsibility which is at once felt and reverenced by the whole community. The notoriety of the proceedings, the solemn manner in which they are conducted, the deep extent to which they affect the reputations of the accused, the ignominy of a conviction which is to be known through all time, and the glory of an

---

[738] Ibid. at 577.

[739] Ibid. at 572 (emphasis supplied).

acquittal which ascertains and confirms innocence,—these are all calculated to produce a vivid and lasting interest in the public mind, and to give to such prosecutions, when necessary, a vast importance, both as a check to crime and an indictment to virtue.[740]

And it puts Congress immediately on the spot—constitutionally, politically, and morally—which is where WE THE PEOPLE'S representatives always should be:

> It is designed as a method of national inquest into the conduct of public men. If such is the design, who can so properly be the inquisitors for the nation as the representatives of the people themselves? They must be presumed to be watchful of the interests, alive to the sympathies, and ready to redress the grievances, of the people. If it is made their duty to bring official delinquents to justice, they can scarcely fail of performing it without public denunciation and political desertion on the part of their constituents.[741]

2) Both in principle and in practice, precedents abound for specifically judicial "Impeachment[s] . . . and Conviction[s]." In principle—

> The offenses which would be generally prosecuted by impeachment would be those only of a high character, and belonging to persons in eminent stations . . . such as . . . *a judge* . . . .[742]

---

[740] 1 J. Story, *Commentaries*, ante note 121, § 688, at 513 (footnote omitted).

[741] Ibid. § 689, at 514.

[742] Ibid. § 761, at 558 (emphasis supplied).

> All officers of the United States ... who hold their appointments under the national government, whether their duties are executive *or judicial*, in the highest or in the lowest departments of the government, ... are liable to impeachment.[743]

> The offense which the power of impeachment is designed principally to reach are those of a political or of a *judicial* character.... *So far as they are of a judicial character, it is obviously more safe to the public to confide them to the Senate than to a mere court of law.*[744]

In particular, judges are subject to "Impeachment ... and Conviction" for their unconstitutional opinions and usurpations—

> [I]f the judges mislead their sovereign by unconstitutional opinions ... these imputations have properly occasioned impeachments; because it is apparent how little the ordinary tribunals are calculated to take cognizance of such offenses, or to investigate and reform the general policy of the state.[745]

> In examining the parliamentary history of impeachments, it will be found that many offenses, not easily definable by law, and many of a purely political character, have been deemed high crimes and misdemeanors worthy of this extraordinary remedy. Thus, ... judges ... have ... been impeached ... for misleading their sovereign by

---

[743] Ibid. § 792, at 577 (footnote omitted) (emphasis supplied).

[744] Ibid. § 749, at 549 (footnote omitted) (emphasis supplied).

[745] 2 R. Wooddeson, *Laws of England* (1792), at 611-12.

unconstitutional opinions, and for attempts to subvert the
fundamental laws, and introduce arbitrary power.[746]

[I]f the usurpation should be by the judiciary, and arise
from corrupt motives, the power of impeachment would
remove the offenders . . . .[747]

In practice, there have been more instances of
impeachment of judges of the General Government than of
other "civil Officers."[748] Were the process of "Impeachment . . .
and Conviction" not so complex and costly, doubtlessly many
more cases would have been pursued.[749] Moreover, precedent
exists for judicial impeachments on a political or
jurisprudential basis: In a private colloquy during the trial of
Justice Samuel Chase before the Senate during Thomas
Jefferson's administration, Senator Giles argued that
conviction of a judge upon impeachment required no proof of
actual criminality or corruption, only Congress's conclusion

---

[746] 1 J. Story, *Commentaries*, ante note 121, § 800, at 584 (footnote omitted).

[747] Ibid., § 394, at 297.

[748] See 3 A. Hind, *Precedents of the House of Representatives of the United States*
(1907), §§ 2319-41 (John Pickering, 1803), 2342-63 (Samuel Chase, 1804),
2364-84 (James Peck, 1830), 2385-97 (West Humphreys, 1862), 2469-85
(Charles Swayne, 1904); 6 C. Cannon, *Precedents of the House of
Representatives of the United States* (1936), §§ 498-512 (Robert Archbald), 513-
24 (Harold Louderback); ten Broek, "Partisan Politics and Federal Judgeship
Impeachments Since 1903," 23 *Minnesota Law Review* 185, 194-96 (1939)
(George English); *Proceedings of the United States Senate in the Trial of
Impeachment of Halsted L. Ritter*, S. Doc. No. 200, 74th Cong., 2d Sess. (1936).

[749] See R. Berger, *Impeachment*, ante note 734, at 166-69.

that he held opinions dangerous to the nation's well-being.[750] Although Chases's escape did render judicial impeachment, in Jefferson's words, almost a "mere scarecrow" thereafter,[751] the acquittal under a general verdict did not disprove Giles's theory of prosecution. Instead, that Chase had been impeached at all supplied a constitutional precedent.[752]

3) The wrongdoing of the Justices in the majority in *Lawrence* fits every applicable paradigm for "high Crimes and Misdemeanors."

a) The phrase "high Crimes and Misdemeanors" embraces a host of improper conduct. As Blackstone explained the underlying principle, "an impeachment . . . is a prosecution of the already known and established law."[753] A Justice's violation of the Constitution—"the supreme Law of the Land"[754]— meets that requirement, as does a derivative violation of statutes punishing such conduct.[755] In addition, the Constitution itself recognizes that an impeachable offense could also be a common-law or statutory offense:

---

[750] See 1 J. Adams, *Memoirs of John Quincy Adams* (C. Adams ed. 1874), at 322. See generally *Trial of Samuel Chase, An Associate Justice of the Supreme Court of the United States* (S. Smith & T. Lloyd eds. 1805).

[751] See 2 H. Adams, *History of the United States of America During the First Administration of Thomas Jefferson* (1889), at 243.

[752] See R. Berger, *Impeachment*, ante note 734, ch. VIII.

[753] 4 *Commentaries*, ante note 158, at 256.

[754] U.S. Const. art. VI, cl. 2.

[755] 18 U.S.C. §§ 241-42. See ante, at 261-62.

> Judgment in Cases of Impeachment shall not extend further
> than to removal from Office, and disqualification to hold
> and enjoy any Office of honor, Trust or Profit under the
> United States: *but the Party convicted shall nevertheless be liable*
> *and subject to Indictment, Trial, Judgment and Punishment,*
> *according to Law.*[756]

So, even if an indictable offense were necessary to satisfy the
requirement of a "high Crime[or] . . . Misdemeanor," at least
two could be charged against the Justices in *Lawrence.*[757]

b) An impeachable offense need not also be a crime,
however.

> [N]o one has as yet been bold enough to assert that the
> power of impeachment is limited to offenses positively
> defined in the statute-book of the Union as impeachable
> high crimes and misdemeanors.[758]

> Congress have unhesitatingly adopted the conclusion that
> no previous statute is necessary to authorize an
> impeachment for any official misconduct . . . .[759]

Rather, "high Crimes and Misdemeanors" can embrace
essentially *political* offenses.[760] As Blackstone pointed out with
respect to *pre*-constitutional English law, "[T]HE first and
principal [high misdemeanor] is the *mal-administration* of such
high officers, as are in public trust and employment. This is

---

[756] U.S. Const. art. I, § 3, cl. 7 (emphasis supplied).

[757] 18 U.S.C. §§ 241-42. See also 18 U.S.C. §§ 1001(a)(2), 1621(1).

[758] 1 J. Story, Commentaries, ante note 121, § 797, at 581.

[759] Ibid., § 799, at 583. See generally R. Berger, *Impeachment*, ante note 734,
ch. II.

[760] See R. Berger, *Impeachment*, ante note 734, at 61 & n.29, 94-97.

usually punished by . . . parliamentary impeachment . . . ."[761]
The reason for this he gave as political: namely, that "it may
happen that a subject, intrusted with the administration of
public affairs, may infringe the rights of the people, and be
guilty of such crimes, as the ordinary magistrate either dares
not or cannot punish."[762] The rationale for impeachment
changed not one whit after ratification of the Constitution,
either:

> The jurisdiction is to be exercised over offenses which are
> committed by public men in violation of their public trust
> and duties. Those duties are in many cases political; and,
> indeed, in other cases, to which the power of impeachment
> will probably be applied, they will respect functionaries of a
> high character, where the remedy would otherwise be
> wholly inadequate, and the grievance be incapable of
> redress. Strictly speaking, then, the power partakes of a
> political character . . . .[763]

> The offenses to which the power of impeachment has been
> and is ordinarily applied as a remedy are of a political
> character. Not but that crimes of a strictly legal character
> fall within the scope of the power . . . ; but that it has a
> more enlarged operation, and reaches what are aptly
> termed political offenses, growing out of personal
> misconduct or gross neglect, or usurpation, or habitual
> disregard of the public interests, in the discharge of the
> duties of political office. These . . . must be examined upon

---

[761] 4 *Commentaries*, ante note 158, at 121 (emphasis in the original).

[762] Ibid. at 258.

[763] 1 J. Story, *Commentaries*, ante note 121, § 746, at 547.

very broad and comprehensive principles of public policy and duty.[764]

> The object of prosecutions of this sort . . . is to reach high and potent offenders, such as might be presumed to escape punishment in the ordinary tribunals, either from their own extraordinary influence, or from the imperfect organization and powers of those tribunals.[765]

Standards such as "offenses . . . committed by public men in violation of their public trust and duties," or "growing out of personal misconduct or gross neglect, or usurpation, or habitual disregard of the public interests," apply word for word to the Justices in *Lawrence*—who, of course, are "high and potent offenders, such as might be presumed to escape punishment in the ordinary tribunals."

3. Nonetheless, one cannot leave unexamined the argument of Raoul Berger, that judges may not be impeached for their unconstitutional opinions in any case, because to do so would unconstitutionally infringe upon the power of "judicial review":

> One case of impeachable conduct in England mentioned by Story, the rendering of unconstitutional opinions, merits special notice. The subservient judges of Charles I had held that the Ship Money Tax was constitutional, a judgment rejected by an outraged [House of] Commons, which later impeached the judges. Under our Constitution, however, the determination whether a measure is constitutional was left to the final determination

---

[764] Ibid., § 764, at 559.

[765] Ibid., § 688, at 513.

of the judiciary. When it was objected in the Pennsylvania
Ratification Convention that the security allegedly provided
by an independent judiciary was dubious because the
judges could be impeached if they declared an act null and
void, the suggestion was flatly rejected by James Wilson:
"What House of Representatives would dare to impeach,
or Senate to commit, judges for the performance of their
duty?" A similar statement was made by Elbridge Gerry;
and that conclusion is inherent in the very nature of judicial
review. Once it is granted that judges are empowered to
declare an act void that is not "in pursuance" of the
Constitution, it defeats the Framers' purpose to conclude
that they authorized Congress to impeach judges for
rendering such decisions.[766]

This passage is a tissue of begged questions, *non sequiturs*, and
fallacies.

a. At the outset, WE THE PEOPLE must demand to be
shown *exactly where and how*, "[u]nder our Constitution, . . . the
determination whether a measure is constitutional was left to
the final determination of the judiciary." As explained above,
although "[t]he judicial Power"[767] authorizes—and the judges'
"Oath[s] or Affirmation[s], to support this Constitution"[768]
require—them to engage in "judicial review" whenever a
constitutional issue is properly raised in a "Case[ ]" or
"Controvers[y]" before them,[769] a decision in any such "Case[

---

[766] *Impeachment*, ante note 734, at 90-91 (footnotes omitted).

[767] U.S. Const. art. III, § 1.

[768] U.S. Const. art. VI, cl. 3.

[769] See U.S. Const. art. III, § 2, cls. 1-2.

]" or "Controvers[y]" applies to only the litigants and their privies, not to anyone (let alone everyone) else in the world, and especially not to the Judiciary's co-equal and coordinate branches in the General Government, Congress and the President, and least of all to the General Government's (and the Judiciary's) creator, principal, and superior, WE THE PEOPLE. That is, "judicial supremacy" is not the necessary consequence of "judicial review"; and if it exists at all must be traced to some other source.

Berger's claim that "judiciary supremacy" follows inexorably from "judicial review"—for which, concededly, he alone cannot be blamed, inasmuch as it is the staple of the contemporary "law-profession culture," in both courthouses and law schools—is the product, not of the Constitution (or, for that matter, of a rational constitutionalism), but of an aggressive ideology aimed at the overthrow of America's political, economic, social, cultural, and even spiritual traditions, through usurpation by an elitist Judiciary of the power to make, unmake, and remake law, in the guise of interpreting it. Were this purpose—which even some members of the bench such as Justice Scalia openly condemn[770]—not enough to indict "judicial supremacy" in the court of public opinion, surely its perverse consequences are. Under "judicial supremacy":

> ➤ A controlling constitutional text disappears, replaced by judicial commentary. Although the Constitution's actual

---

[770] See, e.g., *Lawrence*, 539 U.S. at 602-05 (dissenting opinion).

language cannot be utterly disregarded (if proper form is to be maintained as camouflage for judicial usurpation), it serves only as an occasion and platform for judicial paraphraseology, deconstruction, psychologizing of the Founding Fathers, and other jejune tricks of modern legal rhetoric.[771] The supposed meaning of the Constitution now resides in judicial opinions—in "our cases," the mantra repeated *ad nauseam* throughout the *United States Reports* over the last fifty or more years.

➢ Between the Constitution's text and judicial commentary on it, the commentary reigns supreme. If the text clashes with "our cases," "our cases" invariably prevail. So, in situation after situation, "our cases" license what the Constitution specifically forbids,[772] or (as in *Lawrence*) disallow what the Constitution has

---

[771] As the Court observed in Ex parte *Wells*, 59 U.S. (18 How.) 307, 314 (1856): "It not infrequently happens in discussions upon the Constitution, that an involuntary change is made in the words of it, or in their order, from which, as they are used, there may be a logical conclusion, though it be different from what the Constitution is in fact. And even though the change may appear to be equivalent, it will be found upon reflection not to convey the full meaning of the words used in the Constitution." *Paraphraseology* is the artful judicial technique of employing in opinions *voluntary* changes in the Constitution's words or their order, for the particular purpose of permitting "a logical conclusion . . . different from what the Constitution is in fact."

[772] The classic example is the General Government's authority to emit legal-tender paper currency, as to which the contradiction between what the supreme law requires and what the Supreme Court has said it allows could not be more clear. See E. Vieira, Jr., *Pieces of Eight: The Monetary Powers and Disabilities of the United States Constitution* (2d rev. ed. 2002).

always permitted. And even if one of "our cases" is overruled, the result is simply that another of "our cases" then becomes the temporarily controlling precedent.

➤ Judicial reasoning is plastic, elastic, standardless, result-oriented, and ultimately sophistical. Thus, WE THE PEOPLE are told that "[s]tare decisis is not an inexorable command; rather, it 'is a principle of policy'."[773] So (for example), as a matter of "policy" the Court in *Planned Parenthood* v. *Casey*[774] seized upon *stare decisis* to protect "the right to abortion";[775] whereas, in *Lawrence* the majority eschewed *stare decisis* to protect the new-found "liberty" to engage in homosexual sodomy.[776] The logical thread connecting the two opinions is that, in the former, cultural bolshevism maintained its earlier gains; and, in the latter, cultural bolshevism made new gains—meaning, in practice, that the rule really should read: "*stare* the law-profession culture's agenda."

➤ "Judicial review" is nonscientific. The constitutional correctness of the Court's decision in any "Case[ ]" or "Controvers[y]" is incapable of verification or falsification through any inquiry other than a subsequent act of judicial interpretation—that is, of any inquiry

---

[773] *Payne* v. *Tennessee*, 501 U.S. 808, 828 (1991).

[774] 505 U.S. 833 (1992).

[775] Ibid. at 854-69 (opinion of O'Connor, Kennedy, and Souter, JJ.), 912-14 (opinion of Stevens, J.), 923-24 (opinion of Blackmun, J.).

[776] 539 U.S. at 577.

independent of the Judiciary itself. Moreover, under the doctrine of "the living Constitution" no precedent can ever be "wrong," because "the living Constitution" changes its meaning to fit the needs of the times as the Justices then perceive them. What was appropriate "constitutional law" under the circumstances that prevailed yesterday is merely irrelevant or inapplicable to the different circumstances that prevail today (although it may perhaps become relevant and applicable again under the different circumstances that will prevail tomorrow). So, neither deductive nor empirical reasoning controls the course of "constitutional" decisions.

➤ "Constitutional truth" is situational, relative, even personal: what majorities of then-sitting judges— influenced by their clerks and the "law-profession culture" that molds them all—agree it is, for the time being and the specific purposes at hand.

➤ "Constitutional law" is the exclusive domain of a judicial elite—with, as its members and their partisans like to claim, "life tenure." This elite arrogates to itself power over everyone else, but recognizes no responsibility to listen, let alone answer, to anyone else. Indeed, as in *Lawrence*, it claims autonomy—"the right to define one's own concept of existence, of meaning, of the universe, and of the mystery of human life"[777]—to

---

[777] *Planned Parenthood* v. *Casey*, 505 U.S. 833, 851 (1992), applied in *Lawrence*, 539 U.S. at 574.

separate itself *sua sponte*, not only from the text and time-honored construction of the Constitution, but also from every pertinent reality of politics, economics, and culture that text and construction embody, reflect, or were meant to serve—including "the history of Western civilization and . . . Judeo-Christian moral and ethical standards."[778]

In sum, confronted by these consequences of modern "judicial supremacy," WE THE PEOPLE have ample warrant to ask: Who authorized these elitists to hand down untestable and unchallengeable dictates they admit discovering "in an opposite direction" from "the history of Western civilization and . . . Judeo-Christian moral and ethical standards"? And because no satisfactory answer to this question will ever be forthcoming, WE THE PEOPLE have ample warrant to conclude that "judicial supremacy" not only need not be accepted but also cannot even be entertained as a plausible incident of "[t]he judicial Power."[779] Rather, it must be rejected as an insult and a challenge to every thinking man and woman in this country.

b. Besides the logic of the situation, WE THE PEOPLE can imagine hundreds upon hundreds of possible decisions of judges that no one free to leave a lunatic asylum would dare to defend as constitutional, or to claim that everyone must follow perforce of "judicial supremacy."[780] In such cases, would

---

[778] 539 U.S. at 572.

[779] U.S. Const. art. III, § 1.

[780] See ante, at 177-79.

anyone venture to assert that, notwithstanding the utter illegitimacy of these decisions, nothing could be done about them or about the individuals who promulgated them, save amend the Constitution to put back in what the judicial malefactors have taken out?! Yet, if even *one* such decision would justify WE THE PEOPLE (or their representatives in Congress and the White House) in refusing to follow the judges' ruling, how can "judicial supremacy" exist with respect to *any* decision? Must not *every* decision be subject to the selfsame inquiry—and, if necessary, repudiation—each to stand or fall on its own merits, and not to receive mindless acquiescence (its demerits aside) simply because of its source?

c. History also disproves Berger's claim that judges may not be "removed from Office on Impeachment ... and Conviction" because of their unconstitutional decisions. Surely there was no question under *pre*-constitutional English law that, "if the judges mislead their sovereign by unconstitutional opinions ... these imputations have properly occasioned impeachments; because it is apparent how little the ordinary tribunals are calculated to take cognizance of such offenses, or to investigate and reform the general policy of the state."[781] Rather:

> In examining the parliamentary history of impeachments, it will be found that many offenses, not easily definable by law, and many of a purely political character, have been deemed high crimes and misdemeanors worthy of this extraordinary remedy. Thus, ... judges ... have ... been

---

[781] 2 R. Wooddeson, *Laws of England* (1792), at 611-12.

impeached ... for misleading their sovereign by unconstitutional opinions, and for attempts to subvert the fundamental laws, and introduce arbitrary power.[782]

Berger found this history uncongenial; but he could not deny its authenticity.

In addition, when the Federal Convention debated whether "Impeachment ... and Conviction" should be limited to cases of "Treason & bribery" only, George Mason convinced it to add "high crimes & misdemesnors," arguing:

> Why is the provision restrained to Treason & bribery only? Treason as defined in the Constitution will not reach many great and dangerous offenses.[[783]] ... Attempts to subvert the Constitution will not be Treason as above defined.[784]

One wonders who could be better situated "to subvert the Constitution" than judges riding the high horse of "judicial supremacy," and what could be a "great[er or more] ... dangerous offense[ ]," especially if there were no effective remedy.

d. Berger's own arguments provide no more support for judicial immunity to "Impeachment ... and Conviction" than do logic and history.

1) The contention that, "[u]nder our Constitution, ... the determination whether a measure is constitutional was left to the final determination of the judiciary" is pure *ipse dixit*. The

---

[782] 1 J. Story, *Commentaries*, ante note 121, § 800, at 584 (footnote omitted).

[783] See U.S. Const. art. III, § 3, cl. 1.

[784] *Debates in the Federal Convention*, ante note 735, at 691.

controlling question is whether such "judicial supremacy" as would support judicial immunity from removal for unconstitutional decisions was known to and accepted by WE THE PEOPLE in the late 1700s. For "our inquiry concerns the [legal] standard prevailing at the time of adoption of the Constitution, not a score or more years later"[785]—let alone more than a century and one half later.

Now, as Berger himself correctly admitted, "the matter of Ship Money was a notorious usurpation on the part of Charles I and his 'subservient judges,' and the results, including the deposition and execution of Charles himself, and *the impeachment of many of his followers, were known to, and their lessons understood by, everyone conversant with English history.*" On the other side, though, to and by whom in that era was "known" and "understood" the modern notion of expansive "judicial review," leading first to "judicial supremacy," then to complete judicial immunity from removal for conduct manifestly lacking in "good Behaviour" where the conduct involves perversion of "judicial review" into subversion of the very Constitution the judges are sworn to "support"?[786] This Berger did not reveal.

Doubtlessly because, except to people steeped in or befuddled by the agenda of "the law-profession culture," modern "judicial supremacy" is so extravagant that no liberty-loving American of the late 1700s could be imagined to have

---

[785] *United States* v. *Barnett*, 376 U.S. 681, 693 (1964).

[786] U.S. Const. art. VI, cl. 3.

entertained it—amounting as it does, in light of the difficulty of amending the Constitution, especially upon every error the Supreme Court ejaculates, to effective judicial despotism. After all, the Supreme Court is nothing more than WE THE PEOPLE'S agent. Absent an explicit delegation of authority on that score, a principal cannot be bound by his agent's unilateral, self-interested determination as to the agent's own authority, especially where it is prejudicial to the principal. Also, WE THE PEOPLE have more than one agent in the General Government, all three of which are coordinate and co-equal. The doctrines of separation of powers and checks and balances teach that WE THE PEOPLE have so empowered those agents that, first, none is supreme as to any other with respect to exercise of the powers granted to the others under the Constitution; and, second, none is supreme over WE THE PEOPLE through its administration of the powers granted to it under the Constitution. Modern "judicial supremacy" denies both of these foundational doctrines. To say that Americans in the late 1700s would have accepted that consequence if confronted with the modern notion of "judicial supremacy" is ludicrous.

"Impeachment . . . and Conviction" of judges for their unconstitutional opinions is simply a check and balance that preserves all checks and balances and the separation of powers from a "notorious usurpation"—subject itself to the ultimate check and balance of WE THE PEOPLE'S approval *vel non* at the polls.

2) The comments of James Wilson in the Pennsylvania Ratification Convention do not support Berger's position, either. Wilson actually argued as follows:

> It is said that, if they are to decide against the law, one house will impeach them, and the other will convict them. I hope gentlemen will show how this can happen; for bare supposition ought not to be admitted as proof. *The judges are to be impeached, because they decide an act null and void, that was made in defiance of the Constitution!* What House of Representatives would dare to impeach, or Senate to commit, judges *for the performance of their duty?*[787]

(Berger quoted only the last sentence.) Leaving aside the many lacunae behind this statement,[788] Wilson plainly assumed that the "act [the judges declared] null and void . . . *was* made in defiance of the Constitution," and that in so declaring the judges *were* in "the performance of their duty." *This has nothing to do with cases in which judges declare an act null and void notwithstanding that it is perfectly constitutional; or declare an act constitutional notwithstanding that it is blatantly unconstitutional; or usurp power; or hand down tyrannical opinions.* In those cases, by hypothesis, the judges are *not* in "the performance of their dut[ies]," unless their duties encompass the commission of egregious error, usurpation, and tyranny—which, presumably,

---

[787] 2 J. Elliot, *The Debates in the Several State Conventions on the Adoption of the Federal Constitution as Recommended by the General Convention at Philadelphia in 1787* (2d ed. 1836), at 478 (emphasis supplied).

[788] Wilson was responding to other delegates whose remarks, and even whose names, are not reported in Elliot's Debates. See ibid. at x-xi. For all any reader can fathom from the reports today, a majority of the delegates may have disagreed with Wilson, in whole or in part, on this issue.

Wilson would have vociferously denied. For it is no part of judicial duty to disregard, defeat, subvert, destroy, or simply amend the Constitution through the subterfuge of "construing" it. Even to be honestly wrong, again and again, evidences incompetence, insouciance, or habitual negligence, which do not amount to "good Behaviour." To be grossly negligent, reckless, willfully blind, malicious, or out-and-out criminal is something worse—amounting to a "high Crime[or] . . . Misdemeanor[ ]." The question in such a situation, then, is not, "[w]hat House of Representatives would dare to impeach, or Senate to commit," such judges, but what House or Senate would dare not to?

3) Berger's conclusion that, "[o]nce it is granted that judges are empowered to declare an act void that is not 'in pursuance' of the Constitution,[789] it defeats the Framers' purpose to conclude that they authorized Congress to impeach judges for rendering such decisions" is a *non sequitur*. True, if judges in the course of otherwise proper "judicial review" were to "declare an act void that *is* not 'in pursuance' of the Constitution," they could not for that reason alone be subject to "Impeachment . . . and Conviction," because it is no "high Crime[or] . . . Misdemeanor[ ]"—or *any* species of wrongdoing whatsoever—for anyone in public office to denounce as unconstitutional and refuse to enforce *within the ambit of his own authority* an "act" that *is* unconstitutional. Indeed, to do the opposite would violate the official's "Oath or Affirmation,

---

[789] See U.S. Const. art. VI, cl. 2.

to support this Constitution."[790] The question of "Impeachment . . . and Conviction" relates only to cases in which judges "declare an act void that *is* . . . 'in pursuance' of the Constitution," or declare an act "in pursuance" of the Constitution which is *not*, or engage in usurpation or tyranny—or, as in *Lawrence*, go so far as to repudiate the philosophical foundations and the political result of Declaration of Independence—and, beyond that, claim that their decisions bind everyone else in the world, perforce of "judicial supremacy." Not every mistake made in the course of "judicial review" necessarily warrants "Impeachment . . . and Conviction"; but every assertion of "judicial supremacy" does, whether it arises out of a proper or improper exercise of "judicial review."

---

[790] U.S. Const. art. VI, cl. 3.

CHAPTER 15

A House Resolution that the Conduct of the Majority of Justices in *Lawrence* Constitutes an Absence of "good Behaviour," a "high Crime[ ] and Misdemeanor[ ]," and a Criminal Offense

The practical political problem remains, however, whether there are sufficient votes in Congress to impeach (let alone convict) errant judges because of their wildly unconstitutional opinions, to limit the courts' jurisdiction on key constitutional issues, or to appoint new judges sworn to uphold "original intent" ("pack" the courts).[791] Doubtlessly, any action along these lines would arouse all the forces of cultural bolshevism among the *intelligentsia* and special-interest groups, and throughout the mass media, to terrorize Congress

---

[791] Presumably, were the political climate such that Congress would not take any of these actions, the President would not press for indictments of judges on account of their violations of litigants' constitutional rights, either.

into submission to the present regime of "judicial supremacy." For the cultural Bolsheviks and their hangers-on know how important the presently constituted Judiciary is to the success of their "long march through the institutions." Perhaps, then, the most prudent course the friends of the Constitution could follow would be to seek simply a House Resolution:

➤ declaring that the *Lawrence* majority's misuse of foreign law to construe the Constitution, and its determination that traditional morality will no longer constitute a sufficient reason to uphold a law prohibiting aberrant conduct, are usurpations, "high Crimes and Misdemeanors," and criminal offenses;

➤ admonishing the Justices to cease and desist from such conduct, and to reject *Lawrence* as a false precedent; and

➤ demanding that by a date certain each of the Justices shall advise the House of his or her intent to abide by the terms of the resolution.

With such a resolution on record, no Justice could thereafter claim ignorance (or, in a criminal context, lack of *scienter*), even if they all remained silent.

A bill for this purpose could be introduced by a few stalwarts. It surely has a better chance for passage than a bill of impeachment at the present time. And it would probably garner as much publicity. Moreover, were it well supported, such a resolution could provide a foundation for erecting a proper bill of impeachment later on. On the other hand, if the House of Representatives cannot muster sufficient forces to put through even a basically toothless remonstrance to

Lawrence, it should consider changing the nation's emblem from the eagle to the ewe.

Conclusion

L*awrence* v. *Texas* signals both a crisis and an opportunity confronting WE THE PEOPLE. On the one hand, Justices Breyer, Ginsberg, Kennedy, O'Connor, Souter, and Stevens have puffed up "judicial supremacy" to the outermost bounds of irresponsibility and arrogance—construing the Constitution according to foreign law, striking down traditional morality as a rational basis for legislation, and thereby repudiating the fundamental principles of the Declaration of Independence. If these attacks upon America's "separate and equal station" "among the powers of the earth" and the foundational role of "the Laws of Nature and of Nature's God" in America's legal system go unanswered, this country will suffer increasing insinuation of amoral, globalist principles into her laws, and mounting perversion of those laws into pile drivers for imposing cultural bolshevism on her citizens. On the other hand, the repugnance of *Lawrence* to both the Constitution and the Declaration is so vivid that no patriot can any longer doubt the clear and present danger that "judicial supremacy" poses to the Republic, and the necessity for WE THE PEOPLE to restrict the jurisdiction of, and where necessary remove from office, the incumbent personnel of the Judiciary before they inflict irreparable harm upon the country. Only whether WE THE PEOPLE will succumb to the crisis, or seize the opportunity, remains to be seen.

The Conservative Caucus Foundation Mission Statement

TCCF (The Conservative Caucus Research, Analysis & Education Foundation) was established in 1976.

Since then, TCCF's mission has been to provide unique, nonduplicative leadership in policy battles of strategic importance which offer the possibility of success.

TCCF publications include the monthly *Eye on Bureaucracy* and the twice monthly *Howard Phillips Issues and Strategy Bulletin.*

The FIRST 100 WAYS is an ongoing project to spell out specific steps which can constitutionally be taken by a President of the United States who is determined to end legal abortion, withdraw from the institutions of the New World Order, restore local and parental control of education, eliminate all direct federal taxation, defund the Left, end socialized medicine, and return to a system of constitutional money without a privately-controlled, monopolistic, fractional reserve banking system.

Beginning in the 1970s, TCCF has provided much of the strategic and factual guidance for leaders of key policy battles:

1) providing research and advocacy in the late 1970s in support of a global ballistic missile defense for the United States of America;

2) opposing the unconstitutional provision of federal funds to thousands of Left-wing activist groups—backing up our critique with a major fact-gathering effort, utilizing the Freedom of Information Act;

3) refusing to surrender in the battle to maintain an effective U.S. military presence at the isthmus of Panama;

4) opposing arms control treaties with America's enemies, for whom these negotiated "scraps of paper" are, in the words of Lenin, "pie crusts made to be broken;"

5) beginning in the 1970s, making the case against socialized medicine, whether advocated by Jimmy Carter, Hillary Clinton, or George Bush;

6) introducing "THE FIRST 100 WAYS" project to spell out specific steps which can and ought be taken by a President of the United States to restrict the federal government to its delegated, enumerated constitutional functions and to restore American jurisprudence to its biblical foundations; and

7) making the constitutional case for America to withdraw from the United Nations, the International Monetary Fund, the World Bank, NAFTA, the World Trade Organization, and other organizations to which Congress has unconstitutionally transferred control over the resources of the American people and the public policies which govern them.

There is much more.

In support of priorities thus determined, TCCF relies on a comprehensive range of information sources, including periodicals, newspapers, newsletters, television, radio, foreign broadcast reports, and the Internet.

To advance all of TCCF's work, support from members of the public is earnestly solicited.

THE CONSERVATIVE CAUCUS FOUNDATION
450 MAPLE AVE. E.
VIENNA, VIRGINIA 22180

(703) 938-9626

www.conservativeusa.org